ESCAPE ARTIST

PETER MONTEATH is Professor of History at Flinders University in Adelaide. He is the author of *POW: Australian Prisoners of War in Hitler's Reich* (Macmillan 2011), and, with Valerie Munt, *Red Professor: The Cold War Life of Fred Rose* (Wakefield 2015).

ESCAPE ARTIST

THE INCREDIBLE SECOND WORLD WAR OF JOHNNY PECK

PETER MONTEATH

Pen & Sword
MILITARY
AN IMPRINT OF PEN & SWORD BOOKS LTD.
YORKSHIRE - PHILADELPHIA

First published in Australia in 2017 by NewSouth Publishing, an imprint of UNSW Press Ltd

First published in Great Britain in 2018 by
Pen & Sword Military
An imprint of
Pen & Sword Books Ltd
Yorkshire - Philadelphia

ISBN 978 1 52672 753 4

A CIP catalogue record for this book is available from the British Library.

Printed and bound in England by TJ International Ltd.

Pen & Sword Books Ltd incorporates the Imprints of Pen & Sword Books Archaeology, Atlas, Aviation, Battleground, Discovery, Family History, History, Maritime, Military, Naval, Politics, Railways, Select, Transport, True Crime, Fiction, Frontline Books, Leo Cooper, Praetorian Press, Seaforth Publishing, Wharncliffe and White Owl.

For a complete list of Pen & Sword titles please contact

PEN & SWORD BOOKS LIMITED
47 Church Street, Barnsley, South Yorkshire, S70 2AS, England
E-mail: enquiries@pen-and-sword.co.uk
Website: www.pen-and-sword.co.uk

or

PEN AND SWORD BOOKS
1950 Lawrence Rd, Havertown, PA 19083, USA
E-mail: Uspen-and-sword@casematepublishers.com
Website: www.penandswordbooks.com

CONTENTS

Prologue *xii*

1   Woollahra to Tobruk   *1*

2   Anzacs in Greece   *17*

3   The battle for Crete   *29*

4   Stranded at Sfakia   *50*

5   Captive in Crete   *65*

6   On the run   *77*

7   Special Operations   *92*

8   Farewell to Crete   *110*

9   To Italy   *120*

10   Armistice   *134*

11   The escape artist   *147*

12   Partisans   *164*

13   Guest of the Gestapo   *176*

14   Escape from San Vittore   *189*

15   The SOE in Italy   *199*

16   The doomed republic   *213*

17   Victory   *230*

18   Aftermath   *237*

Notes   *248*

Bibliography   *274*

Index   *280*

ACKNOWLEDGMENTS

It is no surprise that historians before me have been drawn to the extraordinary story of Johnny Peck. Foremost among them was the late Roger Absalom, whom I met a number of times, and who had devoted painstaking research over many years to the stories of Allied POWs on the run in wartime Italy. At that time I knew nothing of the scale of Roger's interest in Johnny Peck – to the extent of meeting him, interviewing him in 1986 and 1987, corresponding with him and weaving some threads of the Johnny Peck story into his wonderful book *A Strange Alliance*. I am grateful to Roger's dedication to his topic and to the tangible outcomes of his industry in the form of his publications and the notes contained in Peck's papers.

Western Australian historian Bill Bunbury also wrote about Peck in his book *Rabbits and Spaghetti*. Bill was kind enough to share with me his experience of delving into Peck's life and to help me establish contact with Peck's daughter Barbara Daniels in the UK. This book would not have been possible without Barbara's own generosity in giving me access to her collection of materials relating to her father and also providing some insightful comments on the draft manuscript. She very helpfully collected also the views of her sisters, to whom I also express my gratitude for allowing me to intrude into a part of their family's history.

For the research on Italy I am deeply indebted to Anna Banfi, who went far beyond the call of duty in tracing leads that did much to cast some light on parts of the story which for a long time seemed frustratingly obscure. The book has gained enormously from her ability to find those Italian sources and understand their importance for the bigger story.

In our resolute dedication to the cause of history, my partner Catherine Amis and I walked in the footsteps of Johnny Peck in Crete, Italy and Switzerland. I thank Catherine for her forbearance in allowing historical research to spoil a good walk (with apologies to George Bernard Shaw).

Space does not allow me to list the particular contributions of others, but let me express my heartfelt thanks – in no particular order – to Katrina Kittel, Elspeth Menzies, Margaret Gee, Deborah Nixon, Josephine Pajor-Markus, Tricia Dearborn, Ken Fenton, Glen Peebles, Federico Ciavattone, Philip Cooke, Richard Bosworth, Giovanni Cerutti, Claudio Perazzi, Gianmaria Ottolini, Luciano Boccalatte, Jürgen Förster, Benjamin Haas, Carlo Gentile, Kris Lipkowski, Kevin Jones, David Lockwood, Matt Fitzpatrick, Peter Stanley, Ian Jocumsen, Ross Jocumsen and Brian Dickey. Without singling out any particular individuals, I also thank the dedicated staff of the Flinders University Library, the National Archives of Australia (Canberra and Melbourne offices), the Australian War Memorial Research Centre, the Bundesarchiv-Militärarchiv Freiburg, the Imperial War Museum, the National Archives (Kew) and the Archivio Istituto Storico Resistenza Novara Piero Fornara.

Research for this project was generously supported by a research grant from the Australian Army History Unit and by Flinders University.

Finally, an unerring source of much practical information

and advice was the irrepressible Bill Rudd, who has done more than anyone else to explore, record and make known the history of those he calls the ANZAC POW 'Free Men' in Europe during World War II. Himself a former POW who had experienced life in Campo 57 and dared to climb to freedom in Switzerland, Bill has also been an inspiration to me and to many others. It is to Bill that this book is dedicated.

Johnny Peck's World War II odyssey February 1940 – December 1944

ROMANIA
YUGOSLAVIA
Black Sea
BULGARIA
Istanbul
Bari
ALBANIA
Gravina
Brindisi
GREECE
TURKEY
Kalamata
RHODES
MALTA
CYPRUS
CRETE
Mediterranean Sea
Tripoli
Tobruk
PALESTINE
Benghazi
Bardia
Alexandria
Jerusalem
El Alamein
CAIRO
Suez
LIBYA
EGYPT

PROLOGUE

On an unrecorded date in late September of 1943, a ragged group of Australian soldiers trudged the last metres to the ridge of the Monte Moro Pass in north-western Italy. As they paused for breath, their raised eyes drank in the sublime beauty of the wall of rock that was the Monte Rosa massif.

Behind and below them craggy goat tracks and smugglers' paths wound tortuously upward from the floor of the forested Anzasca Valley, the ancient home of the Walser people. Behind them, too, were months of privation and misery in the lice-infested POW camps of Libya and Italy.

In front of them was the border that separated fascist Italy from neutral Switzerland. A soaring, gilded statue of the Virgin Mary marked the divide, her halo of snowflakes reminding all those who saw her that they traversed a rarefied world of cold and ice.

One by one the Australians commenced their descent through a jumble of rock and then down a gentle slope to a village, where their Swiss hosts would warm them, ply them with food and drink, and offer them a welcoming home for the months ahead. For these men, the war was over.

Johnny Peck observed these last moments of his charges' liberation. He was their guide, but he was also one of them. He, too, had fought in the Western Desert; he knew all too well the ignominy of capture and the misery of captivity. And he, too, had seized the chance to defy his captors and leave the barbed wire behind.

But Switzerland did not beckon to the 21 year old, at least not at this time. Back down on the plains of Piedmont and around the rice fields of Vercelli, there were hundreds more POWs needing help. Their Italian guards had long since headed home, because the new masters of Italy were Hitler's soldiers. If the POWs were to avoid being snaffled by these Germans and sent north across the Alps to spend the rest of the war in a Stalag, something needed to be done, and quickly. What better man to help them than the elusive Johnny Peck, who had already embarrassed a string of captors and saw no need to stop just yet.

More than that, there were still battles to be fought and a war to be won. After the ignominies of Libya, Greece and Crete, there was at last a chance to turn the tables on Hitler's armies. Stretched to its limits, Hitler's Reich was tottering, and Johnny Peck instinctively knew it.

So with the last of his flock safely over the Swiss border, he drew a deep breath, checked his gear, and descended back into the lion's den.

1
WOOLLAHRA TO TOBRUK

JOHNNY PECK'S FIRST ESCAPE WAS FROM THE FAMILY HOME. At the age of 13 he felt it offered more cruelty than love, and while for a time he hoped things might change of their own accord, eventually he resolved to take his fate into his own hands. In Crib Point on Victoria's Mornington Peninsula it was the local policeman who would return any stray children to the bosom of the family, and as Peck knew he had no chance of outrunning the local cop, he carefully considered his mode of exit. Late one night he stole the neighbour's bike and, without turning his head back in regret, cycled 80 kilometres to Melbourne, where he sought refuge under a fire escape.

Not for the last time in his life, a figure of the law caught hold of him. A Melbourne policeman on his nocturnal urban beat found Peck's hiding place and coaxed him from it. Thankfully, as Peck recalled many decades later, this policeman must have been 'a very very nice man', because he did not bundle him back to an unloving home but allowed the fugitive to join him on the beat for the rest of that night. As the new day began, he then dispensed some fatherly advice, admonishing the young man not to remain in Melbourne but to 'get work on a farm somewhere'. That wise counsel came with two shillings, since the lad otherwise had nothing, and then words of farewell. With that, Peck jumped back on his neighbour's bike and pedalled north towards Sydney, the place of his birth.

Perhaps unwittingly, Peck was following a family tradition of doing things young. When his parents, Bert and Phyllis (Phil), both born in 1899, married in July of 1918, they needed parental permission to tie the knot in St Patrick's Catholic Church in Parramatta. The young couple soon had children, six of them altogether, of whom John Desmond was born third in 1922. The growing family lived in Woollahra in Sydney's east so that Bert, who served in the Royal Australian Navy, was close to his work at the Garden Island base. When Johnny was just seven, his mother Phil died of pneumonia and pleurisy, leaving behind six small children. With their father often on naval duties that took him away from home, the children were cared for by their grandmother in Sydney, at least until Bert remarried at the end of 1931.

Bert's choice of new spouse was unconventional – Jean was the divorced wife of Phil's brother Harold. Johnny's stepmother, then, had been his aunt by marriage. And while that was highly unusual, in Johnny Peck's recollections, at least, Jean was determined to play the conventional role of the wicked step-mother. She brought with her to the marriage a son, Lockie, the same age as Johnny. And when Jean and Bert had a new son of their own, Harry, they became a family of ten. By this time Bert had been transferred to HMAS *Cerberus* so that all lived at Crib Point's Flinders Naval Depot,[1] where family life, as Peck recalled much later, 'wasn't very happy, not for any of us.'[2] Well before Johnny, his older brothers expressed their dissatisfaction with their feet, leaving home when they reached fourteen. When his sisters were packed off to boarding school, there seemed no reason at all to stay.[3]

Though details are sketchy, it is clear that Johnny Peck's pilfered bike did not carry him as far as Sydney. North of Melbourne Peck pulled into Craigieburn, where at the local garage he let it be known that he was looking for work. The proprietor kindly put him in touch with an Irish family, the O'Gormans, who were known to need labour on their property. Before long Pat O'Gorman had collected Peck from town, taken him to his sheep farm and employed him at 10 shillings a week, working from about 4 in the morning to 8 at night.[4]

Though the O'Gormans gave him work and what passed for a family life, it was not enough to hold him forever, and certainly not when war was declared. Johnny Peck was part of that generation of '39ers, eking out a living in an Australia which had never entirely recovered from the Depression, and yearning for new challenges and adventure.

By mid-October he was enlisting at the showgrounds in Melbourne. Records show that at this time he was a farmer, single, born in Sydney, and Roman Catholic by religion. He had no distinctive marks, brown hair and hazel eyes. Next of kin was H Frederick Peck of the Flinders Naval Depot at Crib Point. All of that was true enough, but one piece of information was a blatant lie. Peck gave as his date of birth 16 February 1919, which would have meant that he was 20 years and 10 months – old enough to enlist in the 2nd AIF and be sent overseas. In reality, his date of birth was 17 February 1922. He was just 17.

Three days after his enlistment he wrote to the family back in Crib Point, giving as his own new address: 2nd Engineers, 6th Division, 2nd AIF, 3rd District Military Camp, Ascot Vale. If that was not enough of a shock for the family, more was to follow. His unit was to head overseas in just three weeks – on 6 January. Expressing his hope to see them one more time on his pre-embarkation leave, he signed off, 'Thine Own Des', adding, 'PS I'm broke and that's not a hint!'[5]

The final days before departure were a giddying mix of parties, heavy drinking, route marches in full gear and inoculations. Then, in the early afternoon of 11 January, a few days behind schedule, *Empress of Japan* pulled out into Port Phillip Bay in full view of the thousands of spectators gathered on the wharves. They, like most on board, had no clue as to her destination.[6] And on board was Johnny Peck, still short of his 18th birthday.

The day of that birthday brought with it a landing at Kantara (El Qantara) on the eastern side of the Suez Canal, having stopped in Fremantle to join a convoy sailing via Colombo. To some the destination must have been eerily reminiscent of the first AIF a generation earlier. The outbreak of a war in Europe had brought them for training to the Middle East, and they felt a nagging curiosity about where they might finally join the battle.

Training was to be in Palestine, reached by railway from Kantara, and clothing was issued to match the climate – khaki shorts, shirts and long socks. Peck's unit was the Headquarters,

Australian Overseas Base, and to his surprise he found himself billeted in Jerusalem, a location not without its tourist charms. On Good Friday he witnessed the Stations of the Cross, spread through the Holy City and onto the Mount of Calvary, following the path Christ took as he carried the Cross. Among the pilgrims observing the event was a Belgian priest who told Peck, 'You can thank Hitler for that unique experience anyway.'[7] Later he attended Mass in the Church of the Holy Sepulchre and used a day's leave to take a trip to Bethlehem.[8]

There were challenges too. By May Peck was noting temperatures of 112 degrees Fahrenheit in the shade – and there was not much of that.[9] By September he was moaning, 'The weather is still as hot as hell, the flies are still as troublesome, the tucker is still full of sand, but thank God there is still some beer left.'[10] To slake their thirsts the Australians drank beer, and when the beer ran out they turned to the anise-flavoured local spirit called arak, which they drank as if it were beer.[11]

Through all of that there was still little sense of when the Australians might see action and against whom. While they stayed put, in May the war had moved just a little closer to them. After Hitler's armies steamrolled their way through northern and western Europe, Mussolini decided that the time had come for him to enter the fray. On 10 June, as France teetered, Italy jumped from the fence and declared war on both France and Britain. Mussolini told his chief of staff Marshal Pietro Badoglio, 'I need only a few thousand dead so that I can sit at the peace conference as a man who has fought.'[12] The *Duce* harboured vast imperial ambitions centred on the Mediterranean, and they were to be realised at the cost of his newly declared enemies. It took little imagination among Britain's strategists, as they struggled to cope with the

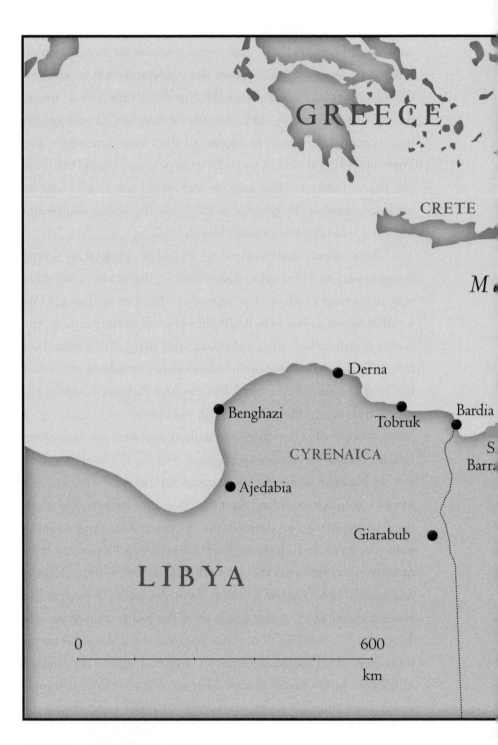

North Africa and the Middle East in 1940

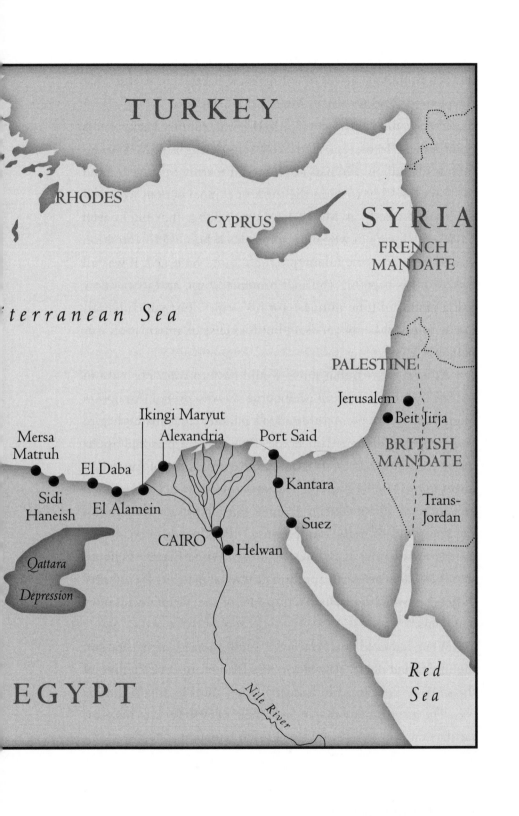

disaster unfolding across the English Channel, to realise that Egypt and Palestine were in Mussolini's firing line.

Even before Italy's entry into the war, Johnny Peck, at this point still in Jerusalem, had been considering a move into an infantry battalion. He had not joined the army to serve behind the front lines but to be in the thick of combat action, whatever the risks. As early as March he wrote a letter that might well have sent shivers down some spines back home. His intention was to transfer to the infantry. 'Don't faint,' he urged, it was all fine with his captain, who had promoted him, and it was now just a matter of time until he got his stripes. Just which battalion he joined was not yet clear, but his sense of anticipation was palpable.[13]

As it happened, that move would have to wait. His ruse in putting up his age back in Melbourne was discovered. An option might have been a premature end to a military career barely begun and an ignominious return home. Peck made a personal application to General Thomas Blamey, the commander of Australian forces in the Middle East, for special consideration. The Gallipoli and Western Front veteran Blamey must have admired Peck's eagerness and offered a compromise – Peck would serve for an indeterminate time as Blamey's batman. When Blamey believed that Peck had reached an appropriate level of maturity for infantry duties, he would be transferred to one of the Victorian infantry battalions.[14]

What followed for Peck were some months of frustration, though devoid of any ill-will towards Blamey. In Peck's telling of the story, he continued to badger Blamey until he finally got his way. The records show that in September of 1940 Peck, to his great satisfaction, was transferred to the 2/7th Battalion.

The 2/7th was established, along with the 2/5th, 2/6th and 2/8th Battalions, as part of the 17 Australian Infantry Brigade, known as the Victorian Brigade, and under the command of Brigadier Stanley G Savige.[15] The 17 Brigade was itself part of the Australian 6th Division. The unit colour patch of the 2/7th comprised a stripe of brown over a stripe of red, so its men were called 'the mud over blood mob'. The battalion's commander was Lieutenant-Colonel Theo G Walker, who was with his men from the time the first volunteers were accepted. He had gathered years of experience serving with the Citizen Military Forces, but at 39 he was Victoria's youngest commanding officer in the 2nd AIF.[16]

Walker and the 2/7th did not arrive in Palestine until May 1940, long after Johnny Peck, having trained at Puckapunyal and then embarked at Port Melbourne on 15 April. They were immediately exposed to the rigours of desert training. Their base was at a village called Beit Jirja, literally 'home of George'.

When Johnny Peck joined the 2/7th after several relatively idle months as Blamey's batman, he had some catching up to do. Through the summer of 1940 the 2/7th had been training for a desert war in the hot, parched conditions of Palestine. When Peck moved with them to a camp at Helwan in Egypt – about 20 kilometres outside Cairo – for more intense training in September, he suffered awfully from the strict regimen imposed on all the fighting forces. After nearly a year on light duties, carrying a full pack while marching across the desert nearly tore him to bits, but it would pay dividends eventually. Though still no-one knew just where and when they would be thrown into battle, they would be expected to do so as an extremely fit, tough, and well-drilled unit.

Indeed, war was edging ever closer. Mussolini's African launch pad was the Italian colony of Libya to the west of Egypt; the strategic prize on offer was the Suez Canal. From Libya the Italian 10th Army rolled across the Egyptian border on 9 September, reaching the port of Sidi Barrani and taking up defensive positions there in advance of a planned assault on Mersa Matruh, 130 kilometres to the east.

Responsibility for halting the Italians' advance and turning them on their heels rested with Lieutenant-General Archibald Wavell, General Officer Commanding-in-Chief of the new Middle East Command. Wavell had to bear in mind that Mussolini also had at his disposal some 250 000 troops in Italian East Africa, and they were equally keen to strike at Egypt and claim the prize of the Suez Canal. But in mid-September Wavell's first priority was to evict the Italian 10th Army, digging in at Sidi Barrani. Among the forces he assembled for that task was the Australian 6th Division, including Johnny Peck's 2/7th. To that end, by the end of October the 2/7th was deployed to Ikingi Maryut near Alexandria; after months of training, practice manoeuvres and speculation, the men now knew that war was close.

The British struck first. Operation Compass was launched on 8 December, and its aim was to use combined British forces to cut off the Italian 10th Army by dislodging them from Sidi Barrani. It was devastatingly effective, as the British destroyed the Italian fortified positions, captured Italian troops by the tens of thousands and forced the remainder into a scurrying westward retreat.

Peck's 2/7th joined the chase. In expectation of turbulent times ahead, Christmas was celebrated early that year – on December 19. All ranks feasted on soup, turkey, roast potatoes, Christmas pudding, fruit salad and cream, all washed down with beer. The spread was complemented with private hampers and delights provided by the Comforts Fund, and the men enjoyed a 'gargantuan feast'.[17] It made sense to savour it, because real Christmas dinner on the 25th would comprise standard army fare of bully beef and biscuits, sprinkled liberally with desert sand.

On Boxing Day reveille was at 4 am, and then the men were marched to Ikingi Maryut Station and loaded on a train heading west, finally stopping at Sidi Haneish in the middle of the night, where they were plied with hot tea and rum as they occupied their new camp. A week later they were moved again, this time to the little port of Bardia. There some desultory Italian shelling announced that their war was about to begin.[18]

Bardia would not be an easy nut to crack. On its landward side its Italian occupiers defended it with a 30-kilometre arc of concrete underground posts shielded by an anti-tank ditch and a series of barbed wire barriers. The posts, some 700 metres apart, were defended by machine guns, while to their rear, clustered around the port itself, heavy artillery was in place to deter any invading force.

It was here that Johnny Peck's 2/7 Battalion and other Australian units were finally to undergo their baptism of fire. As at Sidi Barrani, the challenge was to eject the Italian defenders, now alert to the scale of the danger, from their well-established defensive positions. Bardia was heavily garrisoned, and the landscape surrounding it was a quintessentially western desert landscape, devoid of trees or of features which might offer an attacking force refuge from defensive fire.

For the first days the Australians sent patrols to reconnoitre the Italian defences, before playing their part in the attack which was about to be launched. All of the battalions in the Australian 17th Brigade were to target particular sections of the perimeter, while one of them, the 2/6th, created a diversion at the southern end of the fortress.[19]

Months of rigorous training paid off for the Australians, as three of their battalions were thrown into battle, with the fourth held in reserve. The first stage of the Australian involvement – supported by intense artillery fire from land as well as the pounding of Italian positions by Royal Navy off the coast – began on 3 January. From the west, where Italian defences were thought to be at their weakest, the Australian 16th Infantry Brigade advanced at dawn through gaps blown in the barbed wire and across anti-tank ditches breached with the vigorous use of picks and shovels.

Then it was the turn of Johnny Peck's 17th Infantry Brigade. The Victorians' job was to exploit the breach in the perimeter and to press on to the Italians' secondary defence line, the so-called Switch Line. Together with the 19th Brigade, Peck's 2/7th and other battalions focused their efforts on the southern part of the Italian fortress. When the 16th Infantry Brigade prevailed in the northern sector, not only was Bardia lost to the Italians, but tens of thousands of men fell into enemy hands.

On the night of 5 January Peck's C Company attacked and then just before daybreak finally seized its allotted target, Post 16. Over the following morning hours the other companies of the 2/7th and the other battalions of the 19th Brigade captured all the remaining Italian positions. By then the fighting was done; there remained just to clean out a trove of materials from the Italian positions, among it a mass of invaluable transport vehicles and artillery.[20]

In Johnny Peck's experience it had been a savage battle, fought at times in close combat, bayonets fixed. With little more than some stunted shrubs to protect them from enemy fire, the

Australians did much of their attacking at night, when the desert was bitterly cold. The Italian resistance he thought at best patchy. While the enemy artillery had fought bravely and caused many casualties, many Italians had readily surrendered when they saw that the tide of battle had turned against them.

After the battle Peck wrote of that first battle experience:

> We had a good feed today on captured Dago officers' tucker. Wait til I tell you the real news. Little Me captured an Italian General and his batman. Not bad, eh! And did I souvenir him? He was apparently missed in the general advance and I got him 4 o'clock in the morning in a dugout.

Just hours later, after midnight, he was thrown into the fray again, this time tasked with taking a machine gun nest which had been holding up his company's advance all day. With two other men – Stan and Johno – he was to cut the wire entanglements about 100 yards (90 metres) in front of the nest, then advance on the nest itself. 'You should have seen us three wirecutters. Each with rifle and bayonet slung across the back. Me with a Colt '44 in one hand and the wirecutters in the other. Stan and Johno had wirecutters in one hand and grenades in the other.' In the dark the men lost their way and stumbled into a different nest, whose occupants opened fire on the Australians from point blank range. They were lucky to survive. Stan got one bullet in the thigh, while another ploughed a furrow along the side of his head. 'Another half inch and his brains would have been blown out,' Peck cheerfully recalled.[21]

What surprised him was how few casualties there had been under such heavy machine gun fire. And while the immediate exposure to machine-gunning had been awful, it was not the worst experience he took from that battle. It was much worse, he concluded, to be subjected to the horror of constant artillery shelling and the danger that one's body could be blown to smithereens at any moment. 'You have no idea', he told his parents, 'of a bloke's feelings as the shells are bursting round him and he offers up a last prayer.'[22]

Johnny Peck relished every moment of it. Good fortune had protected him from the ravages of artillery fire; with a sense bordering on invincibility he and his C Company had penetrated into the heart of the Italian positions, his bayonet unbloodied. The discomforts endured were not inflicted by the enemy but by the desert's extremes, which brought almost insufferable cold at night and a daytime thirst which the allocation of a miserly pint (0.5 litres) of water could never slake.

That first battle at Bardia delivered him one of the great lessons of war which, he sensed, would apply universally. It prompted him, as he reflected in an interview many years later, to wonder just what it was that made him and those around him fight so furiously. He drew the conclusion that it had nothing to do with King and Country, and neither was it to be understood as an act of desperate self-preservation. Rather, he recognised, 'the thing that makes people fight and fight hard is their comradeship, their pride; they would rather die than let their mates down.' In the first instance, the kind of loyalty that propelled men through battle and beyond was not a loyalty to anything so abstract as an ideology or indeed even an army, but rather to the members of the section or platoon who were fighting at one's side.[23]

Others, too, had good reason to be satisfied. Within just 56 hours the Australian 6th Division and Allied forces had captured in their entirety the enemy's defences and more than

46000 prisoners at the expense of just 500 casualties.[24] Peck's 2/7th recorded just 76 casualties, eight of them officers. Right after the battle, and while still on Bardia's battlefield, Stan Savige wrote to Theo Walker in glowing approbation of the 2/7th's role in the rout:

> Deprived of tank support, fighting of a severe nature broke out after crossing the start line. The necessary time to clear the situation lost the close support of the artillery barrage. From then on your troops were involved in a fight covering 6000 yards the capture of 14 stoutly defended posts or really forts. Besides that you attacked batteries firing at you over open sights: cleaned up M.G. positions and captured several thousand prisoners. Could troops do more and supported by their own weapons and native resource only?[25]

It was an insight that buoyed him as the 2/7th continued the chase across the Western Desert, towards the Libyan border. The Italians resolved to make a stand at the port of Tobruk, where once again they dug into heavily fortified positions and braced for the arrival of the British with the fearsome Indian, Australian and New Zealand units who fought with them. The dead of Bardia only just buried, the 2/7th for its part moved in brigade convoy to a point 36 kilometres east of Tobruk and readied to strike again.[26]

The assault on Tobruk began on 21 January 1941, and once more it was the Australian 16th Brigade that opened proceedings. As at Bardia, fighting was intense, as attack drew vicious counter-attack, but by the end of the day the Italian position was hopeless; surrender was offered and taken. With that, a precious fort and its equally precious fortifications, still largely intact, fell into British hands, as did some 25000 Italian troops. Like those gathered together after the collapse of Sidi Barrani and Bardia earlier, their war was in effect over. Some of them would soon find themselves on vessels plying the waters of the Indian Ocean, heading to Australia, where they would serve out much of what was left of the war working on farms dotted throughout the countryside. The 2/7th, in contrast, emerged from the Battle of Tobruk almost unscathed; there was not a single loss of life, and just eight men were reported as wounded.[27]

For Johnny Peck and the others of the mud over blood mob, at this point war must have seemed easy. The speed with which they had managed to turn the Italians on their tails had surprised even the most sanguine among them. Moreover, the victory at Tobruk was followed by a period of lighter duties during which they could gather their energy, even as the Italians were chased west across Cyrenaica toward Derna and then Benghazi. Peck's 2/7th was stationed for a time at Ajedabia, south of Benghazi, cooling their heels.[28]

If there was even a hint of complacency, it was soon to be dispelled. Hitler was about to unleash his own dogs of war in North Africa. He could now allow his Axis partner to fail. On 12 February German General Erwin Rommel alighted from an aircraft in Tripoli. The tide of the war in the Mediterranean was about to turn.

2

ANZACS IN GREECE

IT WAS NOT JUST IN LIBYA THAT MUSSOLINI NEEDED HELP from his Axis partner. The Italian campaign in Greece, launched from Albania on 28 October 1940, had gone from bad to disastrous. Not only had Greek forces held up the Italian advance, by November they had turned the Italians back. Thereafter Mussolini's Greek folly had deteriorated into an expensive stalemate founded on the exhaustion of both sides.

There were other developments in the Balkans, too, that meant that Hitler could not ignore what was going on in Europe's south. Italian failure in both Greece and North Africa would present a danger to what the Nazis had long regarded as the main

Greece in 1941

game – that is, the acquisition of *Lebensraum*, living space, in eastern Europe. To launch Operation Barbarossa – the German invasion of the Soviet Union – Hitler needed a secure southern flank.

At first the German aid to Mussolini's Greek campaign took the modest form of transport aircraft ferrying supplies across the Adriatic in December of 1940. A commitment of ground forces appeared unwise through the winter of 1940–41, and in any case would entail a good deal of planning. Then in March 1941 another Balkan state unexpectedly worked its way into Hitler's deliberations – Yugoslavia. Until that time the Yugoslav government was sympathetic to Nazi Germany, but a coup installed a pro-British regime. Hitler's strategic interests could not allow that government to stand, especially in the face of intelligence suggesting that in Greece, too, British influence was expanding. Hitler resolved to invade both Yugoslavia and Greece, and to do so with minimal interruption to the preparations for Barbarossa.

For a time in the first half of 1941 it seemed that Greece and Britain alone held back the tide of fascism as it washed over Europe. In those circumstances it was all the more difficult for Churchill to abandon Greece to the fate of yet another fascist invasion. Historically, too, the British had stood by the Greeks in their battles against foreign oppression. But as the likelihood of a German invasion from the north grew, British planners despaired at the prospects of making an intervention of any significance beyond that of a grand but doomed gesture.

To commit anything approximating the manpower and materiel needed to defend Greece posed a logistical nightmare. Greek forces already had their hands full dealing with the Italian incursion into western Greece; by early 1941 their resources were almost drained. Moreover, a German invasion was an altogether different proposition than the Italians' misadventure. By this time German troops were battle-hardened, superbly equipped and masters of blitzkrieg. With friends in high places in Greek politics, the military and the economy, a German presence was unlikely to provoke the vigorous opposition that had halted the Italians.

To forestall a German invasion from the north demanded the rapid deployment of sizeable forces to the mountainous northern reaches of Greece. Alas, the British had neither time nor the required forces on their side, and they knew it. Yet in weighing the virtues of a political gesture against such harsh realities, Winston Churchill opted for the former. He extended the hand of friendship to the Greek government, offering military assistance which the Greeks themselves were reluctant to accept. Had they known more of Churchill's dealings, the Australian and New Zealand governments too might have voiced their reservations, because they would provide the troops for a campaign which would have little value beyond that of an act of token defiance.

Indeed, it appears that Churchill and his Commander-in-Chief in the Middle East, General Sir Archibald Wavell, did not disclose to the Australians the full extent of the risks involved in any deployment of Australian troops. By early March Menzies went so far as to give voice to his unease, only to be informed that the Australians 'would have a fighting chance' and that the deployment to Greece posed no risk to the forces left behind in Libya to take on Rommel's Afrika Korps on the Benghazi front.[1]

In reality the Australians had plentiful reason to fear that they were being thrown to the wolves. Johnny Peck's 6th Division, having proved proficient in battle in the Western Desert, was earmarked for transfer across the Mediterranean to join British and New Zealand forces on the Greek mainland. Altogether some

100 000 men were assigned a herculean task, which they were to perform under the orders not of the Australian Blamey but a British general, Henry Maitland 'Jumbo' Wilson. In time the Australians and New Zealanders would together form an Anzac Corps, which inevitably provoked memories of the campaign fought by Anzacs a generation earlier, and not so far away.[2] They were unlikely to be pleasant memories, as that campaign, also the brainchild of Winston Churchill, had not gone well.

Blamey was well aware of the perils that awaited the 6th Division. The capabilities of the heavily armed and yet highly mobile Wehrmacht had been on display for all to witness during the lightning campaigns in northern and western Europe. Yet there could be no reversal. While the 9th Division was left behind to defend Tobruk and the other gains in the Western Desert, the 6th Division was quietly recalled to Egypt and dispatched from Alexandria.

As expected, the combined Greek and British preparations were too little, and they were too late. Troops were rushed north to set up defensive positions, the first of them along the Metaxas Line in the far north-east. Sure enough, when Operation Marita – the simultaneous German invasion of Yugoslavia and Greece – was launched on 6 April, the Metaxas Line was defended ferociously but very soon collapsed. To hold it was a hopelessly ambitious brief, because the German troops that poured into Greece from neighbouring Bulgaria were almost immediately joined by others entering via overwhelmed Yugoslavia, who soon exposed the rear of the Greek defences. In one fell swoop, all of north-eastern Greece and the port city of Salonika – Greece's second-largest city after Athens – fell into German hands. The commander of the German 5th Mountain Division commented sardonically, 'It looks like the Greeks are prepared to fight to the last man for England's sake.'[3]

What forces were not trapped at the Metaxas Line abandoned the north-east and fell back south to try to form new defensive lines, each defended with great tenacity, but each soon abandoned in the face of overwhelming German strike-power, especially from the air. To the men on the ground, 'RAF' stood for 'Rare as Fairies' – in another interpretation the 'F' stood for something shorter. Devoid of support from the air, and with neither the time nor the resources to dig in, the campaign turned into a series of humiliating withdrawals.

Peck and his battalion did not finally leave Alexandria until the evening of 10 April, four days after the German assault began, and did not finally disembark in Greece until 13 April.[4] By that time the elements of the 6th Division already in Greece had been chased south from the snowy mountains of the north to the flatter central region around Servia, where desperate measures were being taken to hang another defensive line from one side of the country to the other.

The 2/7th spent a brief time in camp at Daphne and then was ushered north toward the front line. Such a moveable feast was the front at this time that the Australians were delivered too far north, to Larissa, and were almost immediately called back to defensive positions further south at a place called Domokos. Nearby was a pass through which, so the hastily conceived plans ran, the invading German forces would be funnelled on their way further south to Athens. And it was at the Domokos Pass, then, that the 2/7th was to dig in and stop the Germans in their tracks. Under the watchful eyes of the battalion's commander Theo Walker, they did exactly that, preparing for the Germans what they imagined would be 'a hot reception'.[5]

The experience at Domokos turned out no differently from

any of the defensive lines set and then abandoned further north. With total dominance in the air the Luftwaffe could bomb defensive positions at will. When the German artillery rolled within range, it pummelled enemy positions with impunity. Most frightening of all for the men on the ground, no matter how well dug in, were the screaming descents made by Stuka bombers, their noise and speed chasing shivers up and down the spines of the men cowering below. For Peck and for everyone else, the experience was every bit as frightening as the Italian artillery that had hammered them at Tobruk. The difference was that in Greece the work of German bombs and shells rendered close combat almost entirely superfluous. Barely a rifle shot could be fired in anger, let alone a bayonet jabbed at a figure within arm's length.

Domokos had to be abandoned, and in haste. The military situation was now bordering on the impossible. Greek officers – never as devoted to the British Empire as their king – had chosen to negotiate with the Germans and withdraw themselves and their men from battle. The Anzacs were fighting on in the defence of Greece, even when the Greeks had given up.

In the smallest hours of 20 April – Hitler's birthday – the defensive positions at Domokos were cleared, and the men made a hurried retreat to the south, marching the first 10 kilometres through hilly terrain, having abandoned personal gear and a good amount of ammunition. Before the break of dawn whatever vehicles could be found gathered them up and accelerated their journey south.

That new defensive position, occupied on 21 April, was the Brallos Pass. Through the entire day of southward retreat the convoy was subjected to enemy attacks. The 2/7th was to establish itself on a line stretching from the town of Lamia to the Brallos

Road, the main part of it in a deep, jumbled gorge. Theo Walker arranged his men masterfully so as to cover every approach to the gorge; the most optimistic hoped that now, finally, a line had been etched in the rocks.

Constant enemy air activity rendered this new position, too, untenable. Once again it would not come to a direct engagement with the enemy. As before, the most the withdrawing Australian forces could hope to achieve was to slow the German advance by mining tunnels and blowing bridges. At best those tactics could delay defeat, not turn the tide of battle. By this time in any case it was clear that the Greek campaign was lost, and the only option was to effect a rapid and effective evacuation, so that at least the Anzacs might survive to fight again.

Just after midnight on 24 April, the men of the 2/7th climbed out of the rocky terrain that had protected them and onto whatever transport could be found. They were joining a steady flow of men heading south. There would be no further attempt to draw another defensive line, nor even to hold Athens. Instead, they would stream across the Corinth canal and head for nominated evacuation points on the Peloponnese peninsula, from which, so they fervently hoped, the Royal Navy would whisk them to safety in Egypt.

Speed, however, was of the essence, because if the Luftwaffe did not get them, delays would allow German ground troops to thwart the evacuations and condemn the men to spending the rest of the war behind barbed wire. Sure enough, as the Anzacs crossed the Corinth Canal, German troops snapped at their heels.

As Johnny Peck came to realise, the danger confronting him and the thousands of others scurrying onto the Peloponnese was that the Germans were landing paratroops onto the peninsula to block the retreat to the evacuation beaches. So late had Peck's arrival been in Greece, and so rapid the withdrawal, that he and his unit had seen little fighting. At the entrance to the Peloponnese, however, that all changed, as the presence of Germans led to a series of skirmishes. The fighting was more ferocious than anything Peck had experienced against Italians at Bardia and Tobruk; the Germans, he soon learned, were not only superbly equipped but brought to the battlefield a tenacity and confidence derived from an unbroken series of victories. For now, however, his contact with them was fleeting, because the priority was to reach an evacuation beach as soon as possible.[6]

For Peck's 2/7th the target evacuation beach was at Kalamata on the southern coast of the Peloponnese. The plan was that the 2/7th would make their way to Kalamata along with men from other units without delay; they were to wait in allocated zones in the olive groves near the beach until given the order to proceed to the jetty. That the men not only made Kalamata as quickly as they did, but managed in so many cases to carry their weapons with them, was itself a feat of endurance. Brigadier Stanley Savige, who commanded the 17th Infantry Brigade, later wrote:

I consider the feat of [Theo] Walker's mob [the 2/7th] and [Hugh] Wrigley's mob [the 2/6th] withdrawing as they did and travelling 100 miles, ranks as the greatest feat of this AIF, and, other observers say, of the old AIF too … Here is the test of discipline. Every man took his rifle and complete ammunition aboard. Every Bren and anti-tank rifle was dragged aboard by our men, men almost too weary to walk.[7]

At Kalamata the men were to destroy their transport vehicles to prevent them falling into German hands. Royal Navy vessels would approach after sunset, collect as many men as they could board before break of dawn, and sail south at pace toward Egypt.

The official report has it that the behaviour of the men was beyond reproach through the anxious and difficult embarkation in the middle of the night of 26 April. Some of the Royal Navy officers who assisted were veterans of Dunkirk; they were surprised to see many of the Australians still carrying weapons and equipment with them on board.[8] With a disciplined embarkation the convoy was ready to leave at 3.40, able to make its way clear of the coast before sunrise. As if to farewell the Australians, German aircraft attacked the departing convoy as it cleared the coast; later in the morning, too, the Germans descended like vultures on the departing vessels. But no bombs hit their targets, and no damage was done.[9]

Johnny Peck and other men of the 2/7th no doubt allowed themselves a sigh of relief as their vessel, the troopship *Costa Rica*, sailed in convoy into the open waters of the Mediterranean. They were painfully aware that in the two awful weeks of their Greek campaign they had done precious little to halt the German advance, but they could at least count themselves extraordinarily lucky. When a tally was done, it was recognised that from their ranks only three men had been killed and 14 wounded in the Greek campaign. True, 71 were missing, thought to be among the 2065 Australians who would become POWs of the Germans. But for now, at least, the battalion was largely intact, and it had won itself the ability to fight the Germans again.[10]

Any sense of relief or good fortune quickly dissipated at about 2.20 that afternoon. The Germans were not quite done with the

Australians after all. Out of the sun three German bombers, their engines switched off, swooped silently towards the *Costa Rica* and her 2600 passengers. They were barely noticed until they dropped their bombs, not causing any loss of life, but crippling the vessel, which lost power and began taking on water.

The saviours in the precious 40 minutes which separated the attack from the *Costa Rica*'s sinking were the officers of the Royal Naval destroyers HMS *Defender*, HMS *Hero* and HMS *Hereward*, which one after the other pulled alongside the *Costa Rica* and allowed her passengers to leap safely or abseil onto the decks below. Time was of the essence, because *Costa Rica*'s boiler burst and a watery grave beckoned. By the time the last men abandoned her, the *Costa Rica* was listing so badly that they were able to step off the lower bridge of the stricken liner on to the forecastle of the last of the destroyers.[11]

As during their embarkation just hours earlier, the behaviour of the troops on board was exemplary. There was little hint of panic, even if a small group had responded to the initial strike on the vessel by breaking ranks, throwing life rafts overboard and jumping after them. They were fished from the water, but the rescue of the men still on board was hampered, because the destroyers could approach *Costa Rica* only from the starboard side.[12]

Having slept on deck and remained there, Johnny Peck had a bird's eye view of the hurried evacuation. He helped the naval personnel check that everyone had cleared the cabins and moved to positions where they could clamber aboard the destroyers, until he himself jumped onto the third and final rescue vessel.[13]

No lives were lost, but *Costa Rica*'s demise did not augur well. The troops had lost most of their weapons and their personal equipment, all of which they had been so eager to preserve when they embarked at Kalamata. Johnny Peck was one who had nothing on him but the pair of shorts in which he had been sleeping. This might not have been so important if, as Peck thought, they were on their way to Alexandria. Whether he had misunderstood the plans the officers had made for the 2/7th, or whether the sinking of *Costa Rica* had forced a rapid rethink, by the end of the day it was clear that Alexandria was not – or perhaps was no longer – their destination. That was Suda Bay on the island of Crete. Far from being offered the chance to regroup and rebuild in Egypt, Peck and his 2/7th, now unarmed and badly bruised but otherwise largely intact, were being cast from the frying pan and into the fire. Crete, it was assumed with very good reason, would be Hitler's next target.

3

THE BATTLE FOR CRETE

CRETE WOULD BE A TREASURED PRIZE, ITS SIZE AND LOCATION offering Hitler many rewards. To take it would not only weaken the British hold in the Mediterranean, it would strengthen his own lines of supply and communication into North Africa. Moreover, it would deprive the British of any capacity to trouble the imminent Axis strike into Soviet territory. Having overrun combined Greek and British forces on mainland Greece in just three weeks, Crete was the obvious next step, and the British knew it.

Over centuries Crete's insularity alone presented potential invaders with a number of challenges, as did its topography. Nonetheless, history had shown it was not impregnable, and over

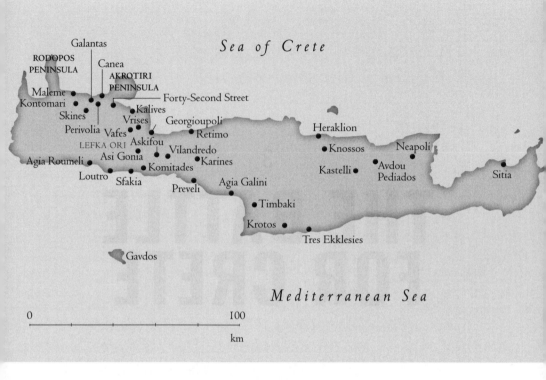

Crete in 1941

many millennia – dating back to the Bronze Age civilisation of the Minoans and their palace at Knossos – peoples from other parts of the Mediterranean had made their homes on the island and lived with changing levels of animosity among the Cretans. More recently, in 1669, the Ottomans had conquered the island and established a regime which by the 19th century provoked numerous bloody uprisings against foreign occupation. Though the Ottoman presence was formally ended in 1908 when Crete declared its union with Greece, the memory of living under the oppression of foreign rule was deeply etched in the Cretan psyche, as German forces were about to discover.

Crete is long and thin, running east–west across the Mediterranean, a series of large peninsulas protruding from its northern coast. Along much of that coast runs a narrow coastal plain which gives way to hills and then a central plain. Atop that plain is a central range with mountain peaks over 2000 metres in height. Imposing a grand presence over the western end of the island are the Lefka Ori, the White Mountains, their peaks capped in snow for much of the year. Along much of the southern coast of the island, the mountain range plunges precipitously into the Libyan Sea.

The major centres of Crete's population in World War II, as today, were on the north coast. In the west was Canea, further east Retimo, and further east still the largest town of all, Heraklion. All of them had picturesque harbours, enduring legacies of the Venetian presence in pre-Ottoman times. For large-scale shipping, however, the favoured port was in the sheltered expanse of Suda Bay, separated from Canea by the narrow stem of the Akrotiri Peninsula. All three major centres also possessed airfields. In the cases of Retimo and Heraklion, they were not far removed from the towns, but the airfield which serviced Canea was a significant distance to the west at Maleme. To gain control of those three airfields, along with the major port at Suda Bay, would be the obvious goals for any invading force. That, too, the British well knew.

The debacle of the Greek mainland notwithstanding, the British were determined to prevent Crete falling into German hands. Churchill issued a characteristically pugnacious message to General Wavell at GHQ Middle East in Cairo. 'It seems clear,' the British prime minister predicted darkly, 'that a heavy airborne attack by German troops and bombers will soon be made on Crete … It ought to be a fine opportunity for killing the parachute troops. The island must be defended.'[1]

On all points Churchill's logic was flawless. Yet, as on the mainland, in the case of Crete there was a yawning chasm between a resolve to defend the island and the provision of resources to achieve that end. There had been a British military presence on Crete since October 1940, when a naval base was established at Suda Bay; from the end of March 1941 it was bolstered by the arrival of formations of the Mobile Naval Base Defence Organisation, but they alone had little hope of repelling an invasion of any scale.[2]

After the arrival of evacuees from Greece from 23 April, there was a flurry of activity to convert the island into the 'Fortress Crete' Churchill had demanded. The centrepiece in the new defence plan was the forces snatched in the nick of time from the evacuation ports on the mainland. Those who were not sent to Egypt began arriving at Suda Bay from 23 April; among 42 000 troops sent from the Greek mainland were some 6500 Australians, including Johnny Peck and his 2/7th Battalion.[3]

Placed in overall command of the combined Australian, New Zealand, British and Greek elements of 'Creforce' was the New Zealander General Bernard Freyberg. Freyberg possessed a Victoria Cross from World War I and a reputation for calmness and resolution under pressure. To hold Crete he would need those qualities in spades, but he would also have to give careful thought to how he best disposed the troops and the equipment Wavell could spare for him. In doing so Freyberg confronted some major challenges, not least the condition of his men. The rapid retreat in Greece against an overwhelming opposition, followed by the hurried evacuations, had done little for morale. Moreover, the casualties suffered in Greece and the parting of evacuees' ways in the Mediterranean – some to Egypt, others to Crete – meant that many of the units were no longer intact; a patchwork of ad hoc formations had to be hastily threaded together. What was available of the 2/2nd and 2/3rd Australian Battalions, for example, was thrown together to become the 16 Brigade Composite Battalion. Rations were scarce, as was anything approaching decent accommodation. After disembarking the already exhausted and undernourished men had to march to dispersal areas, where they found what shelter they could under trees. Those with enough energy formed scrounging parties to go in search of food, while others sought to re-establish contact with friends not seen for days, to swap stories and await further orders. To receive those orders, too, was no easy matter, since the communications system on the island was in a parlous state. Lacking wireless sets, the commander of the Australian forces in Creforce, Brigadier George Vasey, relied on public phones for contact with his superior.[4]

Weaponry, too, was sorely wanting in both quality and quantity. Much had been abandoned prior to embarkation in Greece. Freyberg himself noted that the situation was much worse than he had feared; indeed, 'it was not unusual to find that the men had no arms or equipment, no plates, knives, forks or spoons, and they ate and drank from bully beef or cigarette tins.'[5] A particularly grave deficiency was in the area of heavy weaponry. Some of the guns were Italian weapons recycled from the Western Desert; as many of them were supplied without sights, gunners were expected to aim by peering down the barrel. There were six Matilda tanks, but none had yet been fully refitted – as became tragically evident when the defence of Crete began and they broke down.[6] As for air support, the Australians' dry quip that 'RAF' stood for 'Rare as Fairies' was as true on Crete as on the Greek mainland.

Against all that, Freyberg had one important advantage

over the Germans, and that was in intelligence. The British had cracked German codes and were able to decrypt German wireless messages; the decrypts were known as 'Ultra'. The British were keen that Germans should not learn of 'Ultra', and so the circle of the initiated was kept small. Tasked with the defence of Crete, Freyberg joined this privileged elite, and with the aid of 'Ultra' he gleaned a good deal about the scale and nature of the planned German assault. German intelligence, in contrast, was poor, so that the invading forces had limited knowledge of the size and disposition of the well-concealed defensive forces being set in place. Ordered to remain under cover even as German planes appeared overhead in advance of an invasion, the defensive forces clung to the hope they could lull the invaders into thinking the island was theirs for the taking.

Freyberg prepared for two kinds of invasion, one by sea and one by air. His mistake – perhaps the most crucial one of all – was to misjudge the prospect of an amphibious landing. He had failed to appreciate that the boldness of the German plans lay in the focus on an airborne assault, which would make the initial strikes. Naval forces were assigned a secondary role in which they would consolidate and support the assaults staged from the air. Freyberg seems also to have underestimated the capacity of the Royal Navy to block the combined Italian/German naval force that was to support the initial airborne invasion. And that all meant that in his preparations Freyberg allocated precious manpower and materiel to stretches of coast where he guessed the invaders were most likely to land. In reality, those beaches should have been the least of his worries.

Freyberg disposed the roughly 40 000 men of Creforce along a number of north-coast beaches, around Suda Bay, and at the three airfields. To the western zone around Maleme and its airfield he sent the 5 New Zealand Brigade under the command of Brigadier James Hargest. It was the strongest of that brigade's battalions, namely 22 New Zealand Battalion, that was entrusted with securing the airfield.[7] In that goal it was to draw on support from a couple of anti-aircraft batteries, one of them Australian. Other forces in that zone were positioned in and around Canea and the port just to its east at Suda Bay, while others dug in behind the beaches.[8]

In the central sector forces were allocated wisely to the defence of the airfield at Retimo. The senior officer there was Lieutenant-Colonel Ian Campbell of 2/1 Battalion. Campbell's focus was fully on the airfield, which his men kept in plain view as they dug in. And that in itself was no easy task; with a shortage of picks and shovels they resorted to bayonets and tin hats.[9] Nearby was the West Australian 2/11 Battalion, positioned so as to give itself a view over, and unimpeded access to, the airfield. As for Peck's 2/7 Battalion, it too was in the central sector, but it was west of Retimo in and around the town of Georgioupoli. With a long beach stretching off the east, it seemed plausible that the Germans would attempt to land troops there by sea, in which case it would be 2/7th's job to ensure that the invading force got no further than the beach. It was in Georgioupoli, too, that the Australians' commander George Vasey set up his brigade headquarters.

Heraklion's airfield was on its eastern outskirts. British forces formed the core of Heraklion's garrison, but the 2/4 Australian Battalion was also sent to bolster defences there. Whether they arrived by sea or air, it was crucial that the Germans not be allowed to gain a beachhead. If that was achieved, then the lesson of the mainland was that there would be no stopping them.

German planning to capture Crete began as early as 15 April, when German forces were pouring through mainland Greece.[10] Within a week the plan had gained Hitler's approval, and within days thereafter – on 25 April – Hitler had issued a directive. There would be no turning back.[11]

Designated Operation Merkur, the invasion was audacious in its very conception. General Kurt Student would land the para-troops of his elite XI Fliegerkorps on the island, taking the defend-ers by surprise. Their main targets would be the three airfields at Maleme, Retimo and Heraklion. With the airfields secured, the invasion force would be consolidated by the arrival of an Austrian mountain division – a force which had already been deployed with great success in storming the Metaxas Line on the mainland.[12] Further reinforcement would then be delivered amphibiously, a fleet of vessels bearing German forces having been sent from the mainland. All of this would be carried out under the protection of the Luftwaffe, which would rule the skies over Crete just as it had done over the mainland.

The plan was bold because everything hinged on the German ability to take at least one of the airfields. Without an airfield, the invasion risked quick and embarrassing failure.

The invasion was prepared through several days of bombing of defensive positions around the airfields and Suda Bay. The date for the invasion was set at 20 May. Thanks to 'Ultra', Freyberg, perched in his headquarters on the heights separating Canea and Suda Bay, was not in the least surprised when that day arrived. He was taking his breakfast when the Luftwaffe appeared above the horizon, prompting him to grunt, examine his watch and remark on the Germans' punctuality.[13]

On that first day, in waves of attack that appeared over the northern horizon, the Germans launched their assault on the airfields and Suda Bay. Troops were delivered by parachutes and gliders towed by transport aircraft. In all sectors they received a terrible shock. The island was much better defended than their intelligence had indicated. The period from which their parachutes billowed above them through to their landing on Cretan soil was brief, as they were dropped from as low an altitude as possible, but it was one of awful vulnerability. Defensive forces were able to pick them off mercilessly as they fell toward the ground; for some of the Australians the bloody episode had the bizarre quality of a duck shoot. The defenders were instructed to allow for the invaders' rapid descent by aiming at their feet. As a result, many of the Germans hit the ground as bullet-riddled corpses, their parachutes settling over them as silken shrouds. The occupants of the gliders fared little better. Even if they survived until landing, they were quickly picked off by those who had observed their graceful descent. On that first day alone 1856 paratroopers lost their lives in a bloodbath.[14]

At Retimo Australians stood in the thick of the defensive action. There the attack came in the afternoon, some 160 Junkers clouding the sky to the north to stage their runs. The greatest responsibility for halting the invasion fell to Ian Campbell, who commanded not only his own 2/1 Battalion but also the West Australian 2/11 Battalion and the other assembled forces. He had disposed them and their anti-aircraft weapons sagely, with a clear priority of defending the airfield. The Australians took their first swipes at the aircraft before they had ejected their human payloads. The enemy was so close that the Germans could be seen inside the lumbering Junkers, preparing to jump. At a little over 100 metres above the ground, the aeroplanes were within range of even small arms fire. One of the platoon commanders of 2/1 Battalion watched as paratroopers jumped from already stricken planes, their chutes set alight as they passed through the flames streaming from the Junkers.[15]

Those who reached the ground alive fought ferociously, but they encountered equally vigorous opposition from the Australian, Greek and Cretan defenders perched on the high ground. The defenders could see precisely where the Germans landed and moved rapidly to deal with them, whether individually or in hastily collected units. In this way the defenders held their ground, and the airfield. As the evening set in, there were pockets of paratroopers scattered nearby which would still need attention, but an impressive victory had been won.

At Heraklion it was a similar story. Here the Australian 2/4 Battalion worked together with British forces under the command of Brigadier BH Chappel. As at Retimo, the Germans opened proceedings with an attack from the air, designed to silence the anti-aircraft batteries, and then the Junkers moved in to deliver the paratroopers to their allotted targets. While the Germans had some success in Heraklion itself, the airfield was kept safe, as the defensive forces counter-attacked with speed and determination.[16]

It was the Maleme airfield that provided the major headache for Crete's defenders. Here the attack occurred early and with a heavy concentration of forces. Of all the Cretan airfields, it was at Maleme that the defenders were least favourably disposed to protect a crucial asset.[17] Early in the morning Luftwaffe bombers and fighters pounded the anti-aircraft batteries. When the Junkers appeared, some of them with gliders in tow, it was evident that the early fireworks had not been just another softening-up operation but an immediate prelude to invasion. The sight of enemy aircraft darkening the morning sky and spitting out their human payloads provoked awe and astonishment among those who had the dubious pleasure of observing it. One of them, the New Zealander Eric Davies, later recalled, 'We thought it was bullshit, we couldn't see how they could land thousands like that.'[18]

Indeed, at Maleme as elsewhere, not all of them did land, at least not alive, and in this sector too hundreds were shot as they dangled invitingly from their chutes. But enough of them did make safe landings in the vicinity of Maleme to place the airfield under grave threat, posing a huge challenge to 5 New Zealand Brigade. Alas, much of that brigade had been disposed to defend the beaches east of Maleme in anticipation of a seaborne invasion. The task of holding the airfield was left largely to Leslie Andrew's 22 Battalion. A brutal portent was delivered to Andrew in the Luftwaffe's early morning raid, which killed several of his men and wounded him. 'A wee piece of bomb', he later recalled, had lodged in his temple; it was 'bloody hot and bled a bit'.[19] When gliders later landed in a dry river bed west of the airfield, a platoon of Andrew's men was quickly overwhelmed with superior manpower and firepower, allowing the Germans direct access to the airfield.

All was not yet lost, since the New Zealand 22 Battalion commanded a view of the airfield and a capacity to hold it under fire. But with each passing hour Hill 107 became more isolated, and other defensive positions became heavily compromised. The New Zealanders did what they could to fight back. With communications in a parlous state, much of the initiative was left to local commanders, who grasped vaguely the importance of their efforts but lacked the ability to coordinate them. By the middle of the night, reinforcements having failed to arrive, communications both to his forward companies and other New Zealand battalions broken,

Andrew made the fateful decision to withdraw to the east. With that the Maleme airfield was delivered to the Germans, and they exploited the gift for all it was worth.

Through all this Peck and the 2/7 Battalion sat frustratingly idle, well aware of the raids that occurred throughout the day of 20 May to their east at Retimo and to their west around Suda Bay, Canea and, most vitally, Maleme. There had been no seaborne invasion, and therefore nothing to occupy them around Georgioupoli. The Germans attempted to send reinforcements to Crete with the aid of Italian and Greek vessels loaded with weapons and mountain troops, but that invasion armada was intercepted and brutally mauled by the Royal Navy, fully expecting them, on the nights of 21 and 22 May. Peck later recalled hearing the nocturnal rumblings and seeing over the northern horizon the flashes of the vicious sea battle being played out with great loss of German lives. What remained of the would-be invaders limped back to the Greek mainland; some of the dead would eventually wash up on Crete's shores.[20]

With the attempt to land troops by sea doomed, and with defenders stubbornly holding the airfields at Retimo and Heraklion, the outcome of the battle of Crete hinged entirely on the fate of the Maleme airfield. To save Crete, the New Zealanders needed to reclaim it, just as it was crucial for the Germans to hold it. Only there could mountain troops be landed to aid the decimated, exhausted paratroopers. Early on the morning of 21 May Freyberg learned of the withdrawal of the New Zealanders during the night and devised a plan to reclaim the airfield. The withdrawn 22 Battalion was to be inserted into a solid defensive line between 23 and 21 Battalions. That night, avoiding the attention of the Luftwaffe, the New Zealand 28 Battalion was to retake Hill 107, the point which controlled the airfield.[21] The 28 Battalion, better known as the 'Maori Battalion' because it was comprised solely of Maoris, had already established a fearsome reputation in Africa, so it was hoped that with the support of 20 NZ Battalion it would loosen the German grip on that vital patch of high ground.

The plan at last involved Peck's battalion, albeit indirectly, because it required sending the 2/7th some 30 kilometres west to relieve the NZ 20 Battalion, which would march west toward Maleme to accompany the Maoris in attack. On Crete movement over large distances is difficult at the best of times, but for the 2/7th Battalion this westward shuffle was painstaking. Transport vehicles were scarce, and any movement during daylight hours attracted the attention of the Luftwaffe. In these circumstances the movement had to take place in fits and starts. Had they had their way, the battalion and its commander Theo Walker would have been sent directly to Maleme to join the counter-attack.[22] Instead, they moved to their allocated position near Canea, arriving there so late on the night of 21 May that the New Zealand 20 Battalion did not reach the Maori position until 3 am the next day. About half an hour later, well behind schedule, the most vital battle of the entire Cretan campaign began.[23]

One company of 20 Battalion pushed west, following the coast, and got as far as the airfield, apparently taking the Germans by surprise.[24] On its southern flank, another company of 20 Battalion pushed as far as the village of Pirgos, but there was halted by resolute German resistance. Further south again, the Maoris suffered the same fate, so that by the time day broke they had been pinned down, at best only able to hold the gains they had made. Similarly, two companies from the New Zealand 21 Battalion attempting to claw their way onto Hill 107 met fierce resistance and fell short of their goal.[25] By the afternoon of 22 May it was clear that the counterattack had failed, a fact underlined by the continued landing of German aircraft – and fresh troops – at the nearby airfield.[26] In a tacit concession of defeat, on the evening of 22 May Freyberg withdrew the forces at Maleme to a line further east, conceding the airfield to the Germans.[27]

The fighting was by no means over, not in any of the sectors. Cretans, too, many of them locals lacking military training, joined the fray, alarmed that their island faced the prospect of an indeterminate period of foreign rule. The passion with which they fought incurred the wrath of the Wehrmacht, which soon staged the first of the vicious acts of reprisal which became a hallmark of the German occupation.

Ultimately the commitment of the Cretans and of Freyberg's defenders was no match for the German presence on the island, which swelled by the hour after the Maleme airfield had been seized. Though the forces around Retimo and Heraklion's defences held firm, in the north-west the defenders' presence was confined to a small arc around Canea and Suda Bay. Peck and his 2/7th, for their part, spent three days engaging German forces around Galatas, just east of Maleme, hoping desperately to turn the tide of battle.[28] Faced with unrelenting German attention from the air, the 2/7th pulled back to an area south-east of Galatas on the night of 23–24 May.

With the Maleme airfield to the west now firmly in German hands and allowing a steady influx of German reinforcements, a further retreat to the east was just a matter of time. After holding a position at the head of Prison Valley, they soon pulled back to a new defensive line which ran from the south-western edge of Suda Bay to the village of Tsikalaria.[29]

Even as they dug in to await the arrival of Germans from the west, the fate of Crete was already decided. As early as the evening of 24 May, with the military situation parlous, supplies scarce and the Luftwaffe's presence unrelenting, Freyberg reached an awful but inescapable conclusion: 'I really knew at this stage that there were two alternatives, defeat in the field and capture or withdrawal.'[30] At 9.30 am on 26 May Freyberg sent a cable to Wavell in Cairo, laying out the inevitability of defeat.[31] From that time Freyberg's major task was to perform a retreat following the model provided just weeks earlier on mainland Greece, and leading to the same outcome – evacuation.

Two evacuation points were nominated. The first was at Heraklion, where there was a generous harbour. From there in a series of night-time operations the Royal Navy could embark the forces which had fought valiantly in defence of the city and its airfield. The second was Sfakia, a small fishing village on the south coast of the island. It would be the evacuation point for men in the area around Canea and Suda Bay and east as far as Georgioupoli and Retimo. The plan was that defenders from these sectors would converge at a point just south of Suda Bay. From there they would follow a road that led south across the island, leading up onto the central plain, with the White Mountains to their east. That plain extended almost as far as the southern coast; the final descent to the sea, however, was precipitous and had to be negotiated along goat tracks or through the narrow gorge which commenced at the village of Imbros, feeding down to the village of Komitades. From Komitades Sfakia was within striking distance to the west. And from there landing craft would snatch the men from the village's pebbled beach and take them to Royal Navy vessels offshore. As at Heraklion, the boarding of the vessels had to be completed under the cover of darkness, so that by daybreak the Royal Navy would be well clear of Crete, to avoid the attention of the Luftwaffe.

As on mainland Greece, the success of the evacuation depended heavily on the ability to hold the German forces at bay. A first line was drawn just west of Canea, where the 2/7th dug in with the Australian 2/8 Battalion and other forces. But the exposure to heavy German fire proved perilous, and the Australians' left flank was exposed. Two of Peck's mates in his section, Steve Warner and Arnold Newnham, were killed by bombs exploding in their trenches. Of Warner, it seems, there was nothing left, but Newnham's corpse, thrown several metres into the air before landing on a pile of dirt, was intact and was hurriedly placed in a groundsheet for later burial.[32]

Before the day was out a further withdrawal was ordered, this time back to the east of Canea, to a line just south of Suda Bay's western tip. The line was named '42nd Street' for the 42nd Field Company of Royal Engineers who had camped there earlier.[33] For the locals it was Tsikalarion Road, though in reality it was no more than a dirt track which cut across the strip of coastal plain connecting Suda's port to Canea. To extend eastward their hold on the island, and to block the evacuation of Creforce, the Germans needed to cross 42nd Street.

The defensive line consisted at its northern end of Peck's 2/7 Battalion and 2/8 Battalion. On their southern flank were the 21, 28, 19 and 22 Battalions of 5 NZ Brigade, who had also fallen back from the area around Canea and then dug themselves in with the Australians along 42nd Street. On the morning of 27 May the commanding officers of the Anzac battalions agreed that if the enemy made close contact in that position, their forces would open fire and charge. Orders were given to fix bayonets.[34] Walker's batman noted, 'When this order went out it seemed to lift the tension that had been hanging to us for the past few days. The time had come when we were going to show Jerry a few tricks.'[35]

Peck and his C Company waited anxiously in the line at 42nd Street. The company commander, Major Walter Miller, sent forward a patrol under Lieutenant Beverley McGeoch to locate and observe the enemy. The plan was not to engage at first sight but to observe closely and wait until the Germans would be too close to escape a surprise confrontation.[36]

The enemy force making its way east toward 42nd Street was the First Battalion of the 141st Gebirgsjäger Regiment. Its reconnaissance must have been poor, because it stumbled quite unwittingly into the Anzac line, manned by soldiers who were well prepared to make a stubborn stand.[37] The precise order of the events that followed is difficult to establish, but it seems that New Zealand and Australian troops launched into battle at a similar time. The Maori charge frightened the unsuspecting mountain troops. One witness observed: 'Section after section of the enemy was overrun as the Maoris fanned out and swept around them and then went in for the kill. Some used rifle and bayonet, some threw grenades, and some rushed forward with spandaus at the hip while their mates ran alongside carrying the belt containers.'[38] Of those who had not managed to take flight, close to 100 lay either dead or wounded.[39]

To the Maoris' right were two companies of the Australian 2/7th, including Johnny Peck's C Company, and they too locked horns with the startled Germans. The Australians' commanding officer, Theo Walker, used the cover of an olive grove to allow the enemy to advance within short range, and then the Australians attacked. One source has it that the Australians produced a scream even more spine chilling than the Maori effort and the sight of the Maori Battalion charging with vocal accompaniment sent the whole line surging forward. The forward elements of the enemy did not wait. They threw away their packs and ran. They were shot from the hip and those who hid in the scrub were bayoneted. Some mortar teams that tried to get into action were over-run and dealt with.[40]

Reg Saunders, an Indigenous man from the Gunditjmara people of western Victoria, recalled many years later how he dealt with an enemy soldier appearing in his sights: 'I saw a German soldier standing up in clear view … he was my first sure kill … I can remember feeling for a moment that it was just like shooting a kangaroo, just as remote. After that many Huns appeared and for them and for us it was pretty confused.' In that confusion it became a bloody affair fought at close quarters. It was no longer shots but bayonet thrusts which did the damage. Saunders said, 'We were all obsessed with this mad race to slaughter with the bayonets. It wasn't like killing kangaroos anymore. When we got there they were real men … excited like us and some of them terribly frightened.'[41]

Johnny Peck, too, engaged the enemy when it overcame its initial shock and summoned the will and wherewithal to respond:

They didn't just turn and run, they fought back. You have to be ferocious. 'Come on, you bastards! Let's have a go at you!' I got a bayonet through the arm. Hand-to-hand combat was very frightening. You know without a shadow of a doubt that if you make a fraction of a mistake, then you're dead. The German knew it and I knew it. It wasn't a question of,

'Put up your hands'. No quarter was asked or given. You're dead or you're alive, and if you're alive you move on to the next one. He was fairly big, bigger than me, and he got me through the arm but he was dead very soon afterwards. The German bayonets were nowhere near as long as ours – ours were 18 inches long. I never felt anything, not even relief.[42]

In the heat of the battle Peck felt no pain, the pumping of adrenaline more than compensating for the loss of blood. With momentum secured through the first brutal contact, there could be no letting up. The Germans kept running, and the Australians kept running after them.

Peck had been involved in close fighting at Bardia, but he had not used his bayonet there. It was exhausting work. Though they had practised it in training, nothing could have fully prepared him for this. At training they had been told to scream as they wielded their bayonets, but the instinct that guided him in battle kept him silent. The screaming came later, emanating from the ragged bodies strewn across the field when the battle was over.[43]

Eventually fatigue set in, and the Anzacs' commanders, realising that in their dedication to the pursuit their forces had dispersed, called the men back. Peck recalls the disappointment of the moment: 'The commanders were shit-scared because their troops were scattered everywhere. We were called back to where we had started and we weren't very pleased about it. We wanted to keep them on the run.'[44] The end of the battle was signalled by the sound of a Vickers machine gun delivered to the front line by Lieutenant Wilson Bolton of the 2/1st Machine-gun Battalion. Within moments its burst of fire accounted for many more dead than the frenzied stabbing of bayonets had achieved earlier.

When the dust settled and pulses slowed it was time to count the cost of the battle on both sides. The Anzac forces estimated that some 200 German troops had been killed, and just three taken prisoner; the Germans for their part reached the more modest figure of 121.[45] In Peck's 2/7th Battalion ten were dead and 28 wounded, while the New Zealanders counted 14 Maori dead.[46] Some time later the German commander told Theo Walker – by then a POW – of his admiration for the men who had given his paratroop battalion such a rude shock: 'They are the best troops my men have met. That counter-attack was the only real fight we had.'[47]

Though for sheer bloodletting and release of tension the Battle of 42nd Street would not be replicated, a pattern was set for the following days. With evacuation orders confirmed, fighting units would perform that most delicate operation of buying time by engaging the enemy, while at the same time hoping that they, too, might once more slip the ever-tightening German noose. The trick was to form a line, engage the enemy, and then fall back to a new line when German forces threatened to overwhelm or out-flank them.

That was the challenge set for the 2/7th, which alternated with New Zealanders in forming the Allies' rearguard. As if engaging elite and impeccably trained and equipped German troops were not hard enough, the task was made all the more difficult by a lack of food, water and shelter, as well as by the need to negotiate an unfamiliar landscape. While there was one crude road head-ing south across the island's spine, it stopped several kilometres short of the south coast and its single embarkation point. The skies above were the preserve of the Germans and the Germans alone. Through all that, the men of the 2/7th knew that the number of

Allied soldiers to escape the island would depend in very large part on their skill and tenacity in slowing the German advance. Beyond that, their own survival as a fighting force was at stake.

4

STRANDED AT SFAKIA

AMONG THE WEARY MASSES FLEEING SOUTH ACROSS CRETE'S mountainous spine were the walking wounded, including some with amputated arms, desperate to escape the Germans' grasp one more time. They made their way up the foothills toward the central plain, following paths that led them through the village of Askifou, its well drunk dry, and then they struck onward toward Imbros. From that point there was no road on which to make the steep descent toward the nominated evacuation point, the tiny cove in the village of Sfakia. The best option was to enter the Imbros Gorge, which offered both protection from enemy aircraft and some possibility of moistening parched throats. At the bottom of the gorge was the village of Komitades, and it was in the gullies, groves and caves around Komitades that the men gathered to await word that they should complete the final stage of their journey onto the beach in Sfakia.

Many of those men were unarmed base troops. They lacked the leadership and discipline of fighting soldiers; their mounting anxiety at the prospect that they might be left behind led on occasion to ill-discipline. One officer of Peck's 2/7th Battalion, James Carstairs, gave vent to his frustration at the chaos confronting his infantrymen as they approached Sfakia. 'The whole area', Carstairs wrote, 'was blocked by a teeming horde of leaderless troops. Tommies, Greeks, oddments from far and wide, all milling around in total disorder.'[1] Challenges mounted in arranging a smooth, unpanicked evacuation, since both the officers and their men knew all too well that the Germans were hot on their heels. Adding to the complexities of the evacuation was the reality that the boarding of men onto landing craft had to take place from a small, unfamiliar beach in the depths of night. That process had to be completed well before dawn, so that the launches could deliver their loads to the vessels anchored offshore, which in turn needed to put themselves out of the range of Luftwaffe by first light.

Through all this Peck's C Company maintained discipline to the very last, covering pass after pass, giving their chasers the impression that an overly hasty advance would be met by the kind of determined resistance the Germans had encountered to their horror at 42nd Street. The more stubborn and resolute their defence, the greater the number of men who could be evacuated. Yet an overly ambitious defensive ploy risked the possibility that the rearguard would be outflanked or overrun by an enemy whose strength was growing by the hour.

By the early morning hours of 29 May the rearguard units had reached the village of Imbros, atop the escarpment that plunged down to the sea. Here they were ordered to draw another line, attempting to hold the Germans before Imbros while the evacuations continued from the beach below. Having alternated with the New Zealanders in executing rearguard duties, chance had it that the Australians would be the last to play that role as the evacuations were carried out.[2] Their job done, so the plan demanded, the men of the rearguard would themselves descend to the beach at Sfakia, board the landing craft and live to fight another day.

All this they would need to do on almost empty stomachs. After two days devoid of rations, they now received just two biscuits per man and a tin of bully beef to be shared among six. Reg Saunders, also in Peck's C Company in the 2/7th, described the retreat like this:

> For two days, we ate no food of any kind. I believe some
> boys came to a stream, and literally fell into it with all their
> gear. Some drank so much that they had to be lifted out. As
> we waited above Sphakia, a few of the lucky ones caught
> chickens and ate them raw…entrails and all. Our bunch were
> carrying cans of bully beef and biscuits, but for the last couple
> of days we were without water – and the result was that we
> just couldn't eat.[3]

On 31 May, with their supplies of food, water and ammunition desperately low, the 2/7th was ordered to hold on for another 24 hours. Theo Walker did what he could to boost sagging morale, but his men all knew that their position was no longer tenable. At about 9.30 in the evening the 2/7th began withdrawing from

Imbros, commencing their steep descent towards the coast in the hope of evacuation that very evening. It had to be done speedily, and their commanding officers drove them to the point of exhaustion. From Komitades at the base of the gorge the men struck west toward Sfakia. Eventually, after traversing the unremittingly rocky terrain in pitch darkness, the column approached the beach at Sfakia and began the final descent. Here the challenge of staying together was compounded by stragglers, men who for whatever reason had become detached from their units. Word was out that only intact units would be evacuated, so some of these desperate men sought to break into units of the 2/7th. The platoon sergeants impressed on their men that such impostors were to be rejected; that each man had to know the man in front.[4]

Peck's company was among the last to join the silent masses huddled around the fishing village. The order they had been given was strict and clear: 'Defend the beachhead at any cost but don't provoke an attack which could carry the Germans through to the massed thousands of men hiding in the scrub and among the rocks awaiting the ships.'[5] C Company had also been assured that, their job done, they too as valued fighting forces would be guaranteed their places on the evacuation vessels. 'Last in the line, first in the boats.' That, at least, was the promise.[6]

Arriving at the beach, boots and gear muffled with socks or shirts, Peck and his company joined the rear of the embarkation column. Local guides escorted them down the final slope, urging their charges to keep moving and not lose their place in the line. The urgency of the situation was obvious to everyone, yet through the frustration of the final shuffle towards the last of the landing vessels, Peck's company stuck together.

Not until 3 o'clock in the morning did Peck feel wet shingles under his feet; ahead of him in the dark the head of his column was being loaded onto a barge, while some members of HQ Company squeezed on board. Then another barged moved in, but strangely, Peck noticed, it was not being loaded. A naval beach officer made his way down the line, quietly breaking the awful news: 'Sorry, lads, that's all for the *Skylark*.'[7]

In Reg Saunders' memory he was less than 20 metres from the barge as it pulled away. Among those left on the land was the battalion's CO Theo Walker. One version of the events has it that Walker was among the last of those loaded onto the last of the barges but then chose to step back onto land to stay with his men, if necessary to accompany them into captivity.[8] His men had shown precisely the kind of patience and discipline that had seen them survive the sinking of the *Costa Rica*, but this time their virtue remained cruelly unrewarded. When the Royal Navy delivered its precious human cargo to Alexandria on 2 June, a count revealed that only 72 men from the 2/7th had made it off Crete. Just three months earlier 759 of them, brimming with optimism, had left Alexandria for Greece.[9]

With the departure of that landing vessel in the early morning of 1 June, Theo Walker became the most senior of the officers left in Sfakia. With that came the grave responsibility of negotiating surrender with the Germans, whose arrival was imminent. With his adjutant, Walker made his way back to Komitades, where he surrendered to an Austrian officer. One version of events has it that the Austrian asked Campbell in English, 'What are you doing here, Australia?', to which the Australian replied, 'One might ask what you are doing here, Austria?' 'We are all Germans,' was the retort.[10]

Before leaving his men in Sfakia, Walker had given them some cause for hope. The word he passed on to those gathered forlornly around the village was that they could either await the Germans' arrival, and inevitably enter captivity, or they could strike off in groups in the hope of picking up a boat to spirit them across the Libyan Sea to North Africa.[11]

Neither option was palatable. Surrender was a scenario for which army training had not prepared the men, but which many must have contemplated anxiously before the Royal Navy had whisked them from the Greek mainland. Having endured a tortured trek across the island enduring heat, thirst and hunger, the very thought of a journey back to the north – as prisoners of war – filled the men with unalloyed dread. Yet for most at Sfakia, and especially for the wounded and the utterly exhausted, it was the only realistic option. The rearguard units, including Peck's, had ceased fighting. It was now just a matter of time until the Germans made their own way down the Imbros Gorge and from the heights above Sfakia to declare to the huddled masses who remained there that their war was over. Doctor Leslie Le Souef, the senior Australian medical officer on Crete, surveyed the mood among the men as they awaited the arrival of the enemy. There was, he wrote, 'a certain sullen resignation mixed with consternation and incredulity on every face'.[12]

Of the 6500 Allied forces who fell into German hands at the beginning of June 1941, the biggest contingent came from Sfakia on the very first day of that month.[13] Marched back across the island by their new masters, they were installed in makeshift POW camps until, eventually, they would be transported to the Greek mainland and then Germany itself, where they would serve out their war.

The instinct of those who had not yet succumbed to exhaustion or a sense of utter hopelessness was to grasp at any opportunity, no matter how slim, to retain their freedom. These men immediately faced a series of seemingly insuperable challenges. They needed to feed themselves so as to gather the energy to escape Sfakia before they were trapped. Then they had to find vessels that might carry them as far as Libya or perhaps Egypt, and in doing so they needed to call on seafaring skills of a kind that very few possessed. And if they managed to launch some form of pilfered vessel from a location along the Cretan coast, they would need to avoid the attention of the Luftwaffe as they undertook a voyage of hundreds of kilometres.

Long though the odds of success were, a number of hastily assembled groups managed to bring it off. One of them included some men of Peck's 2/7 Battalion in a mixed party under the command of Major R Garrett of the Royal Marines, who had located an abandoned landing craft. Apart from close to a hundred British officers and soldiers, 25 Australians, eight New Zealanders, three Palestinians, a Maltese and a Greek were loaded onto it. An Australian officer was able to start one of the vessel's engines, so that it pushed out to sea on the morning of 1 June. With heat haze inhibiting the Luftwaffe's ability to detect small vessels, the barge reached the island of Gavdos – Europe's most southerly point – and from there eventually made its way, despite multiple mechanical failures, to the Libyan coast behind British lines. Another landing craft commandeered in Sfakia and skippered by an Australian private, Harry Richards, with some 60 men on board, managed to reach Egypt.[14]

With those landing craft gone, the possibilities of a seaborne exit from Crete – at least from Sfakia – were reduced to next to nothing. Would-be sailors needed to travel to other coastal villages and seize Cretan vessels, large or small. That option demanded a rapid response to a stark choice. With German forces approaching from the north, should the men seek their fortune by tracing the Cretan coastline to the east or the west?

The route west presented seemingly insurmountable challenges, because there was not even the narrowest littoral plain in that direction, and only in places was there a narrow beach, which repeatedly gave way to steep and craggy rock-faces. Nonetheless, at least one group ventured in that direction, perhaps counting on the German assessment that this was the least plausible escape route. Its goal was the village of Agia Roumeli, roughly 15 kilometres west of Sfakia. If no vessel was to be found there, the hope was that the men might be able to stage an evacuation from there with the help of the Royal Navy. The ruggedness of that stretch of coast forced them to strike inland to the north-west, winding their way upward to a plateau on which the village of Anopolis was located. From there they headed directly west, crossing the Aradena Gorge, before descending once more to the coast and finally to Agia Roumeli. Alas, there was no vessel to be found, and no hint that the Royal Navy was seeking to replicate its operations from Sfakia. The members of that group eventually had little choice but to walk up the Samaria Gorge – the longest in Europe – and seek refuge in the isolated highlands of western Crete.[15]

The route east from Sfakia at least offered easier terrain. Most were familiar with the few kilometres that led them back to Komitades at the base of the Imbros Gorge. The danger, though, was that in making their way back towards the east, they would encounter German troops pouring out from the base of the gorge. So if they were to avoid capture, they needed to strike quickly east beyond the gorge. For these men, too, the main hope was that the Royal Navy's retreat in the early hours of 1 June was a temporary setback, and new possibilities for evacuation would present themselves, though they could have no idea when or from where. Failing that, the highlands of central and eastern Crete offered prospects of finding refuge.

A group of men from the 2/7th, including Reg Saunders, was one of those heading east from Sfakia, skirting cautiously past Komitades and seeking refuge toward day's end in an olive grove. There were about 15 of them, who with filled water bottles and whatever rations they could scrounge hoped to slip away before the main body of Germans swooped on them. Their hopes of attracting the attention of the Royal Navy by flashing torches at night came to nothing. This group, under the command of their platoon sergeant Frank 'Blue' Reiter, resolved to travel back across the island to Suda Bay, where they had buried cans of food that they had not been able to carry on their retreat.[16]

To travel in a large group presented difficulties. The larger the group, the more likely they were to be detected, and the more difficult it would be for locals to feed and accommodate them. As they made their way north, the group disintegrated into pairings and groups of three. Fate treated all of them differently. Saunders, renowned for the speed with which he could move over even the most challenging terrain, reached his destination and its buried supplies quite soon. But as an Aboriginal man he faced the difficulty that it would be nigh impossible for him to pass himself off as a local. Later he hooked up with two other Australians – George Burgess and Les Vincent[17] – in the village of Lambini, 9 kilometres north-east of the monastery at Preveli. Here the people insisted that the Australians should eat with them in their homes, while living in hiding outside the village.[18]

There were perhaps a thousand men who took their chances

in this way, avoiding capture and harbouring a vague hope that at some point the opportunity to get off the island would present itself.[19] Among them were men who had never managed to make it to Sfakia in the first place. Others for one reason or another had failed to make it to the north-coast evacuation point at Heraklion, where the Royal Navy had embarked nearly 4000 men, only to be subjected to vicious attacks by German dive bombers – and heavy loss of life – soon after the vessels had left Heraklion harbour.

Among the men who missed out on evacuation were the Australians who had defended the airfield at Retimo. With communication lines west to Georgioupoli cut, they did not realise they were expected to disengage the enemy and join the exodus from the island. When they became aware that Germans had established themselves both around Canea to the west and Heraklion to the east, the situation appeared hopeless. The commander of the 2/1 Battalion, Lieutenant-Colonel Ian Campbell, bowed to the seemingly inevitable. To forestall further bloodshed among his men, Campbell, a regular army officer, performed a textbook surrender, delivering himself and his men into four years of German captivity. But Campbell's counterpart in the 2/11 Battalion, Major Ray Sandover, behaved quite differently. Not a regular officer but an accountant and businessman by profession, the Western Australian gave his men the option of either surrendering to the Germans or joining him in trying their luck by heading into the hills. Those who accepted Sandover's offer fled due south across the island, reaching the coast at the fishing village of Agia Galini. There they encountered a group of British evaders, men from the Black Watch, who similarly had not received the order to evacuate. Together the groups managed to locate a landing barge and prepare it for launching. Skippered by Private Bishop of the

2/3 Australian Field Regiment, it took a full load of evaders – among them 12 of Sandover's men – to Mersa Matruh in Egypt. Their mates farewelled, the remainder of Sandover's men, and the gallant Sandover himself, headed back into the hills.[20]

By nature Johnny Peck was not one to surrender, as was true of many others in the 2/7th. Having fought so hard to allow others to escape, and having been promised passage to Egypt as their reward, to be left behind was a bitter pill to swallow. Not surprisingly then, Peck and others in his 15 Platoon took up Theo Walker's suggestion that before surrender was offered they might leave Sfakia and avoid the German net descending on them.[21] To prepare their flight the men scrounged what food they could, while on the ends of their bayonets they roasted strips of flesh hacked from a newly slaughtered donkey. As they took on as much nourishment as they could, they plotted their next move.[22]

Peck and this group took the westward option, with the idea that somewhere on the coast they would commandeer a boat and sail it to Africa. If that failed, they would head for the mountains. And if that, too, ended in disappointment, then they would trudge north to the area around Georgiopouli with which they were most familiar, where they might solicit the help of locals. By that time, so their reasoning went, those rounded up as POWs would have been on their way to Germany, and the antebellum calm on the island might have been restored.[23]

Two members of Peck's group – he names them as Harry Blake and Dave Pettigrew[24] – swam close to the beach rather than tackling the steep ascent west of Sfakia, and in doing so came across a dinghy which had been used by the barge crews. Like the barges themselves, which had pushed out to sea just hours earlier, it had been hidden in a cave to shield it from German eyes and bombs.

At most the dinghy could carry four, so a coin was tossed to determine who would stay behind. Peck was one of the six unlucky ones.[25] Another was Bill Ledgerwood, who had an especially compelling reason to avoid captivity. His father had fought in the Boer War and become a POW for four devastating years; Bill was eager to dodge that fate.[26] In wishing the fortunate men well, Peck passed to one of them a small Union Jack, thinking it might be useful to identify themselves to Allied aircraft or perhaps even submarines or ships.[27] The chosen four – John Thomson, Jim Gorton, George McMillan and Roy Doran – then managed to row their tiny craft to the island of Gavdos, avoiding the attention of the Luftwaffe. On Gavdos they boarded a Motorised Landing Craft commanded by Harry Richards of 2/11 Battalion. Not far south of Gavdos the vessel ran out of fuel, so a jury mast was rigged with four blankets as a sail. Such was the shortage of food and water that the men conducted a church service on board on 8 June. The next day their prayers were answered, as they made landfall at Sidi Barrani in Egypt, having been at sea for eight days.[28] The Union Jack Peck had given them arrived safely also, eventually finding its way into the collection of the Australian War Memorial.

Peck and his five stranded mates continued toward Loutro, watchful for any sign that Germans might be approaching from the west. Tantalisingly, the only show of military presence came from their own side, as a Sunderland flying boat cruised back and forth along the coast for some time, but there was no way for the Australians to signal their presence.

The next morning the group hiked north towards the barren southern slopes of the Lefka Ori, the White Mountains. To reach the familiar area around Georgioupoli they needed to cut north-eastward in search of their last rearguard position before their descent to Sfakia. From there they could retrace the course of their retreat, all the time avoiding Germans and drawing on the help of local villagers. As they picked their way along paths already twice-travelled by their comrades – first in retreat, then as POWs – they scrounged cigarette butts and any remnants of food.

After some five days they came to the point where the road north met the main road connecting Canea in the west with Retimo to the east. From Vrises they traversed the familiar territory east toward Georgioupoli and came to a halt in a little hollow in the foothills above the town. In his own account Peck gives the location the name Klima. Here there lived just one family, beside a well. In Peck's recollection it was the Venezelos family, comprising the shepherd Papa Venezelos, his wife and five children. Following the Cretan tradition of hospitality to strangers in need, the family conjured a hearty meal from their scant supplies. Relieved at last to be able to eat while seated at a table, the Australians consumed dishes of potatoes and beans smothered in olive oil, followed by a dish of wheat boiled with sour milk called 'misithra'.[29]

The group was invited to stay as long as they wished, but to harbour fugitives posed a massive risk to their brave hosts. Peck could not yet know it, but already German forces were exacting vicious revenge on Cretans suspected of aiding the enemy. As German forces established control over the island, positions close to the northern coast were unsafe both for evaders and their hosts. To harbour as many as six men on the run was to invite calamity, so the Australians moved to a rocky hill called Daphne Corfu, overlooking the coast. There they sought to impose military routine on their daily existence, always ensuring that a guard was posted and that a route to safety was available should a German patrol appear. They reconnoitred the surrounding countryside, carrying out surveillance as best they could on nearby roads and tracks. In this way they gained a good sense of the movement of German troops, especially along the Canea to Retimo road and in vessels plying the waters of nearby Suda Bay.[30]

With the aid of one of the Venezelos sons they re-established their acquaintance with a barber in Georgioupoli they had known before hostilities commenced. Other families in Georgioupoli, too, became aware of the Australians' presence and made clandestine visits bearing food and cigarettes. In pairs the Australians took turns to make return visits into the town, staying with their hosts from dawn until dusk. In these cases, too, offers of long-term shelter had to be rejected because of the dangers to their would-be hosts.[31]

One afternoon Peck was playing cards with Dave Pettigrew when an alarm was given that a German patrol was approaching. Bill and Harry were collecting wood somewhere; if not warned, they risked running into the Germans. Peck found Bill soon enough, and together they moved to higher ground. But Harry could not be located, and worryingly the Germans had split into two groups, doubling the risk that they would stumble upon him.[32]

Peck and Bill separated, the former to watch the Germans winding their way around the hill, while Bill searched desperately for Harry. But it was Peck who was in trouble, as he found himself wedged between the two groups of Germans. If he stayed where he was, the group above would see him on its descent; if he moved down toward the valley, then the valley patrol would nab him.

Compromise offered Peck the best hope. He fell in behind the lower of the German patrols, trying to keep out of sight and earshot. The other patrol descending from above would follow the same track and eventually catch up, by which time Peck needed to have exploited whatever escape opportunity might present itself. His good fortune was that as the gap between the two patrols narrowed, he entered an apparently deserted village, where he frantically tried to open a series of doors, all of them locked. He then turned down a gap in the streetscape into a small square shaded by a plane tree. And there, huddled around the village spring, were Germans, drinking and washing.[33]

With all the calmness he could muster, Peck, who was wearing civilian clothing, stepped up to the spring and spent as much time as he dared quenching his thirst and washing his face and hands. If not suspicion, then curiosity at least would have persuaded the Germans to await the end of Peck's ablution. Having composed himself as best he could, Peck turned to the Germans, who asked him, 'What's your name?' He replied 'Askifou', taking the name of a village on the Sfakia road. When asked where he lived, he gestured airily towards the mountains and said 'Far, far away'. The next question proved much trickier. Noting that Peck was sweating, one of the Germans observed, 'You have been running! What are you doing here?' On one of few occasions in his life, Peck's vocabulary failed him, and he answered, 'I have lost my sheep and don't know where to find them.' The Germans' incomprehension was only deepened by Peck's accompanying pantomime, performed by placing his forefingers to his forehead like horns and bleating 'Baaa, baaa.'[34]

The performance ended when Peck was unable to meet the request that he show his identity papers. When nothing was forthcoming, and when Peck's look of injured innocence failed to mollify his interrogators, his pockets were searched and an Australian Army paybook extracted. The game was up.[35]

5
CAPTIVE IN CRETE

IN FINDING HIMSELF 'IN THE BAG' ON CRETE, PECK WAS joining thousands of other 'British' soldiers – the Germans generally saw no reason to distinguish among soldiers from Britain and the many parts of its Empire – including 3109 Australians.[1] The biggest group were those who had been trapped at Sfakia. To the ignominy of capture was added the cruelty of a march back across the island, ascending its central, imposing spine while in a state of exhaustion, and following in reverse the very route by which they had sought to preserve their freedom just a short time earlier. When they reached the main coastal road at Vrises they headed west toward Canea but then continued on in the direction of Maleme, the airfield where the Germans had established their very first foothold on Crete.

The badly wounded had already been loaded into Junkers aircraft and despatched to mainland Greece for medical treatment. Officers too, entitled to privileged treatment, boarded aircraft for flights to the mainland, where they joined the thousands of British and Commonwealth POWs captured there just a few weeks earlier. Those men had been placed in provisional camps in various parts of the country before transport to a large transit camp, a so-called Dulag, at Salonika in the north-east. From there they were being loaded into cattle trucks and sent by train through Yugoslavia to permanent POW camps in Germany. And what awaited most of them there were four years of frustration and drudgery under the German thumb.

As the Dulag at Salonika was cleared of its hungry, lice-ridden prisoners, space was gradually being created for the newly captured on Crete. In time, when vessels became available, these men would depart Crete for Salonika and then, by September of 1941 at the latest, be shifted by rail into the Reich. In the meantime, they had to cool their heels in a series of provisional camps the Germans set up on Crete's northern coastal plain between Canea and Maleme. Many Australians were detained in a camp at the village of Skines in the hinterland, while others found themselves in a camp on a headland just west of Canea. Wherever they were, conditions were at best rudimentary, typically consisting of barbed wire strung around a small, open area with little protection from the elements.

Peck's first days of captivity were not in one of the camps. The patrol that had nabbed him escorted him on a four-hour westward hike to its base in the coastal town of Kalives. There he faced his first interrogation as a prisoner of war. It was not much of an ordeal, as he was not pressed to divulge any more than his name, rank and number. Thereafter he was placed in a jail cell, where he was well fed and able to rest after the rigours of the preceding weeks. When further interrogations occurred, they did not extend beyond chats about life in Australia and Austria.

On the fifth day Peck received word that he was to be moved on from his Kalives cell, but his destination was not yet settled. The commandant was reportedly contemplating two stark choices. Either Peck would be deposited as a prisoner of war in a camp near Canea, or he would be escorted east to Heraklion for imprisonment as a spy. The issue here was that Peck had been arrested not in his battledress but in civilian clothing. In German thinking, through abandoning his uniform Peck had forfeited the protection offered by the Geneva Convention on the Treatment of Prisoners of War. Without a uniform, he could be subjected to quite a different kind of justice; indeed, might legitimately be treated as a spy or partisan. Peck spent some agonising hours awaiting the outcome of his captors' deliberations, imagining himself as a bloody corpse, smashed on the ground at the foot of a wall in Heraklion. To his great relief, he learned the following morning that his captors' quandary was resolved in favour of the lesser evil. He would formally become a prisoner of war.[2]

The legality of what the Germans did next was dubious in the extreme. The Geneva Convention allowed for the punishment of escaped POWs through placing them in isolation cells for up to a month. When he was captured, however, Peck was not an escaper but an evader; he had not previously been in German hands. On the other hand, dispensing with his uniform in favour of the disguise of civilian clothing was a transgression which might trigger consequences. In any case, his captors were clearly determined to administer some form of punishment.

A truck delivered Peck not to a POW camp but to a jail in Canea, where he was searched, registered and placed in a small, putrid cell. An hour or so later he was transferred to a larger, communal cell full of Cretan prisoners, a mixture of common criminals and others accused of political offences under the new regime of occupation. The only food served there was a single bread roll every morning. Others could have food brought to the jail by family or friends; Peck had to do without, and his protests to the German guards fell on deaf ears. After some ten days he was permitted to make his case to the commandant during the latter's morning rounds. Peck argued that to hold an acknowledged prisoner of war in a civilian jail was illegal. Perhaps the commandant was persuaded, or perhaps the stint in the prison was only ever intended as a stern warning. In any case, three days later Peck was taken to the POW camp near Galatas, about 5 kilometres west of Canea. It was on a small promontory north of the Canea–Maleme road. The camp was bordered on its northern side by the sea and to the south by an administration block and barracks.[3]

One small consolation for his arrival in a formal POW camp was that he was granted the opportunity to write to his parents to advise them of his fate. His brief missive gives some insight into his lowly state of mind: 'Most of my mates were killed here in the battle and I am brokenhearted. There is nothing to write about but I hope you are all OK.'[4]

Arrival in the POW camp did not mean that his punishment had been concluded. Rather than renewing old acquaintances among the prisoners, Peck was immediately deposited in a stockade on a raised piece of ground inside the camp, which had just weeks earlier been the location of a field hospital. Tents which had once served as wards were now prison huts, still bearing the badges of the fierce fighting which had taken place in that area in the form of tears and bullet holes. Peck's own initial accommodation, though, was a cage, offering little protection against the harsh Cretan sun.[5]

Some of the prisoners approached the stockade to solicit information from the new arrival. Peck knew none of them but asked that they let his friends from the 2/7th know of his arrival. Some time later mates from his company approached; both sides updated each other on what had happened since they had parted ways. Peck told of his own platoon's evasion and of the little else he knew of men wandering through the island or hiding out. The news he learned in return was a source of great anxiety. The Germans, he was told, had already commenced sending POWs to the mainland. Peck understood the stark implications of this. If he were to escape, he needed to do so sooner rather than later, because flight to friendly or even neutral territory from mainland Greece seemed an unlikely prospect.[6]

The first challenge was to survive the stockade. During the day he was plagued by hunger, heat, and above all thirst. At night his fellow prisoners would gamely approach to deposit supplies with him to complement the single hunk of black bread and cup of water his captors delivered each morning. One day Peck was so tortured by thirst that he called out to a passing prisoner, 'For God's sake try and get me some water!' Ten minutes later the man returned with a bottle of water. Careful not to encroach into the forbidden zone around the stockade, he hurled it at Peck's cage, but on striking it the bottle bounced off it. As it hit the ground a burst of shots skimmed over Peck's head towards his good

Samaritan, who dashed to the tents. Unfortunately, some innocent men within the tents in the line of fire had become collateral
damage, as Peck heard shouts and cries for a doctor.[7]

The commotion provoked the entry into the camp of a detail
of guards, some of whom approached the tents, the others Peck's
stockade. The offending bottle of water sighted, a guard theatri-
cally removed the cork and poured the contents onto the parched
earth before Peck. More troubling, though, was the possibility
that someone in a tent might have been seriously or even fatally
wounded. That fear appeared confirmed when the wounded were
carted off to the camp hospital. Worse than that, later that day Peck
observed two ranks of prisoners lining up near the entrance to the
hospital, and a guard of honour for a coffin duly emerged, draped
with the Union Jack. Peck could barely suppress his pangs of guilt
as the cortege passed below him, tears streaming down his face
as he stood to attention inside his cage, wishing he were the one
inside the coffin.[8]

The hours that followed were the most abject days of Peck's
imprisonment; to the unalleviated thirst and heat was added the
burden of a troubled conscience. Then the following morning
before dawn he spied just outside the cage a bottle of water and
some food. Attached to the bottle was a note reading, 'After today
it is too risky to talk. Bury the bottle before the Germans see it. All
the wounded are OK. Keep your chin up, it can't last forever.'[9]

For all the discomforts and privations the provisional camps
on Crete inflicted on their prisoners, they offered one consoling
advantage, and that was that escape from them was relatively
simple. In the case of the Galatas camp, the perimeter wire was
flimsy and readily broached. There was no northern escape route,
because the camp was on the coast, and German barracks to the

south discounted that option. An open plain to the west rendered that route too risky. Happily, there was good cover outside the camp to the east, in the direction of Canea. So porous, indeed, was the eastern perimeter fence that prisoners had adopted the habit of making their way into Canea to procure food, returning to the camp to share the spoils. The greatest obstacle was not the barbed wire but rather the seemingly capricious and unpredictable patrolling of the outside perimeter by the German guards.

By the time Peck was finally released from his cage, he had long considered his escape strategy. He sought out his friends in the main camp and found himself toasted like the prodigal son. He was gratified to learn that the shooting incident had indeed led to just three prisoners incurring wounds from which all would recover quickly. The body in the flag-draped coffin was that of a sergeant fatally wounded even before Peck's arrival in the camp. Though this news and the company of fellow prisoners were a welcome filip, it was not Peck's intention to linger in the cold comforts of the camp.[10]

The great challenge was not how to put the camp behind him but what to do next to avoid recapture and a more prolonged detention in the misery of solitary confinement. Some of the others with whom he shared his thoughts placed their faith in the prospect of making their break to freedom after the transfer; certainly from northern Greece neutral Turkey would be within striking distance. Peck was sceptical, not least because he assumed that mainland detention facilities would be more secure than those on the island. But a break from Galatas would not by itself bring freedom. As Peck was politely reminded, his weeks on the run had not allowed him to leave what was now enemy territory.[11]

Those friends might well also have cautioned Peck as to the

dangers of the act of escape itself. The risk Peck faced was illustrated most dramatically in the case of Ken 'Bluey' Atock, from the 2/7th's Intelligence section. Peck did not witness it, but Atock tested his luck on 13 July 1941.[12] He attempted to scale the Galatas camp's perimeter wire at night, only to become the victim of freakishly bad timing and a trigger-happy German guard. A German flare went off just as he negotiated the top wire, creating a silhouette and an easy target. To teach others a lesson, the Germans left Atock's body hanging in the wire. This earned them a stinging rebuke from Leslie Le Souef, who was now the Senior British Officer in the camp. According to one account, Le Souef stormed into the Orderly Room and berated the German commandant for a good half hour. As the commandant was a captain, and thus of lower rank than the Australian, he had to stand to attention and 'cop it sweet'. Nonetheless, it was only when a day had elapsed from the time of Atock's killing that his body was finally cut from the wire.[13] The Germans made a point of leaving Atock's weathered Australian haversack lying on the dust just outside the fence.[14]

Peck's determination to escape was undimmed. He would test his own luck at the barbed wire, and he would confront the challenge of how to get off the island when he left Galatas behind him. Just four days after his release from the stockade he resolved to make his break that night. His plan was to travel light, so he swapped his clothes for nothing more than a pair of khaki shorts and a new pair of boots. On Crete's unrelentingly rocky terrain, no article of clothing or equipment was more vital than a pair of sturdy boots.[15]

The escape combined bravado with a liberal dose of slapstick comedy. At nightfall he arranged for three volunteers to keep an eagle eye on the sentries, signalling any movement to him. Peck's challenge was to negotiate two barbed wire fences nearly 2 metres in height; between them ran a narrow no-man's land. When all was clear, he stepped over the tripwire on the inside of the camp and lay down beside the first fence. When there was no sign that the sentries had stirred, he crawled through the barbed wire of the first fence into no-man's land, where he once more paused to check that all was still in order and allow his heart to cease pounding so furiously. After what seemed hours, he raised his head to scan the exit route through the second fence but saw nothing beyond a shadowy blackness. Then he threw his dice, standing up to part the last wires. But just at that moment a scuffling sound to his left persuaded him to drop back and crouch down. In his own recollection, he was petrified with fear. A shuffling noise came ever closer, appearing to emanate from the space between the fences where he himself was trapped. Then he recognised a dim shape crawling towards him, and his sense of fear evaporated. In hand-to-hand combat, he was confident he could prevail and so braced himself for the fight. When he could make out a human figure clearly enough, he lunged towards where the throat should have been and grappled with his unknown opponent. A silent tussle was transformed into a noisy melee when their writhing bodies rolled onto a sandbag full of bottles and tins, making enough clatter to wake every guard within earshot. The noise brought the wrestlers to a standstill, as Peck realised his rival was a night trader returning from Canea with his goods. The startled trader demanded, 'What the bloody hell do you think you are doing?', to which Peck responded, 'Getting out, you silly bastard.'[16]

A volley of shots twanged off the wire above Peck's head, but he intuitively clambered through the second fence rather than back into the camp. In his panic he gashed his head and neck on the barbs, and ran blindly when he broke free. Only when he believed that he had put a safe distance between himself and the sentries did he slow down to regain his breath and take stock.[17]

His plan was not to follow the coast east into Canea but to strike south, crossing the Canea–Maleme road and heading for the hills. As far as possible he sought the safety of trees, but at times he unavoidably found himself on open ground, at one point even amid tents and huts. After crossing the road undetected, he spent a couple of hours ascending the foothills bordering the thin northern coastal plain. By his reckoning he had put enough distance between himself and Galatas to avoid detection at daybreak, and at that point he crawled wearily into bushes and dozed for as long as the mosquitoes and his aching limbs would allow.[18]

Peck had stumbled across an area where there had been vicious fighting during the Battle for Crete. It was known as Prison Valley for the prison located in it, and it was a short distance to the south-west of Canea. A combination of forces had attempted to hold up the German advances east from the Maleme airfield along Prison Valley Road. It was into this area that Peck's own 2/7th had been sent from around Georgioupoli in a vain attempt to stem the German tide, only to have to fall back to 42nd Street and a renewed bloody encounter there.

When the new day dawned, Peck began to recognise features of the landscape, including slit trenches and bomb craters, and then one of his own company's defensive positions. Familiarity with his surroundings triggered powerful memories of the battle he had fought there, above all the fate of his comrades Steve Warner and Arnold Newnham.[19] Both, he knew, had been killed by bombs the night of the withdrawal. Arnold's corpse had been wrapped in a groundsheet and placed in a nearby vineyard awaiting burial. Though needing to beat a hasty retreat, Peck's curiosity, along with a desire to ensure that his friend had received a worthy interment, persuaded him to look for a grave.[20]

Unable to find so much as a cross, Peck was emboldened to knock on the door of the nearest farmhouse. When a woman in black opened it, he did his utmost in his pidgin Greek to explain his quest. After some minutes of pantomime she surprised him with an invitation to enter, explaining, 'Your friends may be able to help you.' In the gloom of the room inside, four men were taking their breakfast around a kitchen table. One of them looked up from his plate to ask the interloper what he wanted – in German. A moment of mutual recognition seemed to last an eternity, until Peck dived backwards through the door and crashed through the vines on his way to the hills, shots ringing past his ears, his lungs bursting. As he exited an olive grove, he had no choice but to zigzag across an open field, like a rabbit with a dog fast on its heels. On the point of expiring he lunged sideways into a depression cutting across his line of flight and fell gasping into the cold, clear water of a mountain stream. After a brief respite he followed the stream north, keeping his head below the level of the banks. Below the village of Perivolia he dared to raise his head for a glance. When all seemed safe, he scrambled into a clump of bushes and sought to gather his wits and his thoughts.[21]

For three days he beat a path to the east, back towards the familiar territory of Georgioupoli. He was hungry, tired and lonely, but all that was outweighed by his sense of freedom. When necessary he called on the unfailing hospitality of the Cretans. Indeed, had he accepted every offer extended to him, the journey would have taken weeks. His destination once more was the Venezelos family in the hills behind Georgioupoli, and when he arrived they gave full vent to their delight, plying him with food and drink as he recounted his adventures since his capture. They themselves had received many visits from Germans since then, but they had not been molested.[22]

The next day Peck was reunited with his comrades, by now inhabiting a hideout with tight security arrangements, including a 24-hour armed guard. Life continued much as it had before Peck's capture, the Australians' Cretan friends supplying them with food and news. Yet their mere survival at liberty was not fully satisfying, and all asked the perennial question of how they might get off the island. They pursued baseless rumours that boatmen might take them to Egypt or Turkey. They hatched a plan to steal a German motor torpedo boat anchored off Georgioupoli, and they considered commandeering a more modest Cretan vessel, but not even a rowboat could be spied on that part of the coast.[23]

Then, at last, a piece of news delivered by Papa Venezelos gave them cause for hope. A British officer, he learned, had been delivered by submarine to a place on the south coast of the island at Preveli, almost directly south of Retimo.[24] Bitter experience had taught the Australians to exercise scepticism, but there was truth in what they were told.

6
ON THE RUN

ONE TALE ALONE CONVEYS THE SCALE OF EFFORTS BEING made by men like Johnny Peck to avoid capture through the summer of 1941 and beyond. It has it that an unnamed Australian private was making his way toward Crete's southern coast, dressed in Cretan garb, and hoping to catch a boat or submarine to Egypt. At one point he needed to cross a major road held under tight German surveillance and decided that the best way to do so without attracting attention was to assume the guise of a shepherd. When he came upon a small flock of sheep he offered the shepherd a monetary inducement so that he might be permitted to escort the sheep across the road. The shepherd, heavily shrouded in a bundle of rags, offered no reply, and even after repeated offers did no more than raise his head sharply in the Greek sign of refusal.

Exasperated by the Australian's persistence, the bundle of rags finally proclaimed in a Glaswegian brogue, 'Gae and find yer own bluidy sheep. I've spent half a day getting this damn lot.'[1]

There were hundreds of men, Anzacs and others, in the same predicament as the hapless Scottish shepherd. The numbers were fluid, because as more men escaped from the German camps around Canea, others were rounded up by patrols and dumped in the very same camps before transfer to the Greek mainland and eventually to the Reich.[2] Still others could not cope with the heavy burdens of freedom – constant hunger and thirst, a peripatetic life in a harsh and unfamiliar environment, and the constant threat of being found by a German patrol. For them the prospect of medical care, a half-decent feed and the company of friends was enough to persuade them to hand themselves in.

British authorities in Cairo knew that men had been left behind, but they had no way of knowing how many had evaded the German net. After the evacuations staged by the Royal Navy at the end of May, men continued to turn up on the North African coast in an assortment of vessels. They brought with them news that their mates had headed into the Cretan hills, each one of them hoping that there might still be some possibility of getting off the island.

This was not a new problem. Heroically a hastily assembled armada had managed to evacuate British forces from the beaches of Dunkirk after the fall of France, but others had been stranded and, strewn across the French countryside, struggled to keep out of German hands. In those months of 1940 and later, airmen bailed out over or crash-landed on enemy territory and did all they could to evade capture, make their way back to Britain, and fight another day.

For men in precisely those harrowing circumstances the British had created an agency called MI9 as early as December 1939. It was a department within the Military Intelligence Directorate, and it was placed under the leadership of a veteran of World War I, Major (later Brigadier) Norman Crockatt.[3] The acronym revealed something of its origins and its institutional identity – Military Intelligence. The agency devoted much of its wartime work to attempting to stop men falling into enemy hands in the first place by training them in the art of evasion. And if they were nonetheless captured, they could draw on their training to escape. After all that, should they manage neither to escape nor evade, MI9 still saw benefit in cultivating clandestine links with men in POW camps, because they were potentially useful sources of information about what was going on behind enemy lines.

The most prominent candidates for training in evasion and escape were airmen, highly valued because they had been prepared for their roles at great expense and could, should they manage to return to Britain, play crucial roles in the war in Europe's skies. In contrast, army personnel – especially those among the Other Ranks, like Johnny Peck – had been woefully prepared for evasion or captivity and relied above all on their own wits and instincts. Nonetheless, MI9 did not wish to leave them in the lurch, and certainly not as it seemed they might still make a useful contribution to the war just when Germany was in the ascendancy.

MI9 was not well prepared to deal with men on the run after the debacles in Greece and Crete, campaigns no-one had expected to fight. Moreover, by late June 1941 Winston Churchill and his advisers had more pressing matters on their minds. Operation Barbarossa, the German invasion of the Soviet Union, was launched on 22 June, and it soon appeared that the Soviet defences would crumble entirely within a matter of just weeks. At that point, as seemed inevitable, Hitler would resume his arm-wrestle with the British.

Nonetheless, it was in June that the first tentative steps were taken to rescue the men on Crete. By their own estimates the British suspected that there were 'probably over 1000' men spread across the island, but mainly along its southern coast.[4] A formal commitment to get them out came as early as 17 June.[5] But it was a commitment made with very little preparation and with precious few resources supporting it. MI9 had not established a presence in the Middle East until the end of 1940.[6] The key figure was the South African–born Lieutenant-Colonel Dudley Clarke, whom Archibald Wavell had brought to Cairo to help conduct 'irregular' forms of warfare in the Middle East. Clarke would go on to earn the title 'the greatest British deceiver of World War II'.[7] In Cairo he set up 'A Force'; for the sake of preserving secrecy and some discreet distance from GHQ, its headquarters were set up in a brothel, its workers continuing to practise their profession in the parts of the building Clarke did not require.[8] The part of A Force which was to carry out the MI9 brief of aiding evaders and escapers through the Middle East – including Crete – was called 'N section'.[9]

After the initial commitment was made in mid-June, it was more than a month until the first practical step was taken to get the men off Crete. An agent was smuggled onto the island by submarine, tasked with contacting evaders and escapers and arranging their evacuation. He was Francis 'Skipper' Pool, a middle-aged ex-Merchant Marine officer, who in his pre-war civilian career had run the Imperial Airways flying boat station at Spinalonga on the eastern end of Crete.[10] On 27 July 1941 the British submarine

Thrasher delivered Pool to Preveli on the island's central southern coast, almost due south of Retimo.[11] Pool's landing site was adjacent to the Preveli monastery, which would be crucial to the success of his mission.[12] Sure enough, on its return voyage – without Pool – *Thrasher* had 73 men on board, as he set about collecting another 130.[13] Within days of Pool's arrival the Cretan version of the bush telegraph – it became known as 'the Cretan wireless'[14] – spread word that rescue operations were to commence. When it reached people like Johnny Peck and Reg Saunders, word was vague, but the gist was clear. They needed to make their way to the vicinity of the south coast, where submarines would collect them and whisk them to Alexandria.

Johnny Peck knew nothing of MI9, let alone Commander Pool, but when he learned that clandestine evacuations would take place, he and all those like him made their way to the south coast to get more precise information.

To avoid German patrols, the track Peck and another Australian named Alan (Peck does not provide Alan's surname) followed toward the southern coast steered them away from major roads and population centres and into bare ranges with dry watercourses and rocky crags. The only sound was the tinkling bells of goats. So ragged was the landscape that the men did not walk at night for fear of falling over a cliff or into a ravine from which there would be no way out. At first they slept under whatever shelter nature provided, and ate from the stores with which Mama Venezelos had sent them on their way.[15]

In time, though, they had to turn to locals for food, accommodation and advice, so as they approached the village of Asi Gonia, halfway across the island and south of Georgioupoli, they resolved to risk making contact. The first person they came across was an old man with a fantastically bent stick, perched atop a large stone as he watched a small flock of sheep and goats. In his best Greek, Peck bade him good afternoon and enquired whether there were Germans in the village but elicited no response. A second query about the existence of a local hotel or café was also greeted with silence, prompting Peck to mutter to his companion, 'Let's find a more intelligent bloke than this crazy old bastard.' But as they continued on their way, they heard an American voice shouting from behind, 'Say, boys, how would you like a little drink?' As they spun around they saw the old man holding a gourd of wine and beckoning them with the stick. He explained, 'I just wanted to make sure that you were not Krauts. Those sons of bitches have been going around dressed as British soldiers and then shooting the people who help them.'[16]

Stick, gourd and American accent belonged to Demetrios, who instructed the interlopers to call him Jim. He had lived for 30 years in the United States before returning to Crete just before the outbreak of war. In accordance with the unswerving Cretan tradition of hospitality, he invited the men to his modest home, where his sister Maria poured them wine and served up a steaming dish of beans and oil. Demetrios cut bread with a viciously hooked clasp knife of the kind every Cretan male seemed to possess. Through all this he regaled his visitors with tales of his life as a train driver in the United States.[17]

It was Peck who broached the subject nearest his heart: had Demetrios heard any rumours of a visit to the south coast by a British submarine. 'Sure boy,' came the answer, 'you have come just to the right place. We are collecting all the wandering soldiers and keeping them here until the time comes for the march to the coast when the submarine returns.' On pressing from Peck,

Demetrios explained that 'we' meant the men of the village who had 'pledged to freedom', and who had received a visit from an English officer organising an evacuation. That officer had instructed the villagers of Asi Gonia to gather together men on the run, while he made final arrangements. Demetrios had himself met the officer in question – Commander Pool of the Royal Navy – whom he described as 'a big fat man with a red face'. With that description Peck's scepticism evaporated, at least for now, and the repast ended on a more hopeful note than any in recent weeks. The men were guided through a densely wooded hill on a steep slope to a rocky outcrop with a commanding view over the surrounding area. The challenge, it seemed, was to keep out of harm's way for a time until the mysterious Commander Pool delivered on his undertaking.[18]

Peck and Alan took up residence in a well-concealed cave. Fortified with blankets, food and wine provided by Demetrios and Maria, they awaited word on when to make their next move toward the coast. An almost idyllic existence was punctured one day by the arrival in the village below of a German patrol, prompting them to abandon any complacency about their clandestine existence. The greater concern, however, was that the keenly awaited word of a submarine did not arrive. The only change Demetrios signalled was that the two Australians would soon be joined by three New Zealanders from 22 Battalion, on the run since they, too, had been stranded at Sfakia. Their presence was welcomed, especially as it appeared to signal that final preparations for an evacuation were being made. Yet after two more weeks the group of five still had no positive news, and Peck's mood was sliding into pessimism.[19]

He chose to leave the group and to strike out alone, pushing further south to the coast. His parting from Demetrios was painful, but his generous host acknowledged tacitly that Peck was not equipped for sitting idle. He set him on a safe path to the next village, shook his hand vigorously and kissed him on both cheeks in a sign of genuine affection bred over a time when Peck's well-being rested entirely in the hands of Demetrios and Maria. And with that, Peck set off to chance his luck elsewhere, striking a south-easterly course, and relieved to be taking his fate into his own hands.[20]

By the following morning he was hopelessly lost. On reaching the outskirts of a large town he took the chance of reorienting himself by entering a *kafeneon* and ordering a raki. That first drink fortified his sense of bravado, so he ordered another, and then a third. At that point the proprietor sought to satisfy his own curiosity and asked him, 'Germanos?' Taken aback, Peck answered, 'No, Australianos', which caused a couple of other customers to choke on their drinks and huddle around him. In hushed tones they explained to him in the simplest and clearest Greek they could summon that the town in which he found himself contained a German outpost; he was in the gravest danger. With that, Peck was shepherded from the *kafeneon* and into the nearby house of a new-found friend. And it was on consulting a map there that he realised how far he had strayed from his intended path, instead stumbling into this village of Argiroupolis, much frequented by Germans. Not wishing to endanger his hosts, he left at the first opportunity, and spent that night sharing a mountain hut with a young shepherd.[21]

His mental compass recalibrated, the next day he headed south as far as the village of Vilandredo, in an isolated mountain region. There he was soon made welcome by villagers, who ushered three other Australians to meet him. They too, as Peck soon learned, were on a submarine hunt, so the four of them decided to travel together for a time towards the south coast.[22] Their next destination was the village of Alones, just a few kilometres from the coast as the crow flies. On the way there they joined up with two New Zealanders and a Scot, only to find on entering Alones that their own motley crew was far outnumbered by a group of about 30, impatiently awaiting the arrival of a submarine, but no-one knew either where or when.[23]

After many false starts the group got the word to move. The submarine was about to arrive. Peck, who had survived for the previous days on a diet of boiled potatoes and raw onions, was so excited at the thought of escape that his appetite evaporated. At dusk the group set off down a long and winding path to the beach. Three times they took short breaks from the cracking pace set by the guides, yet each fresh start brought the awareness of how much their legs ached and how much steeper and more perilous the terrain became as the coast beckoned.[24]

By dawn the group was holed up in a wood within striking distance of the sea; word from the guides was that a short march that evening would deliver them to the beach. When dusk fell again they set off at breakneck speed to a tight coastal plain, the smell of the sea by now in their nostrils. About midnight they halted a short distance from a monastery perched upon a craggy hillside overlooking the sea. It was Preveli Monastery, whose foundations dated back at least as far as 1594, during the Venetian occupation of Crete, and the activities of a feudal lord who went by the name Prevelis. Later, during the Ottoman occupation, the monastery was destroyed, though the monks managed to save their own lives and engage in acts of resistance against their Ottoman foe while the monastery was painstakingly rebuilt.

It was there that, hour by hour, expectation soured to anti-climax; the men were awaiting a submarine signal which never came. By four o'clock it was apparent to all that this would not be the day of their departure. When the lead guide returned from the direction of the monastery, he was accompanied by a monk who broke the bad news in flawless English: 'I am sorry my friends. The submarine has not been able to come tonight as the Germans are patrolling the sea in strength so you will have to wait until tomorrow night. In the monastery we have some hot food prepared for you before you return to the mountains.'[25]

The descent down to the monastery at the tail end of that deflating night at least focussed the men's minds; so narrow was the path and so sheer the drop on both sides that a weary misstep could easily have caused tragedy. In hindsight Peck was glad that he had negotiated the way at night, oblivious to the dangers beneath him. There was at least a warm meal at the end of the perilous trek, taken in the solicitous company of bearded, dark-robed monks. The refectory, as Peck later described it, had 'more of the appearance of the devil's pit than the eating place of holy men'. The monks served a stew from two steaming cauldrons, ladling it into a variety of bowls and calabashes, and placing in their weary guests' hands pressed tin cups of raw Cretan wine.[26]

There followed three days of dashed hopes passed in the hiding place above Preveli. On the fourth, the danger of collecting so many men in one location was considered too great, so they were dispersed into the surrounding countryside. The Cretans, who appeared every bit as disappointed as Peck and his comrades, advised them to head east, but to remain within striking distance of the coast until more auspicious news could be spread. Peck set off with a small group into the nearby foothills, from where they could stare hopefully at the sea and exercise whatever patience they could still summon.[27]

Twice in the following fortnight they repeated their dash to the sea, only to trudge back to their redoubt. As time passed, more men on the run gathered nearby, straining the already scarce supplies of food. On one desperate occasion Peck's group, having searched in vain for food, climbed back over a mountain to devour the potato peelings they had dumped in a pond days earlier.[28]

Two of Peck's little party – an Australian and an Irishman – lost their chance of escape when snaffled by a German patrol after they had taken a meal in a small village. Peck and his remaining companion, a New Zealander named Noel Dunn, narrowly managed to avoid the patrol themselves. They did not, however, escape witnessing the consequences for the hapless family who had fed the two captives. When Peck and Noel sought out the house, it was already a place of mourning, both father and eldest son shot dead as punishment for aiding the British. The Germans had also sought to burn parts of the village, but not entirely successfully. They threatened to be more thorough on their return. Peck felt helpless when confronted with the weeping widow and crying children. He left his Egyptian bribe money with the village priest to hand to the family after his departure. To hand it to them directly made it seem too much like blood money.[29]

Peck and his companions had been desperately unlucky. There had indeed been evacuations from Preveli, or at least from Limni beach, below the monastery. Pool had done his job well, benefitting from the generosity and above all the bravery of the monks at the monastery. In particular it was the abbot, Father Agathángelos Langouvardos, who risked everything in aiding the British, because in effect the monastery functioned as a marshalling yard for escapees.[30] One of the Australians who had already managed to escape Crete by submarine from Limni beach was the West Australian Geoffrey Edwards, a member of the 2/11 Battalion which had fought with distinction at Retimo before fleeing into the hills. Years later he described the difficulties that both rescuers and rescued faced in the middle of the night:

> I pulled myself along the rope to the sub. Halfway out there the soldier in front of me panicked as he couldn't swim a stroke and he started splashing around and shouting out. A sailor quickly quietened him with a terrific punch to the jaw and then guided him along. As I climbed down the conning tower I got the old claustrophobic feeling but couldn't do much about it as someone just above me was pushing me down, so down into the sub I went. We were packed in like sardines but the crew were marvellous.[31]

Nearly a month later, on 22 August, Limni beach was the site of another evacuation. This time it was HMS *Torbay* which took 130 men on board, creating a record for the number of people jammed into a submarine.[32] One of the evacuees happened to be Major Ray Sandover, the West Australian who had led many of his men across the island from Retimo. And this time there was a sprinkling of men from Peck's 2/7 Battalion as well – but no Johnny Peck.[33]

After that, Preveli had to be struck from the list of possible evacuation points. Word had reached the Germans about what was afoot at the monastery, and on 25 August they paid a visit. Fortunately there were no escapers or evaders to be found there, and the abbot himself had gone into hiding. But the remaining monks were punished for their efforts by having the monastery stripped of all its livestock and supplies, while a German outpost was established nearby.[34] Eventually the abbot was spirited to Cairo; he would never see his precious monastery again. Neither would the monastery experience another evacuation, though a third had been planned for September.[35]

Scenes of disappointment were played out at other points along Crete's rugged southern coast in the following weeks. On one occasion the acuteness of the men's frustration, and the release from it they sought in alcohol, was observed by a British officer infiltrated onto the island. Xan Fielding came across what seemed like an Anzac encampment near the southern seaside town of Treis Ekklisies (Three Churches), some distance east of Preveli:

> The chorus of *Waltzing Matilda* filled the dusk as loudly as
> a wireless switched on at full blast against a background of
> yowling, spluttering atmospherics composed of typically
> Antipodean sounds of revelry; and through the open door
> of the village coffee-shop I saw a horde of frenzied giants in
> tattered khaki and slouch hats. All these men had hoped to
> be evacuated from Three Churches two days before and were
> now, understandably enough, drowning their disappointment
> – an easy feat in Crete, where wine and raki were both more
> plentiful than food.[36]

For Johnny Peck and the men like these who were left behind, the sole option was to trust that the submarine they missed would not be the last. They could not, however, bide their time in large groups on the south coast but needed to disperse inland in small clusters, avoiding German patrols while awaiting word of when and where the next sub might make its appearance.

The saving grace in their awful predicament was that as they waited they could at least draw on the help of locals. For Johnny Peck, as for countless other men on the run, the traditional Cretan *filoxenia* – the love of strangers – proved more than just legend.[37] Even as the Cretans suffered the privations of a harsh occupation, the men on the run could be certain of one thing. Peck put it beautifully:

> As long as the Cretans had anything they would give it to us. When we went hungry we knew that they were going hungry too. Even when they had no food to offer someone always invited us in for a glass of wine or ouzou. They would share their last piece of bread with us and we would all sit around the table dipping the hard crust into a cup of olive oil and vinegar, and if we were lucky, crunching away on a piece of raw onion. Sometimes the host, with vast ceremony after the repast, would bring out his only cigarette and, solemnly cutting it into three, would pass the pieces around with the air of an ambassador handing out cigars after a banquet.[38]

This hospitality was based on a system of mutual obligation; it imposed a mode of behaviour on the guest with which Peck could not always readily comply. Many a time, he recalled,

> We watched the children peering hungrily around the table at us. We knew the whole family would go to bed with empty bellies that night and sometimes we openly rebelled until the head of the house pleaded with tears in his eyes not to shame

him before the world. Having fought together in defence of their homeland brought a sense of unity and comradeship to the Cretans and the Allied soldiers. They were determined to succour and sustain those unfortunates who were left behind after the evacuation and no risk was too great for them to take in hiding and feeding the hundreds who were wandering the mountains in search of ultimate freedom.[39]

Peck sought to ease the burden on the poorest by turning first to the more prosperous looking among the villagers. Generally he and those in his circumstances avoided the shame of asking directly for food; the opening request was typically for a glass of water or the sewing of a button. Usually, then, by the time the glass was drunk, the meal invitation was extended. A simple and seemingly innocent request for directions, too, could set in train events which worked to the traveller's favour.

7
SPECIAL OPERATIONS

THE LOSS OF PREVELI AS AN EVACUATION POINT DID NOT bring the evacuations to an end. Whether under their own steam or with the help of Cairo, Australians and others would continue to find ways to get off the island.

The award for the most circuitous of them, begun in August 1941, goes to a group containing Charles Jager of the 2/2 Field Regiment. After much travelling across the island, the nine Australians and New Zealanders made their way to the very tip of the Rodopos peninsula in north-western Crete. They had heard that Greek vessels – caiques – were staging secret runs between the mainland and the island, and on a return run might deliver them to the mainland. The plan was to seize a boat as it headed north to the Peloponnese and force it on a southerly course to Egypt. Instead, having boarded a caique they sailed as far as the Peloponnese, where they remained in hiding from Italian occupying forces. Eventually the group – which by now had swelled to 17 – seized a boat and sailed it to Africa, finally arriving there on 15 October.[1]

The settlement to the east of Preveli called Treis Ekklisies was the site of a major evacuation on 23 November 1941. This time the vessel was not a submarine but the converted trawler HMS *Hedgehog*, which managed to take 86 escapers and evaders to safety. They had been brought together under the leadership of an Australian, Lieutenant James De Mole Carstairs, an officer in Peck's 2/7 Battalion.[2] Though those numbers were never repeated, *Hedgehog* in the following year performed other daring operations to get men off the island.[3]

As for Reg Saunders, life was difficult as he patiently awaited his chance. While others were able to don Cretan garb and pass themselves off as locals, as an Aboriginal man Saunders could not, and so remained in hiding. But for his loyalty to his mate Arthur Lambert, Saunders might have made it off the island on *Hedgehog* in November. The pair hid near a village within a short distance of the coast, where Lambert contracted yellow jaundice. In choosing to stay with him, Saunders forfeited the chance to board *Hedgehog* at that time.[4]

By the middle of 1942 the evacuations were drawing to an end. At that point there were very few known Anzacs left on Crete, among them the two Australians Tom Spriggs and Norm Scott. Spriggs had made his way with the New Zealander Wally Swinburne to the eastern end of the island, the Lasithi province, which was occupied by Italians. There they joined a band of partisans until they were eventually evacuated by a motor torpedo boat in September 1943. That meant that the sole Australian left on the island since the battle of Crete was the luckless Norm Scott, a giant of a man from the 2/8 Battalion. Like Peck, he had experienced the attack on *Costa Rica*, and like Peck he had found himself in a German POW camp for a time. After escaping it he hid in a cave with some other Australians, until in September 1941 he became completely paralysed from the neck down, and quite incapable of getting himself – or being carried – to one of the evacuation points. That he survived at all through the winter of 1941–42 was a miracle in itself, but also testimony to the humanity of the local villagers, who risked German patrols and endured miserable weather to trek to Scott's cave to bring him food.[5] At one point he received a visit from a British agent, who expressed his admiration for 'the fortitude with which he bore the discomfort and humiliation of total immobility, [and] the steadfast courage with which his protectors attended to his needs'.[6] Only much later – after he had been taken as a POW in Germany – was Scott diagnosed with beri beri, caused by severe vitamin deficiency. After 34 months in his cave the Australian was captured on 11 April 1944, the day before his 27th birthday.[7]

The sad truth was that there were severe limitations to the resources that GHQ Middle East could allocate to getting men off Crete, though MI9 did the best it could, and the men were never forgotten. The other factor which meant that evacuation slipped down the list of British priorities was the increasing focus on supporting the Cretan resistance to German occupation. And that was not the job of MI9 but of an organisation called the Special Operations Executive, SOE.

SOE was a more recent creation than MI9, having been formed in July 1940, soon after the fall of France. In time it would expand exponentially, sending agents into occupied countries in Europe and beyond, where they would collaborate with local resistance elements to undertake acts of sabotage and espionage. As Churchill put it with characteristically feisty pithiness, SOE's job was to 'set Europe ablaze'.[8] It had to achieve that, though, under a cover of strict secrecy, and during the war SOE was referred to by such names as the Baker Street Irregulars – a reference to its London headquarters, and to the street urchins Sherlock Holmes occasionally used as informants – Churchill's Secret Army, the Ministry of Ungentlemanly Warfare or simply the Firm.

In the case of Crete, the work of MI9 gradually and almost seamlessly transitioned into the sorts of operations that fitted SOE's brief. In part this was because MI9's activities required contact with Cretans who opposed the German occupation and so were well disposed to helping Allied forces in whatever way they could. It was also because of the way that MI9 and SOE operations were set up in Cairo. In September 1941, when the scale of the task of bringing men out of Greece and Crete became clear, Dudley Clarke recruited to his A Force Major Anthony Simonds, who headed a small unit called N Section – in effect, the Cairo arm of MI9. Simonds had already served a stint with SOE and knew its modus operandi intimately. Under his watch, MI9 would continue to do what it could to recover men from Crete, but increasingly the focus shifted to SOE's core business – gathering intelligence, fomenting resistance and making life difficult for the Germans.

The limited intelligence the British did have about Crete at the time of the German invasion was due in large part to the efforts of JDS Pendlebury. Like many of the SOE officers who followed in his footsteps, Pendlebury was an erudite Hellenophile and a fluent speaker of Greek. By profession he was an archaeologist, and in a short time he built an invaluable network of contacts in and around his Heraklion base. At the outbreak of war Pendlebury returned to Britain, enlisted in Military Intelligence and was drafted into Military Intelligence (Research), one of the forerunners of SOE. He returned to Crete in 1940 as a British Army captain to organise resistance in advance of the expected invasion. Pendlebury would leave his glass eye on his desk in Heraklion to signal that he had left on Intelligence business in the hills, cultivating his Cretan contacts. Tragically, Pendlebury was killed by German forces outside Heraklion shortly after the invasion commenced.[9] An apocryphal story has it that after being captured and placed before a firing squad Pendelbury's last, defiant words were, 'Fuck you.'[10]

With Pendlebury's early death it was all the more crucial during the war to build on the contacts established by Francis 'Skipper' Pool, the MI9 operative of whom Peck had heard rumours, who had been infiltrated into Crete in July to round up evaders and send out feelers to the local resistance. Sure enough, when MI9's evacuation work subsided, Tony Simonds exploited the contacts Pool had made among Cretans bold enough to help the men on the run. These were precisely the sort of people who would form the germ of the Cretan resistance, since to harbour Allied soldiers was by itself a courageous act of defiance. One such man with whom Pool had made early contact delighted in the sobriquet Captain Satan; several others followed as Pool travelled through the island, forming alliances with Cretans determined to rid the island of what was proving to be a brutal German occupation regime.[11]

In another important way, too, the tasks of MI9 morphed into those of SOE. A number of men recruited in Cairo to do work for SOE on Crete and on the mainland had themselves spent time in German-occupied territory as evaders and escapers, and they were willing to go back. That they volunteered to do so speaks volumes for the courage of the individuals concerned. At the same time, there were very sound reasons why SOE beat a path to recent evacuees. One was that if captured during SOE operations, such men could plausibly claim that they were POWs still on the run. In theory, at least, the worst fate they could suffer would be to be taken into captivity as a POW and treated accordingly. More-over, such men were familiar with the island and its people, having spent weeks and even months there, and they had a keen sense of which locals they could trust with their lives.

One man recruited for SOE work was the Englishman Jack Smith-Hughes, who was captured by Germans and held in the Galatas camp on the northern coast of Crete near Canea until his escape with a group of friends.[12] Smith-Hughes was evac-uated from the south coast with the help of Pool and was then recruited by SOE in Cairo and infiltrated to Crete by submarine on 9 October 1941.[13] He was accompanied by a wireless operator, Ralph Stockbridge, who had evaded capture on Crete and made his way to Egypt.[14] Back in Crete, Smith-Hughes and Stockbridge together sought out contact with the nascent Cretan resistance. Their first steps were reinforced six weeks later when a caique landed the SOE agent Monty Woodhouse on the island to take over from Smith-Hughes. It was a sign of the growing commit-ment to the Cretan cause that Woodhouse was accompanied by four prize students from SOE's training school in Haifa.[15]

There were men from the AIF, too, who volunteered for

infiltration back into enemy territory. A report lists two Australian Other Ranks employed by MI9 to carry out escape work: William Maynard Bazeley and Francis Neil Tudor Brewer.[16] Records show that both were POWs, and then both were employed on 'intelligence duties' from November 1941.[17] What exactly they were asked to do was shrouded in some mystery, though a confidential report divulged that they 'had made outstanding escapes, and had volunteered to go back to carry on escape work to rescue those left behind'.[18] In recognition of their bravery the men were awarded Military Medals.[19]

Then there was an officer, Lieutenant GJ Greenway of the Western Australian 2/11 Battalion. Greenway missed the early evacuations and, in a group of 15, remained on the run along the Cretan south coast for two months, at every opportunity signalling out to sea in the hope of attracting the attention of a sub. On the night of 28–29 August they finally had success and swam out to a British sub which took them to Alexandria. When asked to volunteer for special duties, Greenway did not hesitate, despite the extreme hardships he had just endured. Rather than being infiltrated back into Crete, however, Greenway was sent to Greece, where he helped establish an evacuation line through the Greek islands to neutral Turkey, a feat which earned him – on the recommendation of MI9 – a Military Cross, even before he went on to perform courageous service in New Guinea.[20]

SOE's operations on Crete are best known for the work of senior officers such as Patrick Leigh Fermor, Xan Fielding and Billy Moss. Over a period of years they did what they could to make life difficult for the Germans on Crete by encouraging and collaborating with local resistance elements. There was no unified resistance movement on Crete, so the British operatives had to perform the often delicate task of winning the confidence of a wide range of groups spread across the island. Communication was a perennial problem, not least because of the island's unrelentingly rugged topography. For their capacity to communicate not only with one another but also with sympathetic locals, the SOE agents were dependent on Cretan 'runners', most famously a young shepherd by the name of George Psychoundakis. In his memoirs *The Cretan Runner*, Psychoundakis gives gripping insight into the hardships faced by Cretans and British alike when confronted with an enemy which was determined to impose its authority over the island, and which did not shy from acts of indiscriminate violence to achieve that end.[21]

By the end of 1941, SOE was ramping up its work on Crete. The officers it assembled for infiltration onto the island became known as Force 133. They were instructed to 'concentrate on preparations for an outbreak of guerrilla warfare combined with the formation of a Fifth Column in anticipation of our invasion'.[22] Even with that priority in mind, and as MI9 through the following year wound up its operations on Crete, SOE agents counted among their tasks rounding up the stragglers who, for whatever reasons, had not managed to get off the island. One of them was Johnny Peck.

After the disappointments of missing the Preveli evacuations, Peck and his companion of the time, the New Zealander Noel Dunn, instinctively headed east to keep clear of German patrols. With rare highlights such as gorging on a roast goat with a shepherd celebrating his birthday, the food situation had become parlous. Mostly they lived on carob beans and boiled weeds, supplementing that meagre diet with the offerings that Cretan villages conjured for them.

One day while on the move the two men approached a stream, where they saw a man sitting on a donkey. As the man appeared, in Peck's words, 'fat and affluent', they decided he was the sort of person who might grant them a favour. They greeted the stranger with '*Kalimera*' and bent down to drink from the stream with cupped hands. Yet something uncanny in the stranger's ruddy complexion triggered Peck's curiosity, and then something clicked. Without consulting Noel he blurted involuntarily, 'You're Commander Pool.'[23]

The hunch was correct. A startled Pool soon recovered his wits to confirm his identity and then added some words of gentle admonition: 'You want to be careful who you tell that to young feller.' Then he made a statement which mortified his new-found companions, 'It's a pity you were not nearer the coast the night before last. The submarine which originally brought me here took off a large group of your friends.' It was a bitter pill to swallow, and one which Pool immediately sought to sweeten. Before long, he told them, another sub would come. But before then, Pool continued, he wondered if they might be prepared to do a job for him. They agreed.[24]

The problem Pool faced, as he went on to explain, was that he alone could not possibly travel to all those places where men were in hiding. His request, then, was that Peck and Dunn should return to the places through which they had already travelled, re-establishing contact with people there, and telling them to make their way to a place called Timbaki, where the Cretan underground would pick them up and hold them in a group until evacuation. His final words of advice were delivered in a generous spirit, but they contained a dire warning: 'Remember that if the Germans catch you your only punishment will be a beating and prison, so tell them nothing. If you involve the local people they will certainly be shot and their villages destroyed.'[25]

With that caveat new plans were put in place. Peck would go back north across the island as far as Georgioupoli, while Noel would head to a village near Sfakia. For a short distance the two travelled together with Pool, but then he handed them each some Greek money and waved them on their separate ways. In five days Peck was back at Klima, outside Georgioupoli, finding some 20 men along the way and advising them to head to Timbaki. He was happily reunited with the Venezelos family, who undertook to pass on the crucial message to head south. Peck advised them to be careful of spies and Germans dressed as British. He was very conscious of the tense atmosphere that had descended over the area. Just as they had done at Kontomari, near Maleme, back at the beginning of June, the Germans had continued to commit vicious acts of reprisal against villages thought to be abetting the enemy. People in the villages around Georgioupoli who contemplated offering refuge to soldiers on the run were taking an enormous risk, especially as German patrols had become a regular occurrence.[26]

Accompanied by young George Venezelos, Peck went down into the town of Georgioupoli. It was by now empty of men on the run, but Peck made contact with the barber, Peter, and other acquaintances who would spread the word about Timbaki. With George acting as a scout, the two men were able to set up a network which would enable stragglers still in that district to be funnelled through Klima towards Timbaki, a trek of several days to the south-east. Peck himself led a group across the island, swelling in size as it went. Soon they were an organised troop, with dedicated scouts and a rearguard. With a military efficiency imposed by Peck, they reached their schedule in good time and met up again with Pool as planned.[27]

Noel had not yet returned from his mission in the region of Sfakia, and Pool decided that before an evacuation could take place there would be time for Peck to carry out one more task. The Englishman explained that the submarine which would perform the operation – HMS *Thunderbolt* – would land weapons on the island before it evacuated stragglers. As an infantryman, Peck was well qualified to train local resistance fighters in the use of those weapons. Though he felt a pang of regret as the men he had shepherded across the island now headed towards their coastal evacuation point, Peck 'bucked up' at the offer of a new job and was greatly pleased at the praise heaped on him by Pool for the successful completion of his first job. He immediately agreed.[28]

Over the following days Peck accompanied Pool on his travels, frequently acting as a courier. Having already travelled hundreds of kilometres by foot across the island over the preceding months, and having picked up more than a smattering of the local language, he was well equipped for the task. At one point Pool introduced him to one of the leading resistance figures on the island, Manoli Bandouvas. The extravagantly moustachioed Bandouvas was once described by the SOE's Xan Fielding as 'a dark burly man with sad ox-eyes and a correspondingly deep-throated voice in which he was fond of uttering cataclysmic aphorisms such as "The struggle needs blood, my lads."'[29]

The Cretan's heavy welcoming embrace almost crushed the Australian. As Pool moved off to other duties, Peck remained for a time in the care of Bandouvas and his band. The fearsome-looking Bandouvas was, Peck noted, quick-tempered but also just. He was also, as Peck later learned, unable to read or write, and yet was an enormously charismatic, courageous and effective leader.[30]

Through these days of carrying out Pool's wishes, the plans for the promised evacuation remained imprecise. This was in part for security reasons, but it was also because they were extraordinarily difficult to put into place. As intended, a large body of men had been gathered at Timbaki, and when freed from his liaison duties with the Bandouvas band, Johnny Peck joined them. The New Zealander Noel Dunn, too, took his place after carrying out his tasks for Pool. But when the prospects of evacuation again dimmed, the entire group was moved further inland from Timbaki to shelter under a giant overhanging rock called Megala Petra. There they passed the time as best they could, playing cards and delousing themselves. The tedium of the wait was relieved by the arrival of locals bearing food, and by occasional excursions into the nearby hills and valleys.[31]

It was on one such foray, while the group accepted a woman's offer of a meal, that Peck felt he was being drained of all energy. His bones ached, he felt cold, and his appetite disappeared. A feeling of nausea gave way to uncontrollable shakes. No number of blankets and coats piled on top of him would dispel them. Such was the concern for his well-being that a local healer was fetched, and he proceeded to administer a potion of herbs. When that had no effect, the decision was made to 'bleed' him. To this end a series of raki glasses were produced and candles lit, while the healer produced a dagger. Peck baulked, but his comrades sided with the healer and urged him to submit himself to the proposed cure, which for them appeared a source of great mirth.[32]

Peck had no choice but to undergo the operation. The healer, dagger at the ready, sat astride his legs and prepared to operate on his now unclad back. The women held upturned glasses over the candle flames, while in the background his companions made sympathetic noises. Peck wore a suitably martyred expression for the little children peering from the shadows, at least until a sharp stab drove all else from his mind, followed by the sensation of a red-hot glass being applied to the spot. He tried to resist his torturers, but soon the strength of many strong arms – Cretan and others – drove him back down. For the next hour more cuts were made, and more glasses applied, but at least the pain seemed to ease when he became accustomed to the process and he was fortified with raki. By the time the operation was concluded, the cuts seemed little more than tickles. When he finally calmed down, it was long past sunset.[33]

Not only was it late, but Peck did not have the strength to return to Megala Petra. He urged his three friends to go, as he would not forgive himself if they were to miss the evacuation because of him. Eventually they departed, leaving Peck to sleep the sleep of the exhausted. The following morning he was pampered by the womenfolk, so that he did not return to his camp until that afternoon. As he took a meal there, Noel appeared, with an expression on his face that said everything. The sub had come and gone without them.

Noel revealed the painful details. The men had lost their way on their return to camp after sunset, not reaching it until after midnight. When they found it deserted, they rushed around in vain to find someone to guide them to the evacuation point. As day broke, they were still scrambling, unguided, toward the coast. The first people they met were guides returning from the landing place. It was a terrible kick to the guts; there was nothing to be done now but to return to the boredom and frustration of another wait.[34]

For Peck the news only got worse. Three days after the missed evacuation, his shivers returned, followed by a ferocious high fever. He and Dunn were on the move at the time in the hills, so they took shelter under rocks and spent the most abject of nights there. By now Peck knew that there was something seriously wrong with him, and that without proper medical attention he would die on Crete. He struggled to a small hamlet, where the locals extended him their customary hospitality and sympathy. When a fresh episode of the shakes set in, the cuts treatment was administered again. That, too, would be to no avail. A discussion of those gathered around led at last to a correct diagnosis – Peck had malaria.[35]

What he desperately needed was quinine, but it was scarce enough in the big towns of Crete, let alone in an isolated mountain village. To make matters worse, by now winter was setting in, the village was cold, food was in short supply and the Germans were sending foraging parties to collect whatever they could get their hands on. Twice they visited the village where Peck lay desperately ill, and on each occasion he was bundled from house to house to avoid detection. On the second occasion, as he was later told, he was hidden in a large wooden box, well past caring what happened to him, and a German sat on it to drink his stolen wine.[36]

The Cretans, too, struggled through that winter of 1941–42. It was during those months, as George Psychoundakis later recalled, 'that the snail kingdom suffered the fiercest inroads. Every night, armed with oil dips and torches, the villagers would set out in hundreds in search of the priceless treasure which was the most luxurious fare to be found in house or inn.'[37]

Waking one day from an attack of the shivers, Peck found a stranger in city clothes with a neatly trimmed beard and glasses bending over him. It was a doctor from Heraklion, who had come to administer a shot of quinine filched from the Germans. After a series of injections over the next day the doctor's supply of the precious medicine was exhausted and he departed, but soon the malaria attacks ceased. When he became alert to the world around him again, Peck realised that Noel was no longer with him. The word was that another evacuation was planned, this time still further to the east, where another gathering of stragglers was being organised.[38]

Peck, however, proceeded in a different direction, heading back toward Georgioupoli in the hope of getting more quinine. His need for it was confirmed by another attack of the shivers, but neither he nor his Georgioupoli friends could get hold of any. Moreover, the area around the town posed a huge security risk; the German presence was heavier than ever before. Following the advice of a local member of the resistance, Peck headed east towards the village of Vafes, between Georgioupoli and Canea. A British agent had allegedly established a hideout in the hills outside Vafes, and Peck's hope was that that officer might have quinine. He was getting sicker by the day and knew that, despite the dangers posed by the German presence in the area, he had no other option. He was piloted to the home of a British sympathiser by the name of Vandoulakis. So accustomed had Vandoulakis become to sheltering men on the run that his home had earned the informal title of the British Consulate.[39]

In time the British agent did turn up. It was Xan Fielding, the SOE agent who on Crete went by the name of Aleko, and who spoke perfect Greek. Fielding could offer no quinine, but he expressed confidence that he could get Peck onto the next submarine or boat. In the meantime, Peck was hidden in a little hut in the Vandoulakis vineyard. The weather, at least, was brightening, but against that, in the absence of quinine Peck's health was in rapid decline. Moreover, after so much travel across the rocky Cretan terrain, his boots were in a parlous state. On both counts, any march across the island to an evacuation point would be torture.[40]

As Peck's despair deepened, Xan Fielding arrived to announce Peck would be taken to Amari to catch a submarine.[41] With Fielding was George Psychoundakis, the young shepherd from the village of Asi Gonia, already established as an invaluable courier for the British. Fleet of foot and high of humour, Psychoundakis with his local knowledge was able to cover prodigious distances across even the most challenging landscapes. Peck was keen to see him, having already encountered him on two fruitless sub chases. Psychoundakis gave an honest assessment of the task that awaited them. It was a long way to the evacuation point, and time was short. To get there in time, they would need to travel at night along the most direct route, and that meant passing through villages with a German presence.[42]

Psychoundakis set a cracking pace, placing a severe strain on Peck, who in a semi-conscious state staggered along as best he could, his feet blistered. Psychoundakis drove him on remorselessly until Peck's feet were raw and every step agony. One day they could not reach the nominated destination, as Peck collapsed on the stony track, and in utter exhaustion fell into a rough bunk that Psychoundakis fashioned in the nearby scrub.

Years later Psychoundakis, too, remembered that day and his efforts to help 'Johnny'. They had narrowly dodged a German patrol, but despite all George's efforts to help the Australian on his way, he could go no more. Half an hour short of the village of Karines, Peck said, '*Okhi allo, Yorghi. Poly arrostos. Edo ypno!*

(No more, George. Very ill. Here sleep.)' Psychoundakis observed Peck fall asleep almost before he lay down in his makeshift bed. He also saw what a pitiable state Peck's feet were in, mangled by his boots and the jagged terrain. Had he been the Australian, he thought, he would not have been able to walk at all.[43]

The next day, Psychoundakis was struck by the 'great sadness' in Peck's face and did what he could to lift his spirits. '"Never mind, Johnny", I told him, "everything will be all right when you get to Egypt", and laughed, telling him various amusing tales. But all in vain. All he did was to say: *"Panayia Mou! Kako paidi! Ego pathaino kai esy gelas."* ("All Holy Virgin! Bad boy! I die and you laugh!")'[44]

Eventually they descended from the central plain toward the south coast, entering a village which was George's destination. There they found a barn half full of hay. So shattered was Peck by this point that his guide hoisted him through the entrance, lay him down, covered him with grass and warned him not to make any noise for any reason until he returned. Peck would not see Psychoundakis again, at least not for a very long time. To him it seemed that he had been left there to die, a prospect which, such was his physical state, he welcomed with a sense of relief.[45]

In place of Psychoundakis another George arrived to take his charge on the last part of the journey. In the short time they were together, the second George became Peck's guide, philosopher and friend. The most illustrious of the SOE agents on Crete, Patrick Leigh Fermor, tells us that this was George Tyrakis, one of the best helpers of the British mission, who would later distinguish himself further during the kidnapping of the German General Kreipe.[46] On Tyrakis's watch Peck remained in a dazed state for much of the time. Later he vaguely recalled 'being half carried in strong arms through the cold night, arms that were so protective that I knew I was still in friendly hands'. In time the malarial cycle – shivers, high fever, and then blessed sleep – worked itself out, and Peck was able to propel himself towards their final goal, the evacuation beach. In time they could finally hear the sound of the sea. There were people about, and George engaged them in animated conversation. At the end of it George returned to Peck, placed his arm around his shoulder and told him the news: 'I am very, very sorry Johnny, the boat sailed away just over an hour ago.'[47]

What happened next is not entirely clear from the record, but it seems that Peck was captured once more by Germans, this time in the vicinity of the south coast, and perhaps in the aftermath of his failed evacuation. At Timbaki the Germans had established an aerodrome on territory that was strictly off limits to all but the Germans themselves. Perhaps Peck unwittingly stumbled into forbidden territory; in any case, he later reported that he was captured and held at the aerodrome on 12 February 1942. The circumstances of his capture, the conditions of his captivity and the means of his escape are unknown. It is merely recorded that his escape was effected two days after his capture 'by Cretan villagers'.[48] After the narrow escape from the German net in early June of the previous year, and then the breakout from the Galatas camp, this was his third escape. There would be more.

8

FAREWELL TO CRETE

WHILE PECK WAS BITTERLY DISAPPOINTED TO HAVE MISSED the boat, he was consoled once more with the assurance that another evacuation was being planned in the near future. In preparation for it he was guided to another group of evaders impatiently awaiting evacuation. They were concentrated in caves and huts in the mountains north of Treis Ekklisies; Peck himself was assigned to a tiny shepherd's shelter. It was not an ideal resting place for a man in Peck's condition, as the wind whistled through gaps in the wall and the earth roof dripped in multiple places. He shared it with an Englishman who had sustained a serious wound in the Battle of Canea, and whose days, like Peck's, seemed numbered.[1]

Their Cretan hosts were well aware of how desperate the two men's plight was, so a new plan was devised to save them. It entailed sending a mission to the north of the island to see if there might be doctors with the necessary knowledge and medicine. In Peck's assessment it was a foolhardy enterprise, but in about a week the Cretans returned in the company of two doctors. One of them was British – Major Arnold Gourevitch, the Paris-born son of Russian émigrés. Like the Australian Leslie Le Souef, Gourevitch had eschewed evacuation from Sfakia and stayed with the men in his care. But where Le Souef was taken to Salonika and then Germany, Gourevitch was eager to escape while he still had the chance. His identity as a Jew and the possible consequences for him after arrival in Germany might well have factored into his thinking. In any case, Gourevitch got out of Galatas by climbing the camp's perimeter wire and heading for Canea.[2]

Gourevitch's escape partner that night was the Australian surgeon Kiernan 'Skipper' Dorney, a Melbourne doctor who had enlisted in December 1939.[3] In Canea the two men were given refuge and civilian clothes by a dentist, and then they headed into the hills to spend the following months inhabiting caves and shepherds' huts. It is not known where they were when they got word to make their way to Treis Ekklisies, where their medical skills were desperately needed, and from where they, too, hoped to get off the island.[4]

The two doctors arrived at Peck's hut with neither quinine nor medical instruments, but their presence alone made him feel better. As for his sick English companion, they performed an operation on him using a razor blade in a piece of wood, and with no anaesthetic. A few days later the patient was found wallowing in the sheep pen – the operation had failed.[5] Efforts were made to fly in medical supplies, but the drop was poorly aimed and did not reach its target. When the by now large group of men moved down into Treis Ekklisies in readiness for evacuation, another operation was attempted, this time with instruments borrowed from a doctor in Heraklion. Peck records that it was performed on a church altar, the men by this time having taken refuge in the village's churches, but he does not record the outcome.[6]

While the delicate state of Peck's own health again scotched any chance of his evacuation, the good news for him was that a boat had landed some distance down the coast and had brought with it supplies. Among them, to his enormous relief, was quinine. Almost as welcome were tins of Players cigarettes, the first whiff of which made him pass out. Arnold Gourevitch departed to tend to his English patient, while Kiernan Dorney stayed in the church with Peck. When a German patrol approached, Dorney hid. The expectation, if not the hope, might well have been that the Germans would take Peck with them. Formally taken into captivity once more, he might have received proper medical attention. Instead, they seem to have calculated that the dying man represented a burden they preferred not to bear, so they gave him bread and wine and left him to die in peace.[7]

When the Germans moved on, chasing down the elusive stragglers, Dorney returned, heaved Peck onto his back, carried him back into the hinterland and, when settled, administered massive doses of quinine. At every point along the way locals took him in to give him refuge for the night. For part of the way he travelled by mule. On one more occasion Peck was halted by Germans, but when they observed more closely his skeletal thinness, his ragged clothes and his matted beard, they let him go. Eventually he and Dorney reached the northern side of the island once more and found refuge with a Cretan family in the village of Avdou Pedia-dos, about 40 kilometres east of Heraklion and not far from the new German aerodrome at Kastelli. The village had a proud history of resistance to Turkish occupation in the 19th century, and its inhabitants were determined to treat the German presence with a similar disdain.[8]

It was the Knarakis family which took him in and undertook to nurse him back to health. Though Peck felt ashamed of his lice and filthiness, he was washed and, for the first time since Cairo, was able to sleep in a proper bed with sheets. As he edged back toward normal health, he went on walks, dressed as an old woman to deceive Germans and any collaborators. The local deacon, the *diakos*, became a great friend who taught Peck much about the history of Crete, and in particular its resistance to occupiers over many centuries.[9]

After several weeks he felt sufficiently well to free his hosts of the awful risk of being caught harbouring a fugitive. He moved into a cave shared by several other men on the run. It was there that, for the first time since the Battle of Crete, he was able to hear via radio the gloomy news of the time. Days dragged by as they all awaited news of another sub chase, but no word came.[10]

It was at this time that Peck renewed his friendship with the New Zealander Noel Dunn. As relief from the monotony and bickering that could at times beset their gloomy troglodyte existence, Peck and Dunn abandoned the safety of their cave to trek into Heraklion, where their suspicions that the Germans had tightened their grip on Crete's largest town were confirmed. Only by the skin of their teeth did they evade capture at the archaeological site of Knossos, just outside Heraklion, the site of a Bronze Age palace complex built by the Minoans. From the beginning of the 20th century the famed British archaeologist Arthur Evans and his team had been excavating and partially restoring the site. Misdirections had sent Peck and Dunn to the vicinity of the Villa Ariadne, built adjacent to the Knossos palace to accommodate Evans as he dug his way into the history and culture of the Minoans. With the arrival of the Germans in 1941, the stately villa was confiscated and repurposed as the headquarters of the German occupation regime – 'Fortress Crete'.[11]

Countering the German presence in the area where Peck was hiding out were *andartes*, resistance fighters, most prominently Manoli Bandouvas, as well as their British SOE partners. Peck and the other men in hiding maintained contact with the SOE agent in the Heraklion area, at that time most likely Monty Woodhouse, in the hope that he might at some point impart some encouraging words about their prospective evacuation. For weeks on end he had to disappoint them.[12]

The situation was not entirely hopeless, as the fate of two other men still stuck on Crete reveals. Kiernan Dorney, the doctor who in all likelihood saved Peck's life, at some point in early 1942 made his way back to the south coast of the island, where further evacuations were still taking place. Records show that two occurred from the beach at Trofalos below the village of Krotos in Crete's central south. They took place on 22 May and 6 June 1942. On the first of those evacuations, carried out by the trawler *Hedgehog*, was Kiernan Dorney.[13]

Also aboard *Hedgehog* was Reg Saunders from Peck's 2/7 Battalion. Like Peck, he had been living on the run for over a year by this time, and was still alive and at liberty only because of the uncompromising kindness of the Cretans. Saunders and the other evacuees had been gathered on the beach during the night and told

Above Johnny Peck in Jerusalem, May 1940.

Australian War Memorial Peck Collection

Below Australian troops advancing into Bardia.

Imperial War Museum photograph E1573, Australian War Memorial 069221

Above Bardia. A group of diggers with some of the stragglers they had rounded up from the holes about Bardia.

Australian War Memorial 004905. Negative by Frank Hurley

Below Tobruk. Italians leaving the town to surrender to the Australian forces attacking Tobruk.

Australian War Memorial 005407. Negative by Frank Hurley

Above Kalamata, Greece, 26 April 1941. Exhausted Australian troops resting under trees in the Kalamata area while awaiting embarkation during the withdrawal of the Allied forces from Greece.

Australian War Memorial 069888

Below Suda Bay, Crete, May 1941. Troops of the 6th Division landing after their evacuation from Greece.

Australian War Memorial 074445

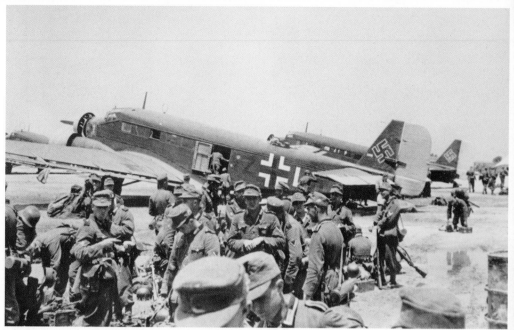

Above Milos, Greece, 20 May 1941.
German mountain troops waiting to
board their Junkers 52 transport aircraft
for the invasion of Crete (captured
photograph).

Australian War Memorial 069215

Below The village of Sfakia, situated on
the southern coast of Crete. Sfakia Cove,
visible in the midground, was the site of
the Allied withdrawal from Crete over
four nights, beginning on 28 May 1941.
Over 12 000 Allied troops were evacuated
in a series of naval convoys.

Australian War Memorial PO4067.005

Above Crete, 20 May 1941. German parachute troops over Suda Bay during the invasion (captured photograph).

Australian War Memorial 128433

Right The Forty-Second Street sign, near Suda Bay in Crete. The name came from a group of sappers from the 42nd Field Company, Royal Engineers, who had bivouacked beside the dirt lane. On 27 May 1941 it was the scene of a bloody battle between German forces and combined Australian and New Zealander units, including Johnny Peck's 2/7 Battalion. Taking the form of a bayonet charge, this was the last offensive action by Anzac forces.

Australian War Memorial P03731.001

Right In Crete German forces acted viciously against civilians suspected of aiding the enemy. The murder in cold blood of the men of Kontomari on 2 June 1941 was the first of a series of reprisals. Photo by Franz Peter Weixel.

Bundesarchiv Bildarchiv 101I-166-0525-30

Left 'The Cretan Runner', George Psychoundakis, who aided Johnny Peck, and an unidentified Cretan *andarte*.

SOURCE *WWIIinColor, photographer unknown*

Right The Union Jack Johnny Peck gave to the four men who escaped Sfakia on a small rowing boat. Peck had obtained the flag as a souvenir from a Greek girl who had made it to welcome the British to her country. Peck handed the flag to the four in the boat, stating that it would be best for them to have it as it might allow them to identify themselves if they encountered British forces on their way to Egypt. Having left Crete on 1 June 1941 the party finally reached their destination on 11 June, after suffering severe privations through shortage of food and water. The flag is in the

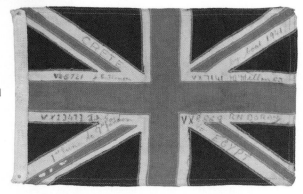

collection of the Australian War Memorial. The flag was later sent by one of the men – John 'Jack' Thomson, one of the signatories – to Australia, and it was subsequently carried by his brother as a lucky charm while serving in New Guinea.

Australian War Memorial RELAWM20230

Above Gruppignano in north-eastern Italy, c. 1941. The main entrance to the Italian Prisoner of War Camp PG 57 (Campo 57) in northern Italy with a Carabinieri guard on sentry duty. By October 1942 there were more than 1200 Australians and 1000 New Zealanders held in this camp.

Australian War Memorial P02793.001

Right One of the most famed and feared of the Cretan partisans – *andartes* – Manoli Bandouvas, photographed with his brothers Yiannis and Nikos. The British SOE agent Xan Fielding described Bandouvas as 'a dark burly man with sad ox-eyes and a correspondingly deep-throated voice in which he was fond of uttering cataclysmic aphorisms such as "The struggle needs blood, my lads."' (Xan Fielding, *Hide and Seek: The Story of a War-time Agent,* Secker & Warburg, London, 1954, p. 194).

National Library of Scotland 13338/622-625/F.520 Permission courtesy Artemis Cooper.

Photograph taken in Vercelli, 1943, after Peck's release from Vercelli jail. The spectacles helped him to assume the identity of a local businessman. Taken for the purpose of gaining an identity card, the photo came back to haunt Peck. Held on file by local authorities in Vercelli, it was used for 'Wanted' posters when Peck was being sought for his role in assisting POWs on the run.

Australian War Memorial Peck Collection

VERCELLI. 30/10/43.

Dear Boys?

    I have just recieved word that there are some of our chaps still in
the bush hiding out. This letter is really an introduction as the man who is
taking me out to you is a bit scared of me being a spy and as he wants some
garantee that I am a fair dinkim Aussie I hope you acknowledge this letter as
soon as it is given to you .

    Surely some of you know me and as I am half-pissed I wont waste time
with writing a long letter. My name is JOHNNY PECK., VX.9534. 2nd./7th.BATT.
6.th.DIV. A.I.F. Home Adress. CRIB POINT VICTORIA. AUSTRALIA.and thats basta
for me .

    When you receive this note I will not be far away from you so dont
keep me in suspenders ,send a reply back immediately as I will we waiting
for it

    I will tell you the news when I see you.

        All the best

Everything O.K
2/1.Batt all know above named   Yours Sincerely,
A.I.F Cpl. A.J. Sedgman
Pte. A.J. Forde
Pte. J.H Parker 2/24th Btn *Johnny D. Peck*
Pte. W Squires   *VX. 9534.* *X. P.O.W.*

Above An example of a note sent by Peck
to POWs hiding out in the Vercelli region
after the Italian armistice.

Australian War Memorial Peck Collection

Left The Australian Claude Webb, like Peck a former
POW, was part of the escape network Peck ran in
Vercelli. In March 1944 Webb was captured and sent to
a POW camp in Germany.

Australian War Memorial Peck Collection

Above Dr Anna Marengo, a Vercelli paediatrician and member of Peck's escape network, is arrested in January of 1944.

Australian War Memorial Peck Collection

Below Johnny Peck and Oreste Ferrari in the guise of Italian businessmen. The photo was taken in Luino in December 1943. Ferrari arranged guides to take escaped POWs to the Swiss border. He was captured and reportedly sent to concentration camps in Fossoli, then Mauthausen.

Peck family collection

Above A vicious war. The body of Douglas Smedley, a farmer from Corryong in Victoria, murdered by fascists on 24 April 1944. The Australian and two New Zealanders, JT Clark and Leslie George Batt, were hiding out with other men on the run in a farmhouse near the Piedmontese village of Andorno Micca. The three appear to have been shot as they tried to exit the building; all had fractured skulls. Smedley is buried in the Milan War Cemetery.

The National Archives (Kew) WO 235/324

Right Theo Saevecke, the Gestapo head of the Milanese prison where Peck spent some time.

Bundesarchiv Bildarchiv 183-BO221-0056-001

Above left The Queenslander Frank Jocumsen. Jocumsen, who became known in Italy as *'il Australiano'*, was very close to the Italian communist partisan leader Cino Moscatelli.

The National Archive (Kew) HS9.798/4

Above Peck, his hair still growing back after a stint in Milan's San Vittore prison, while recuperating in Wil in Switzerland in July of 1944.

Peck family collection

Left The most influential of the partisan leaders in north-western Italy, the communist Cino Moscatelli, addressing a gathering in Novara in 1945.

Instituto per la Storia della Resistenza

Above Willi Tensfeld, who led German and fascist forces in the brutal war against partisans in north-western Italy, with Italian fascist and German officers.

www.mymilitaria.it/liste_04/ss_scotti_baveno.htm

Below In the city of Domodossola, capital of the freshly proclaimed 'Free Republic of Ossola', September 1944. From left to right are Johnny Peck, Paul Ghali (an Egyptian-born, Berne-based reporter for the *Chicago Daily News*), Frank Jocumsen and the Irishman Pat Cottington, a member of Jocumsen's staff.

Australian War Memorial Peck Collection

Above Dionigi Superti, one of the most avid supporters of the Free Republic of Ossola, had overall command of Peck's Valdossola Division during the defence of the Republic.

Australian War Memorial Peck Collection

Below In the doomed battle to save the Free Republic of Ossola in October 1944, Peck's forces try to hold off the enemy.

Australian War Memorial Peck Collection

Above Partisan forces of Peck's Valdossola Division create a defensive position in a railway tunnel near Mergozzo, using granite blocks and machine gun apertures.

Australian War Memorial Peck Collection

Above left Peck, with an unidentified man, at Mergozzo on the shore of Lago di Mergozzo, scanning the lake shore for signs of enemy activity on the eve of the battle to save the Free Republic of Ossola.

Giorgio Armanini

Above right Johnny Peck as British Liaison Officer and Commander of Operations on the Central Front at Mergozzo in the defence of the Free Republic of Ossola, September–October 1944.

Australian War Memorial Peck Collection

Above Photograph of Peck in uniform when he was commanding forces in the Valdossola Division during the defence of the Republic of Ossola.

Peck family collection

to strip by three agents with clipped British accents, 'Most of you chaps are thick with lice. We've a trawler coming in at dawn, and we don't want to take lice on board.' When *Hedgehog* pulled in at dawn, the men waded out to her to help unload supplies, which were carted from the beach by donkeys. When Saunders, Dorney and the others boarded, they were given their first fresh clothes for what seemed an eternity, along with copious supplies of fruit and rum. When they finally reached the Egyptian coast at Bardia, now garrisoned by British forces, they were nursing hangovers.[14]

As for Johnny Peck, he had remained on the north of the island to the east of Heraklion, where he was attracted by rumours suggesting that boats or submarines might still evacuate remaining stragglers from the beaches at the very eastern end of Crete. As the quinine did its work, Peck dared to hope that he might yet make a successful sub chase, but this time by heading east, not south.

Crete was divided into four prefectures, or *nomoi*, and the easternmost of them, Lasithi, was not under German but Italian occupation. As on the Greek mainland and in Yugoslavia, the Axis powers had agreed to share occupation duties. The commander of the Italian zone was General Angelo Carta, whose regime was less brutal than that of the Germans in the three prefectures to the west. Nonetheless, the Italians, too, remained alert to the possible presence of Allied soldiers on the run and to the prospects of partisan activity, spurred along by British special forces.

Despite those dangers, and despite the advice issued by Dorney and Gourevitch to nurse themselves back to full health, Peck and Dunn resolved to head east into Italian-occupied Lasithi. They bade farewell in Avdou Pediados and, their Cretan rucksacks – *sakoulis* – stuffed full with supplies, they took off toward Sitia, near the north-eastern tip of Crete. Even before reaching Lasithi they were surprised by a German patrol, which shot at them but did not capture them. Their *sakoulis*, though, with their precious contents, were discarded in the act of flight. After hiding all day, they headed for the mountains at night.[15]

That narrow escape soon had a sequel. It seems that their discarded *sakoulis* had been identified by the Germans, who made arrests in the nearby villages on the suspicion that the locals had been aiding men on the run. On entering a village, Peck and Dunn were held by armed locals, determined to hand them over to the Germans. It seems that the population was divided over what to do with the interlopers, who were able to exploit the dissent to make a break for the hills, German patrols on their heels. Once again, however, Peck managed to give the Germans the slip, as became clear when his chasers' aimless and desultory shooting faded to silence.

Although Dunn and Peck had been heading east out of the prefecture of Heraklion and toward Lasithi, they were still in the territory of the renowned *andarte* Manoli Bandouvas, and soon became reacquainted with him and his band. Peck and Dunn stayed with the Bandouvas group for a while in an arrangement which suited both sides. Through Bandouvas the Anzacs had ready access to food and drink; they, for their part, were able to train the partisans in the use of the British weapons which were being smuggled onto the island with the help of the SOE.[16]

After the hardships of the trek it suited Peck to rest for a time. His malaria had been checked, but older wounds were causing him grief. During the escape from Galatas he had scraped his head and neck on barbed wire, and a piece of metal had lodged at the base of his spine and would not settle. Dorney had warned him that it was likely to play up until removed altogether, but in the meantime Peck had to resort to cruder measures to relieve the pain. The Cretan cure for the wounds on his head and neck was to apply a poultice of red-hot onions, but Peck would not let the locals near his spine.[17]

This was in the spring of 1942, and high in the hills south-east of Heraklion the nights were bracing. With the shepherds they encountered on their journey east they lit fires to keep warm. They saw planes flying overhead, some of them British, heading toward Kastelli airport to drop their lethal loads. But on one occasion a drop occurred much closer to where they were, and with much friendlier intent. Parachutes descended bearing radios and other equipment. With the help of shepherds they gathered together as much of the equipment as they could and hid it. They took the radio to a shepherd's hut, where they were given hot milk, cheese and raki. The drop, they feared, might draw the unwanted attention of occupiers, and as they had by now penetrated as far east as Lasithi, that would mean that Italian patrols could appear at any moment.[18]

One did. It was very early in the morning of 28 April. Inside their hut Peck and Dunn heard the sound of feet on nearby rocks. They at first assumed it was the shepherds returning from their nocturnal sweep of the surrounding countryside in search of parachutes, but it was an Italian patrol. At first Peck and Dunn sought to bluff their unwelcome visitors that they were shepherds. When they could produce no identity papers, they insisted that they had left them in Heraklion, but that, too, fell on disbelieving ears. Then one of the Italians chose to souvenir a brightly coloured woven blanket and found the radio underneath. And with that it was clear that the two men needed to be escorted to headquarters in Neapolis for questioning.[19]

It was a routine with which Peck, at least, was already familiar. When captured by a German patrol outside Georgioupoli, his interrogators had been reluctant to believe that he was an Allied soldier on the run. In asserting their scepticism on this occasion, the Italians were no less harsh than the Germans had been. On the contrary, as Peck stuck stubbornly to the line that he was entitled to be treated as a POW, and therefore in accordance with the terms of the Geneva Convention, he was struck across the face by the incredulous Italian officer. Peck at the time was handcuffed, while the Italian inflicted his cruel blow with a riding crop.[20] Italian captivity, the Australian would soon learn, meant unrelieved hardship and privation. Further interrogations followed after transfer to the prison at Ay Yiannis. Both Peck and Dunn, it was resolved, should be sent to Rhodes to be tried as spies.[21]

Chained to the mast of the caique that was to deliver them to Rhodes, there was no chance of escape. The caique touched at several islands on route to its destination, where the men were immediately despatched to a prison at Kalithea on the north-eastern coast of the island, just south of the capital Rhodes. They were not alone there. In their cell was a man Peck later identified as Frank McCaskey, who had been sentenced to death, and a New Zealander by the name of Roy Natusch. The latter, stranded at Kalamata, had spent the best part of a year on the run with an Australian sergeant named Johnny Sachs in the Peloponnese before Italian occupying forces had nabbed them.[22]

The next morning the men were taken from Kalithea to the town of Rhodes and deposited in a jail there. In the cell next-door was a group of Czechs, in all likelihood Jews, fearful that the Italians would serve them up to their Axis masters.[23] Peck and his cellmates were confronted with a similarly stark fate – a tribunal had allegedly sentenced them to death as spies. The men volubly protested the breach of the Geneva Convention and pleaded with their captors to check with the Germans in Athens to confirm that they were indeed POWs. Like the Czechs in the neighbouring cell, however, Peck and his co-condemned were not hopeful that a more positive outcome was in prospect. More importantly, like the Czechs next door, they were not inclined to wait around to find out.[24]

9

TO ITALY

THE AEGEAN ISLAND OF RHODES, OVER 300 KILOMETRES TO the north-east of Crete, was an entirely Italian possession, a small part of Mussolini's dream of *mare nostrum* ('Our Sea'). Its population was mixed, drawing from the surrounding nations, including Turkey, visible on the eastern horizon. For the men plotting their escape from a jail near the north-eastern coast of Rhodes, the proximity of neutral Turkey was a godsend, and it became the centrepiece of their plan. That plan came to fruition when, soon after their arrival in the island's capital, they made a nocturnal break from their prison, knocking out the guard, scaling a wall and scurrying to the beach. There they seized a boat with the aim of sailing it to the Turkish coast, just 18 tantalising kilometres distant.[1]

It was at this point that things went fatally awry. The tiny vessel was barely seaworthy; when a sudden storm blew up, its fragility was cruelly exposed. Despite the passengers' frantic efforts to hold it together, the boat sank, and all five of the Czechs on board drowned, as their knee-length boots filled with water and dragged them to the bottom. Only Peck and Dunn managed to keep themselves afloat as they swam toward Turkey, until an Italian destroyer plucked them from the sea, hauled them aboard and returned them to Rhodes in a state of exhaustion.[2]

This was not the first time Peck had cheated death by drowning – the Luftwaffe's assault on *Costa Rica* had already taken him to the brink. And it was not the last time that he would be saved by Italians. While he and Dunn no doubt cursed their misfortune in not reaching neutral Turkey, they could at least be grateful that their lives had been spared.[3]

Though Peck did not speak of it when later in life recalling his interlude on Rhodes, the records from close to that time suggest that he spent several days – from 16 to 21 May – in the Rhodes hospital.[4] Then he was despatched to a more secure camp in the centre of the island, near the village of Apollona. The one abiding memory Peck had of it was the abundance of beautiful butterflies in the nearby Valley of Butterflies. At the end of the wet season every year, towards the end of May and so just when Johnny Peck was there, thousands of butterflies emerge from the pupal stage and overwhelm the valley. To Peck they offered a fleeting reminder that there was a world outside the war that had engulfed him. Apollona was, however, at best a temporary abode. Peck and Dunn were returned to the coast and prepared for another voyage. In case the sirens urged them to escape their island-hopping westward voyage, they were once more bound, Ulysses-like, to the mast. This time their destination, reached on 1 June 1942, was Italy.[5]

Though the starting point was unusual, voyages to Italy were almost a commonplace for Anzac POWs in the Mediterranean theatre of war. Some 2000 Australians were captured in North Africa. At first there was just a trickle of men taken prisoner by the Italians in the first days of 1941. Far more commonly it was Italians who were being captured by Anzac and other British forces and packed off to such places as India, Canada and Australia. But after Rommel and his Afrika Korps arrived in Africa from February of 1941, the desert war was turned on its head, as the Germans pushed the Allies back across Libya towards Egypt. At Tobruk and other points of the Western Desert through the middle months of 1941, Australians and their various allies were captured by Germans and told that their war was over.

Almost always the tasks of processing, detaining, feeding and accommodating these men were left to the Italians. This wounded the pride of many Australians, whose crushing victories in the Western Desert had taught them to question the worthiness of their Italian adversaries. Whether they liked it or not, Australians captured by German forces in Libya through 1941 were given over to the Italians and placed in rough holding camps, the biggest of them in Benghazi. When the time was ripe, they were loaded into the dank, stinking holds of Italian vessels and delivered to the Italian mainland.

A year later, and around the time that Johnny Peck was being taken to the port of Bari from Rhodes, history repeated itself in North Africa. By the middle of 1942 Rommel was on the march again, and at pace. Once again Australians were among the Allied forces that blocked Rommel's path to Cairo, most famously at

El Alamein. Their desperate efforts came with a great cost in lives and in numbers of men who found themselves POWs. On a single night – from 26 to 27 July 1942 – at a place which military map-makers had labelled 'Ruin Ridge', Allied forces made a desperate effort to break the Axis lines. The Germans conceded ground early, but within hours had recovered from the early shock and hit back hard. To their horror the men of the West Australian 2/28 Battalion realised with the dawning of the new day that they were completely surrounded by German tanks and artillery. In one fell swoop, 490 of them were captured.[6] Like those caught earlier in Africa, and all those still to be seized until victory at Alamein finally halted Rommel, their fate was to be handed to the Italians, placed in crude lice-ridden holding camps and sent to Italy.

The most perilous experience for these POWs was the voyage across the Mediterranean. The sea was infested with Royal Naval submarines with a brief to disrupt Axis shipping; from the murky depths cargo ships loaded with POWs could hardly be distinguished from any other vessel. The single event which cost most Australian POW lives in Europe was the accidental sinking of the *Nino Bixio*, an Italian vessel carrying a load of some 3000 POWs to Brindisi. Two days out from Benghazi, on 16 August 1942, *Nino Bixio* was struck by two torpedoes fired from the British submarine HMS *Turbulent*. The first torpedo killed about 200 men on the spot when it exploded in the tightly packed forward hold. Others died of wounds or drowned when they jumped overboard. The survivors were those who stayed put, since *Nino Bixio* stayed afloat long enough to be towed to the Greek coastline.[7] By that time over 300 men were dead, 41 of them Australians and 118 New Zealanders.[8]

A variety of fates awaited those who arrived in Italy. The Italians had established a camp system which stretched across the mainland and which was designed – as the Geneva Convention dictated it should – to hold the officers separately from the Other Ranks (ORs). Thus a number of camps for officers were established, the most important of which for Australians was PG 78 at Sulmona, not far from Rome.

As for the ORs like Johnny Peck and for Non-Commissioned Officers (NCOs), the first camp was commonly PG 75 at Bari, a hot and dusty holding camp located near the port at which most arrived. Peck was there from the beginning of June through to the middle of July 1942.[9] It was only six weeks, but it was enough for him to make another escape attempt. A wound needed attention, so Peck was transferred to the camp hospital. Only his own brief notes attest to what happened next: 'Escape from hospital. Recaptured in café.'[10]

After that he spent a similar time – until the beginning of September – at PG 65 Gravina. Like Bari, it was in the Apulia region of southern Italy, and like PG 75, it was also a transit camp. From there he and other POWs were sent on to other camps, usually in northern Italy. In small numbers they were scattered across a number of camps, where in most cases they were outnumbered by men of other nationalities.

The most common destination for Australian and New Zealander POWs was PG 57 Gruppignano. It was located in the province of Friuli in the very north-east corner of Italy. The nearest city was Udine, just 15 kilometres to the west. In the other direction, just a few kilometres away, was the border with Yugoslavia, a large swathe of which had been annexed to Italy. The nearest railway station was at Cividale; from there the men were walked the 3 kilometres to the camp and to their forbidding new homes.

The camp had little to recommend it. Before Johnny Peck's arrival it was undergoing an expansion to accommodate the swelling numbers of men being shipped from Africa. Of the 1600 men recorded there in July 1942, nearly 1000 were Australians, mostly ORs and 70 NCOs.[11] By October the Australian population of Gruppignano had reached its apogee of 1200, just outnumbering some 1000 New Zealanders.[12] Prisoners bemoaned the shortage of decent food, the lack of recreational facilities, the confiscation of musical instruments and the omnipresence of vermin. Red Cross parcels aside, the food was universally regarded as abysmal. Accommodation, too, was at best rough. At least the initial forest of tents had been replaced by huts, offering some shelter against the icy winds which swept down from the Alps in winter, and the baking heat of summer.[13]

The discomforts were aggravated by the personality of the camp's commandant, Colonel Vittorio Calcaterra, who in the POWs' view appeared to take a perverse delight in causing his charges discomfort and pain. A known disciplinarian, Calcaterra may have been given the duty of supervising Anzacs precisely because their reputation for fractious behaviour went before them. The Italian military's assessment, founded on fascist propaganda and on close encounters in the Libyan desert, was that Australians were so prone to looting and ruthlessness as to require firm handling.[14]

Calcaterra's authoritarian streak set the tone of life in the camp, infecting the attitudes of the guards who served under him, and producing contempt and resentment among the prisoners. Numerous sources have it that Calcaterra adorned his office wall with a quote from Mussolini which ran, 'The English are accursed, but more accursed are Italians who treat them well.'[15]

Ultimately the tensions in PG 57, never far from the surface, had fatal consequences in May 1943. On one awful day, one of the Australian POWs, Edward William 'Sox' Symons, was shot dead by one of Calcaterra's men.[16] As a postwar trial revealed, Symons had been drinking and had threatened an Italian guard, Corporal Soddini, with a beer bottle. Soddini was in no mood to accommodate the Australian's bawdy behaviour and shot Symons dead at point-blank range.[17]

Johnny Peck arrived in Gruppignano in September 1942 after his stints in camps at Bari and Gravina. Gruppignano was no work camp; the men spent their days passing their time as best they could. Though many might have contemplated escape, in reality PG 57 was well guarded, and escapes were rare. Peck took a longer-term view, determined to win his freedom once more, but persuaded also that in Gruppignano he needed to prepare himself as best he could for the day his opportunity arrived. That meant devoting himself to acquiring Italian, above all from the guards.[18]

These were bleak times for Johnny Peck. There had been an escape attempt while he was there, but the men who managed to get out were soon recaptured, and security was tighter than ever before. He despaired at the woeful prospect of making a successful break, telling his parents in a letter that he would 'sell my soul to be home right now'.[19]

A ray of hope arrived unexpectedly after more than six abject months in PG 57. Italian authorities had elected to draw on POW labour to fill some yawning gaps in Italy's rural workforce. Well over 1000 of PG 57's prisoners were transferred out of Gruppignano to new sites hundreds of kilometres away in Italy's far

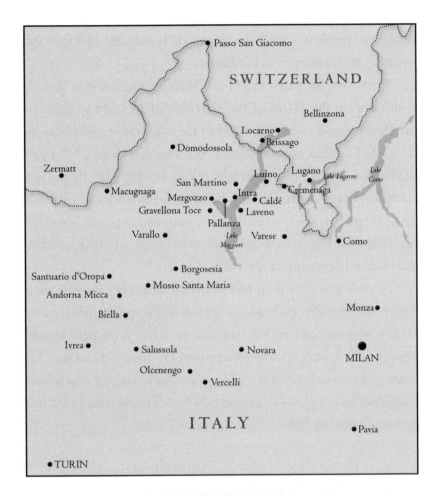

The parts of Piedmont and Lombardy
which Johnny Peck came to know well

north-west.[20] Though they might have felt ambivalent about the prospect of lending the enemy a helping hand, many could see that the move would liberate them from the misery of Gruppignano and deliver a boost to their mental and physical health. So it was that in April of 1943, Johnny Peck and 821 other Australians found themselves huddled in cattle cars heading westward by rail across the north Italian plains, through Lombardy and into the north-western province of Piedmont.

They were delivered to PG 106 Vercelli. The town of Vercelli is situated on the plains of the river Po, about halfway between the Piedmontese capital of Turin to the south-west and Milan to the east. The area around Vercelli is renowned above all for rice production. Unlike PG 57 Gruppignano, PG 106 Vercelli was not a single, heavily guarded camp but a series of work camps, 29 of them altogether. These were typically state-run or privately owned rice farms, the largest of which took up to 100 men to help with the planting or harvesting of rice crops.[21]

In most cases the men had few complaints, because life on a farm was generally more pleasant than at Gruppignano. Johnny Peck was no exception. He was sent to a rice farm just outside Vercelli called San Germano Vercellese. He soon noticed that his hosts and co-workers were more sympathetic, and the conditions altogether less oppressive. His sense of relief is palpable in a letter he wrote home in May:

> Since I've been here, about a month, my health and spirits
> have improved a 100%. There are forty-seven of us in this
> camp and we are growing rice on the plains of Piedmont
> in the North of Italy. It's much better than being locked up
> behind the barb-wire for 24 hrs a day, year in-year out, as we
> do get a certain amount of freedom out here. We rise at 6.30,
> have a cuppa' tea, start work at 8AM. Work till noon, home
> for dinner, usually rice and then work till 5PM. We then walk
> 4 miles back to camp and eat again, more rice.[22]

Though of course he made no mention of it, there was another reason his mood had leavened: the possibility of escape was now vastly greater than at PG 57. Security arrangements varied from detachment to detachment, but most commonly the men were housed within some kind of makeshift camp within the farm, to which they would return every evening after their day's work. Typically, a fence would be strung around one or more buildings crudely converted for POW accommodation. Guards were posted to each of the sub-camps, and civilian supervisors were present as well. But they had their work cut out containing men whose eyes were experienced in detecting the flaws in the security arrangements. In the event of an escape, they could telephone PG 106 headquarters in Vercelli, but by the time help arrived, the escapees would be well on their way.[23]

Perhaps even more valuable for the intending escaper were the opportunities that work camps created for prisoners to form contacts, even friendships, with civilians outside the camp. Such was the everyday reality of farm labour that Australian prisoners tilled the soil, harvested the crops or perhaps worked machines immediately alongside Italian workers. In time, some of them began to feel at home there.

Not so Johnny Peck. Giorgio Nascimbene, an Italian historian who explored the habitual elusiveness of the Allied POWs, has it that within the first few weeks of his arrival in Vercelli Peck had sought to escape three times, but without success.[24] Then, on the night of 13 June 1943, Peck finally made good his disappearance.[25] 'Climbed the wire fence at dusk', was his pithy description of this exploit.[26] With him were three Victorians: George William 'Bomber' Brown, John Thomas (Jack) Giles and Douglas Andrew Brook. Their destination was Switzerland.[27]

Peck's view, as he explained many years later, was that he had a duty to get back and fight again, but he knew that to do so from deep inside enemy territory was a tall order. From the start he dismissed the notion that the four of them might bamboozle people they met by pretending to be Italian; instead, the plan was to travel by night, heading north-west as fast as they could, and avoid the local populations entirely.[28] From the plains around Vercelli this seemed feasible enough; after all, the distance to the Swiss border was only about 100 kilometres as the crow flies. After the first third of the journey, however, the flat lands gave way to pre-Alpine hills, and then to a landscape of steep mountains and plunging valleys. The closer the Swiss border was, the more intimidating appeared the prospect of reaching it.

For four or five days the men made good progress, managing to scrounge enough to eat and drink while strictly avoiding contact with locals. Then, however, Brown became ill and could not go any further, and Giles chose to stay with him to surrender to the authorities. After eight days of freedom, Brown and Giles were recaptured at Varallo.[29] Peck and Brook, however, pressed on.

There is no surviving account of the precise route the men took, except that Peck spoke many years later of trekking up the Val Anzasca, a valley that wound its way from the pre-Alpine region of Ossola up to the famous Monte Rosa massif, which straddled the Swiss–Italian border. In all likelihood the men entered the Anzasca from the south, and might at some point have gleaned that at the top of the valley was a steep but negotiable path up the border, which ran along a craggy ridge. The starting point for that precipitous climb to the border was in the vicinity of the picturesque village of Macugnaga, nestled in the upper reaches of the valley. From the narrow, winding valley floor it was possible to ascend in a northerly direction toward the Monte Moro Pass, reaching the border markings as the track levelled out, and then descending into Switzerland. To the people of the valley, intimately familiar with the landscape and the fluky conditions which could render it lethal in a flash, it was known to be one of the easier crossing points, much favoured by smugglers. To foreigners without as much as a map and suffering sustained undernourishment, it was a severe test, worth taking only because of the precious reward at the end of it.

By Peck's own reckoning, Doug Brook and he reached the border – indeed, crossed it – on 1 July. The Australians had been on the run for 18 days, the last three of them without food. On that auspicious day they had scrambled from the tiny village of Pestarena in the valley floor – just before Macugnaga – to the border ridge. They crossed it, and stared down the other side into Switzerland, and freedom.

Many times before, Peck's bids for freedom had been cruelly thwarted. But never had his freedom seemed more tightly in his grasp than now, and never had it presented itself with such a beautiful visage. As he looked down into Switzerland he spied a scene that would have done any box of chocolates proud – 'range after range of snow-covered mountains', as he reminisced decades later.[30]

Sublime beauty alone did not, however, fill the bellies of the famished escapers. With no prospect of feeding themselves, and faced with a daunting trek down cavernous valleys and up sheer mountains, the men turned back into Italy to seek supplies. They appealed to the kindness of a local whom they took to be a shepherd. Perhaps, indeed, he was, but he was not well disposed to these strangers. The Italian wandered off to gather supplies for the weary travellers, while Peck and Brook hid behind a rock.[31] When the shepherd returned, instead of food he had a posse of uniformed men. Brook and Peck were promptly arrested. They spent some rueful hours in the village of Ceppo Morelli before being returned unceremoniously to Vercelli.[32]

In Italy as elsewhere, a standard punishment for escape from a POW camp was a month in prison, and that was Peck's fate when he was returned to Vercelli. Unlike the established camps like PG 57, the Vercelli camp did not have its own prison facility for this purpose. He served his time in great discomfort in what appears to have been a converted silo. At least, though, he was able to let his parents know what he had been up to. On 18 July he wrote:

> As the old saying has it, if you could only see me now. I'm
> just back from an unofficial tour of the Alps and as the
> result am doing thirty days in a jail within a jail. It's rather
> a curious calaboose in its way although it's pretty effective
> and does the job. It's got no bars, no doors, no barb wire,
> no windows and only one wall and that's cement. I won't
> hold you in suspense with the answer to that riddle, so here
> it is. We, that is, my mate Dug Brook, from North Carlton,
> who did the midnight flit with me, are now taking the place
> of ensilage in a silo. They just chucked the chaff out and
> chucked us in, and here we stop until the penance is thought
> to have expiated our crime, to wit, leaving without notice
> our hosts' lodging for one of our own choosing in a better
> and far away land. Alas, luck played us false and we stop
> here till the right time comes for you to see your vagabond
> son, Des.[33]

At the end of July he was released, but not back to his original San Germano sub-camp. According to one source, at least, his new place of work was the Cascina Dallodi farm.[34] Security might well have been tighter than at his first work camp; Peck in any case regarded his new home as a punishment camp.

Clearly the new regime did not suit him. Without divulging details, he would claim that he 'fell out' with the camp commandant. As punishment this time he was given a stint of solitary confinement. By early September he was vegetating in a civilian jail in Vercelli, the castle of Beato Amedeo.[35]

10
ARMISTICE

AS JOHNNY PECK SAT OUT HIS TIME IN A VERCELLI PRISON, fundamental changes were afoot in the wider world. The successful Allied invasion of Sicily – Operation Husky – began on the night of 9 July. For Italy the military calamities in Greece and Africa had been bad enough, but the presence of Allied troops on Italian soil heralded drama in Italian politics. By alienating a coterie of leading fascists, Mussolini had unwittingly engineered his own downfall.

When the Fascist Grand Council met on the night of 24–25 July, Mussolini was savagely attacked by his opponents, painfully aware that not just Sicily but the entire war was lost. A majority favouring an ignominious but rapid exit, together with the immediate deposition of the *Duce*, got its way. The King was called upon to resume control of the armed forces, and, when he had done so, used his powers to have Mussolini arrested.

The running of the government was placed in the hands of a monarchist general, Pietro Badoglio. The message to the Italian population, and above all to Italy's Axis partners, was that Italy would continue to prosecute the war. Secretly, though, Badoglio planned an armistice with the Allies. Negotiations produced a text which was signed as early as 3 September, a short time before the Allies were to launch their invasion of the mainland. For several days the Armistice and its terms remained confidential, until on 8 September, as the pusillanimous Badoglio appeared to be having second thoughts, the Allies announced the Armistice to the world.

From as early as May Hitler had been preparing for the possibility that Italy would not just withdraw from the war but defect.[1] Under the pretext of bolstering Italian defences in advance of a likely Allied invasion of the Italian mainland, German troops had been streaming south through the Brenner Pass since 25 July. Within hours of the announcement of the Armistice, thousands more followed. By the end of August seven German divisions had established themselves in Italy without deigning to solicit the permission of the Italian General Staff.[2] Hitler would do everything in his power to stop Italy falling into Allied hands.

Sure enough, the German response to the Armistice announcement was swift and savage. The Germans had not forgotten what they regarded as Italy's treachery in World War I, when the Italians, after much prevarication, had opted to join the Triple Entente against the Central Powers. To Hitler's mind the Armistice was a second betrayal and could not go unpunished. On the Mediterranean island of Kefalonia the Italian garrison of 5000 was brutally murdered by German forces when it offered resistance.[3] On Crete, whose easternmost province was occupied by Italian forces, the German takeover was less bloody, though no less forceful. The German mood was all the sourer because British SOE officers had managed to persuade the Italian commander, Angelo Carta, to deliver himself to them and be spirited off to Cairo.

In Italy itself confusion reigned. The Allied intention was that the Armistice would coincide with a full-scale landing. However, as the vacillating Badoglio did little to prepare for either a dramatic announcement or an invasion, a crucial component of the Allied plan – a large-scale airborne invasion of the capital, Rome – had to be abandoned at the last moment.[4] Instead, on the day after the Armistice was proclaimed to the world, Allied forces staged a seaborne invasion in the south to establish a beachhead at Salerno in the Gulf of Naples. The rest of the country, including Rome, remained entirely at the mercy of German forces who were in no mood to exercise restraint.

Such had been the expansion of the German presence that even the relatively modest Allied goal of establishing a beachhead in the very south was heavily contested. As for the rest of the country north of that tenuous toehold, German officers arrived at Italian army headquarters by 8 pm on 8 September to deliver a stark choice: the Italians must either surrender within the hour or guarantee immediate cooperation.[5] Indecision reigned, because amid his hurried departure from Rome, Badoglio had failed to give firm instructions. Most of the Italian armed forces were unsure as to whether they were supposed to fight the Germans, their erstwhile allies, or join them in resisting the Allied invasion.[6] With that, all hope harboured by the Allies that the Italians might act to loosen the German grip on their country evaporated. Confronted with overwhelming and well prepared German adversaries, in most cases Italian forces meekly surrendered and, for the time being, were allowed to go home. Wherever they dug in their heels, they soon felt the full wrath of the Germans; then, and over the weeks to follow, they were taken prisoner and deported in cattle trucks to Germany to serve as slave labourers.[7] Altogether some 600 000 Italian officers and men were captured in this way. Deprived of any meaningful leadership, the Italian army dissolved, creating a vacuum which the Germans filled at lightning speed.[8]

Within just a couple of days of the announcement of the Armistice, there was not much of Italy left for Badoglio and his government to rule. As the state and its armed forces crumbled, the King, Badoglio and leading officials fled Rome to seek refuge on the Allied beachhead. A precarious new seat of government was established in Brindisi, later in Salerno, as the King entrusted Badoglio with consolidating the so-called Kingdom of the South.[9] On 13 October the government, its die well and truly cast, declared war on Germany as it assembled five divisions to fight side by side with the Allies. As a durable reminder, though, of their recent errant ways, the Italians were not acknowledged as 'Allies'; they had to make do with the lesser title of 'co-belligerents'.[10] As far as the Allies were concerned, there was still some penance to be done before the Italians could be viewed on an equal footing.

Everywhere north of the Allied beachhead, too, the Italians had largely lost control of their country. Wehrmacht units were dispatched southward at pace to halt the Allied advance. Behind the Wehrmacht's operational zone the Germans established a regime of occupation which was every bit as brutal as those it had imposed on Greece, Crete and numerous other parts of Europe.

While the German occupation was deeply resented, it was not without Italian collaboration. Despite his humiliating dismissal, even Mussolini's exit from the political stage proved a temporary affair, since Hitler could still see symbolic value in engineering a political reincarnation. Mussolini had been held under arrest at a ski resort in central Italy's Gran Sasso massif. In the confusion that surrounded the Armistice announcement, the Badoglio government failed to carry out the promise to deliver Mussolini to the Allies.[11] On 12 September a team of German commandos under Otto Skorzeny staged a spectacular assault, using gliders to fly onto the mountain, freeing Mussolini without firing a single shot.

Though the former *Duce* might have preferred an exit from the political stage into genteel retirement, Hitler had other plans for him. Mussolini was informed of them – and saw no option but to agree to them – when he was whisked to the Wolf's Lair in Rastenburg for a meeting with Hitler.[12] Within two weeks the reluctant Mussolini was installed as the puppet leader of a new fascist government based in the town of Salò on the shores of Lake Garda in Lombardy. German 'minders' were appointed to keep a close watch on the revived state. Nominally, at least, Mussolini was the leader of *Repubblica Sociale Italiana,* or RSI, yet real power rested with his saviour Hitler.

What did all that mean for the roughly 80 000 'British' POWs like Johnny Peck, detained in camps and prisons dotted all over Italy, but mainly in the north? They had not been forgotten in the course of those tumultuous events leading to the Armistice. Indeed, one of its articles explicitly imposed an obligation on the Badoglio government: 'All prisoners and internees of the United Nations shall be immediately handed over to the Allied Supreme Commander and no one of them shall be now or in any moment transferred to Germany.'[13] As Badoglio manoeuvred to save his own skin, however, he failed to convey that obligation to those who might have been able to meet it. As it happened, an order to the effect that POWs were to be released was sent out to Italian commandants by the Italian War Ministry on 6 September, but with little effect other than to add to the sense of confusion.[14]

On the British side as well, there occurred what soldiers and military theorists alike term 'a monumental cock-up' which cost thousands their freedom. The word that was sent to POWs across Italy in advance of the announcement of the Armistice was that they should stay put. MI9, which had done its utmost to extend assistance to POWs on the run in Crete and elsewhere, had decided that POWs in Italian hands should remain in their camps and await the arrival of Allied forces. Order P/W 87190, stemming from MI9 head Norman Crockatt and issued as early as 7 June 1943, stated: 'in the event of an Allied invasion of Italy, officers commanding prison camps will ensure that prisoners of war remain within camp. Authority is granted to all officers commanding to take necessary disciplinary action to prevent individual prisoners of war attempting to rejoin their own units.'[15] Instructions were issued to the Senior British Officers (SBOs) in Italian camps via a popular BBC weekly program. Instead of the usual 'Hello' or 'Good evening', the show opened with the words 'Good evening, forces' – a signal that a message would be embedded in the following words of Christian comfort.[16]

The fear driving the instruction was that with a lack of weapons the POWs could hardly be expected to make a military contribution to the impending occupation. Indeed, if on the loose behind enemy lines they risked being subjected to severe reprisals. The safest path, it was assumed, was for the POWs to expect the arrival of liberating Allied forces. Sure enough, in most cases the SBOs did as instructed, ordering their men not to leave their camps, even after Italian guards had laid down their arms and disappeared. In one camp, for example, PG 21 in Chieti, the SBO threatened to court-martial any POW who left. When that provoked a near mutiny, the SBO appointed his own phalanx of guards to man the watchtowers. German paratroopers on their arrival at the camp were astonished to discover the prisoners still milling around inside the compound.[17]

In certain circumstances British policy did allow the officers to adopt a different course of action. In the event, Crockatt had written, that it was impossible to defend the camps, then the commanding officers should 'set at liberty all the white prisoners but keep the blacks in prison. Facilitate their escape either to Switzerland or along the Adriatic coast to southern Italy.'[18] Only at the very last moment, on 8 September, was there a change of heart at the War Office in London, which belatedly sought to convey the news that the Italian authorities would be releasing POWs so that they might make their way to Switzerland or an Adriatic port.[19]

It was little wonder, then, that mixed messages led to a variety of responses when news of the Armistice reached Italian POW camps on the evening of 8 September. What happened next depended on the attitude of the camp commandants, their guards, and on the POWs themselves. There were those who jumped through the window of opportunity the very moment it was prised open. Then there were those whose capacity for individual initiative was stifled by years behind barbed wire and who preferred the seemingly safer option of staying put. To the ultimate regret of most, they trusted that Allied forces would descend on them at any moment and whisk them to safety. They could not know that the Allied landings were confined to the south, typically hundreds of kilometres away and soon halted by fierce German resistance, or that plans to take a port such as Genoa or stage air assaults in the north had been scotched. Rumours abounded, and there was no way to confirm or deny them.

In most cases the men stayed put.[20] At Gruppignano, in any case, the speed of events gave them little chance to make good an exit. True to form, Colonel Calcaterra was determined that order would prevail. News of the Armistice was read to the men at parade on 9 September, and indications were given that they would be guided from the camp. By the evening, however, Calcaterra announced that no POW was permitted to leave the camp, and Italian guards were positioned around the camp's perimeter fence. On the afternoon of 10 September the commandant made it clear that he remained in charge and escape attempts would not be tolerated. For two more days order was imposed over an increasingly restive population, until early on the morning of Sunday 12 September German troops arrived by truck. The men's hearts sank as the regime changed before their eyes. By the following day the men were escorted under threat of violence to the nearby railway station, where they were loaded into cattle cars and sent to Germany. Within a whisker of their freedom, as it seemed, most were destined to another 20 months behind barbed wire.[21]

Most of the Australian officers had been in PG 78 at Sulmona, outside Rome, but had been transferred north to Campo PG 19 in Bologna in July 1943. Unusually, the SBO in Bologna, Brigadier Ronald Mountain, had chosen to ignore the 'Stay put' order and arranged for a breakout. Unfortunately, a nearby German garrison got word of the plan and nipped it in the bud.[22] The Germans loaded the prisoners onto what became known colloquially as 'the Moosburg Express', named for one of the German POW camps for which they were headed. A couple of decades later the scenes of disconsolate men finding themselves suddenly prisoners of the Germans and embarking on long train rides north would be recreated in the movie *Von Ryan's Express*. The only men to escape spending the rest of the war in the Reich were those who managed to smash their way out of the moving cattle cars on their journey towards the Alps.[23]

By the middle of November the Germans had snatched some 24 000 of the almost 80 000 Allied POWs in Italy at that time and transferred them into the Reich.[24] By the end of the year more than double that figure – some 50 000 men – had been added to the population of the Reich's Stalags and Oflags. Most of them would spend the rest of the war working for the Germans, while officers and most NCOs could do little but adapt to the boredom and privations of their caged routines.[25]

At work camps like those scattered around the province of Vercelli, it was quite a different story. Commonly the guards and prisoners celebrated the Armistice together, and when all had nursed their hangovers, the guards abandoned their posts. The commanding officer at PG 106, Sergio Rigoni, had instructed his subordinates at the many work detachments to that effect.[26] Most had lost all taste for a war which, as they saw it, had brought only misery and ignominy to Italy. The guards fled, most of them heading home, before the Germans arrived in the district to attempt to round up the POWs.[27]

That happened on 10 September, just two days after the Armistice was announced. The Germans collected all those whom apathy or indecision had confined to their work detachments. By 20 September the whole Vercelli district was firmly under the German thumb. As a sure sign that a new regime was in command, the Vercelli newspaper *La Sesia* announced in plain language 'the

German orders in Italy'. One of them related quite specifically to Allied POWs: all prisoners escaped from camps were to be delivered to the German military authorities, who would give 1800 lire in exchange for every prisoner.[28]

Of those men on the loose in the Vercelli countryside, not yet nabbed by Germans or betrayed by Italians in exchange for their reward, the highest percentage were Australians, with New Zealanders and South Africans making up smaller numbers. Initially, at least, there were perhaps 1800 of these men spread around the work detachments.[29] Commonly it was the local peasants, the ones who had the least to spare, who were the first to offer them food and shelter.[30] As in Crete, it was often the poorest who displayed the most extraordinary generosity – and courage – in extending a helping hand. They took unimaginable risks in welcoming the Australians and others into their homes, or finding a hut in a secluded spot where they might hide, doing whatever was needed to keep 'their' prisoner alive. In some locations peasants vied with each other to 'capture' one of the men on the run, so that some 'found themselves being plied with several gargantuan feasts in a single day'.[31]

Reflecting many years later on this phenomenon, which he had both witnessed and personally experienced in Italy as in Crete, Johnny Peck pondered the motivation behind such risky altruism. Perhaps, he speculated, their positions on the lowest rung of the social scale meant that they 'could appreciate to a greater extent the vicissitudes of somebody on the run. And were naturally against authority anyway, and were more likely to help you than hinder you. And coupled with the innate sympathy of these sorts of people, and particularly the women ... ah, then they were more prone to give you a helping hand.'[32] What was especially astonishing in the case of Italy was that the peasants were risking their lives for the benefit of men who, until the very recent past, had been their enemies. In not much more than a blink of an eye they discarded the image of Australians as barbarians to be mocked or feared and saw them as pitiful fellow creatures in desperate need of help.

The Australians and other POWs in the region faced quite a quandary. They might remain with the people who offered them shelter and succour, albeit at great risk. Or they could hope to avoid the Germans and their Italian fascist minions by seeking refuge in more isolated areas, moving when necessary from one hiding place to the other, but always relying on the almost unfathomable kindness of strangers. Two such Australians were Esca Riordan – like Johnny Peck, a survivor of the sinking of the *Costa Rica* – and Neil Sloane. They moved from one area to the next, sleeping in haylofts, farm huts or animal stables, collecting food where they could and receiving it gratefully from their bold and discreet benefactors when nothing else was to be had. At times that meant bread dipped in oil or wine, plates of polenta, or even frog legs in cold rice. On one memorably miserable winter evening they were served a stew featuring the hindquarters of a cat. Thankfully it could be quickly washed down with red wine.[33] Riordan and Sloan were among some 2000 former POWs in Italy who did not emerge from their hiding places until the war was over.[34]

An alternative was to try to leave Italy altogether. From around Vercelli there were several options. To strike south toward the Allied beachhead was a possibility, but it was fraught with peril. It took men into unfamiliar territory with no known sources of support. At some point it would require crossing through German lines, and with that the high risk of recapture.

From Vercelli they might also strike out in a south-westerly direction and make for France. Eventually, a year and more later, there were some who did precisely that, making their way via the Val d'Aosta or a flatter, more southerly route across the border. But in late 1943, and for most of the year that followed, France was enemy territory and still an inauspicious option.

The most attractive prospect in September 1943 was Switzerland, but, as Johnny Peck well knew, it was also an imposing one. From Vercelli the men had to head north-west, from the Po plains into the pre-Alpine foothills, and then follow one of the valleys that snaked toward the Monte Rosa massif. The rigours of the trek were a challenge for even the fittest of climbers, let alone for men who were undernourished, unfamiliar with the landscape, had no easy access to food and needed to keep out of harm's way. There were some who, having headed towards the border, were so intimidated by the scale of the challenge before them that they turned back. And if the climb into the Alps was not commenced before the winter set in, they might as well have stayed put. It was a triumph of endurance and determination, then, that sooner or later 412 Australians made it.[35]

For these and other POWs attempting to flee Italy, MI9 did its best to redeem itself for the 'Stay put' bungle which had seen so many POWs meekly swap one set of guards for another by following British orders. That mistake having cost so many men their chance at liberty, MI9 hastily plotted schemes to aid those men who had had the pluck or good fortune to avoid the first cast of the German net. The situation was not unlike that which had prevailed in Crete when the evacuations finished at the end of May 1942. Around the countryside were thousands of POWs urgently seeking help, guidance and a path to freedom. In Italy, as in Crete,

MI9 commenced its work from an abysmally low starting point. Before the Armistice most Italian POW camps were well guarded, so there was precious little for MI9 to do, and indeed, little was done.[36] With no-one on the ground in Italy in September 1943, the organisation scrambled to throw some lifelines. Once more it was Tony Simonds in Cairo, on the orders of Churchill himself, who was ordered to attempt to extract as many of the prisoners as he could.[37]

The people he gathered together for the task were called 'A Force' or 'IS9'.[38] Simonds' plan was to infiltrate parachutists at various points up the Italian coast, where they were to contact POWs and guide or direct them to predetermined rendezvous points on the coast, from where they would be embarked on commandeered Italian fishing vessels at prearranged times.[39] Three boatloads of POWs were plucked from the Italian coast in the Marche region in late 1943 and the first part of 1944. A further group was extracted from the mouth of the Tenna River in April 1944.[40] But for northern Italy – where the Australians were – MI9's insertion of a handful of agents was almost entirely useless.[41] Those who were determined to escape would have to use all the courage, strength and guile that they themselves could muster. And while MI9 in this instance was very unlikely to provide their knight in shining armour, they could at least rely on the goodwill of others. In Italy, as in Crete, local goodwill was present in spades.

11

THE ESCAPE ARTIST

JOHNNY PECK WAS ONE OF TENS OF THOUSANDS OF ALLIED POWs in Italy confronted with the same Armistice conundrum – was it better to stay put or flee? If the latter, where to? Yet Peck's particular circumstances at that time were extraordinary. Instead of being in a POW camp or work camp like almost everyone else, as a result of earlier misdemeanours he was cooling his heels in a civilian jail in Vercelli.

Liberation came on 9 September, when Australian and British POWs from nearby work camps arrived at the jail.[1] The good citizens of Vercelli, too, had an interest in throwing open the doors of their local prison, and were present when Johnny Peck staged the most leisurely of his escapes and strolled out through the front gate.

The first temptation for Peck at this point was naturally to repeat his trek to the Swiss border. Whether by themselves or in small groups, others were already beginning to do exactly that, hoping to get clear of Vercelli before German forces rolled in to impose a new regime. Peck's chances of reaching the border were good. He knew the way, having been there just three months earlier. And though the summer had passed, the season was still good.

But Peck rejected the option of the quick getaway. Mixed into his thoughts, in all likelihood, were his memories of Crete, when courageous people had risked their lives to help people like him, abandoned in the heart of a foreign country about which they knew next to nothing. While he did not abandon the idea of striking out for Switzerland, his impulse was to place his knowledge of the countryside at the service of his fellow POWs. They were milling around the Vercelli work detachments in their hundreds, wondering what on earth to do next. If he could round up at least some of them, then he could perhaps engineer their escape as well as his own.

In this plan he won the support of a couple of other newly liberated POWs. One of them was the Australian Claude Webb, with whom Peck lived in hiding in Vercelli for a time after his release from jail. Like Peck, the Victorian Webb had adjusted his date of birth on enlistment, in Webb's case from 1923 to 1919.[2] Webb had the distinct advantage that, as another Australian put it, he spoke Italian, looked Italian, and allegedly was protected by false papers issued by the Commandant at Vercelli. Soon he had another reason to remain in Vercelli, and that was his Italian girlfriend, with the result that for several months after the Armistice Webb was still doing what he could in Vercelli to help his fellow Australians, until eventually, it seems, the Germans got hold of him and packed him off to Germany.[3] The other freshly self-liberated POW who chose to stay in the town of Vercelli and work with Peck was a South African by the name of Freddie Muller.[4]

It says something about the character of Johnny Peck that he was also able to gain the crucial support of Italians, who would not only lend their hands to assist the men on the run, but would risk their lives. These were perilous times in the town of Vercelli and the surrounding province. Not only were the Germans establishing a military presence – politically, this was still fascist territory. While many Italians had grown weary of the war and welcomed the apparent political demise of Mussolini, there was no shortage of Blackshirts, and the local administration collaborated with the new masters in town. To voice an antifascist sentiment, let alone to abet the enemy, was to court disaster.

The locals' display of courage began by hiding Peck and others at various sites in the Vercelli province. Provided by his liberators with a set of civilian clothes, and drawing on a geniality conveyed in his by now fluent Italian, Peck began contacting other locals audacious enough to help him locate other POWs in hiding and plan their trek to freedom. They came from all walks of life, both women and men. Foremost among them was Adele Maschietti, whom Peck later extolled as 'a beautiful, young, working class woman who worked in the railway station bar; brave, resourceful and immensely helpful'.[5] In time he would develop a 'brotherly' relationship with her, but on first acquaintance she sprang to Peck's aid, helping him to make contact with, as he put it, 'some business men and two priests in the town who were willing to help feed and clothe the POWs in the neighbourhood'.[6] Another was a young obstetrician at the Vercelli hospital by the name of Anna

Marengo, who in this way signalled that she was throwing in her lot with the antifascist resistance – and indeed would stick with it to the very end.

That was true also of the Vercelli schoolteacher Ermenegildo Bertola, whose leading role in organising aid for men on the run would eventually lead to his arrest.[7] Added to the growing circle of helpers were the housewife Clia Paglierini, the shop assistant Salvatore Grassi, the maid Maria Pozzati, and the river boatman Silvio Nascimbene. To find clothes for the men on the run Peck drew on the help of Giuseppe Baralle, while Aldo Pensotti, a tailor, was able to do his bit to kit out both Johnny Peck and Claude Webb. Pina Gamba, who became a close friend of Peck's for about a month, also helped him procure clothes and, later and more daringly, an identity card. Piero Camana was one of the men with local knowledge who helped take up contact with the POWs who had wandered off into the hills around Vercelli, just as Volmano Dall'Orto searched the farms in the district for POWs unsure what to do next. Later he went so far as to help Peck find weapons, and when the Germans closed in on Peck, found him a place to hide. A concealed space in Vercelli's Basilica di Sant'Andrea, used over the course of about a month by Peck, was found by Vittoria Cerutti, the sister of a priest who had come to detest the fascists.[8] From just outside Vercelli, Filippo Bonardo of the municipality of Borgo Vercelli came to the attention of the Peck group when he lent a helping hand to some POWs he encountered. Having cast aside his own military uniform, Bonardo, known as Nino, felt an empathy for men wanting to start afresh and soon became a valued member of Peck's burgeoning network.[9]

As the circle of helpers expanded and they set about their tasks, Peck formed a committee to coordinate activities. On it served Anna Marengo, Luigi Mastroviti, Pino Agrati, Nando Dell'Orto and

Oreste Barbero.[10] The last was a local businessman who owned a café and cake shop, and who began his work with Peck with a modest offer to look for POWs in the woods outside Vercelli, but soon went on to become a driving force in what had become an impressive web of courageous locals.[11] Together they found safe hiding places at which the would-be escapers could gather in advance of their departure, and they scraped together the food and clothing to prepare them for the journey ahead.[12] To their eternal credit, all of them had more to fear from the discovery of their clandestine operations than the men they were seeking to help.

Before the end of September Peck took his first group of about twenty POWs to Switzerland, following the route which he had taken in June. They crossed into Switzerland at the Passo di Monte Moro, under the watchful eye of the Madonna of the Snow and their secular saviour, Johnny Peck. By now he had resolved not to accompany his charges on their descent into the Saas Valley, where they would be received by Swiss authorities, fed, clothed and accommodated.[13] Instead, he would walk back to Vercelli and round up another batch of men to be guided to their freedom. Much more than that, on his return journey he recruited guides and helpers who agreed to receive and send forward future parties. Winter was not far away, and a trek across the border was about to become even more taxing than it was already. Worryingly, too, the arrival of Germans in northern Piedmont meant that the most easily negotiated of the passes at Monte Moro were about to close. Peck would need to find new routes and expand his network.[14]

At first Peck's field of operation was in the region of the labour camps around Vercelli. His challenge was to conquer the hesitations of all those paralysed by inertia. The men were inclined to trust rumours that Allied armed forces would arrive soon, or they preferred the familiarity of the farms where they had worked and the people who took them in. The prospect of a climb through unfamiliar terrain to an unknown destination, made with minimal resources and often in a compromised state of health, was daunting. Peck would need to be compelling in his bid for their trust.

How he managed this is eloquently revealed in a letter that survives in Peck's papers at the Australian War Memorial in Canberra. Dated 'Vercelli. 30/10/43', it reads:

Dear Boys,

I have just received word that there are some of our chaps still in the bush hiding out. This letter is really an introduction as the man who is taking me out to you is a bit scared of me being a spy and as he wants some guarantee that I am a fair dinkum Aussie I hope you acknowledge this letter as soon as it is given to you.

Surely some of you know me and as I am half-pissed I won't waste time with writing a long letter. My name is JOHNNY PECK, VX.9534 – 2nd/7th BATT. 6th.DIV. A.I.F. Home Address. CRIB POINT VICTORIA, AUSTRALIA. And that's basta for me.

When you receive this note I will not be far away from you so don't keep me in suspenders, send a reply back immediately as I will be waiting for it.

I will tell you the news when I see you.

All the best,
Yours Sincerely,
Johnny D. Peck VX. 9534. X. P.O.W. 2/7. Batt A.I.F.

The note must have laid its bearer's fears to rest. Scribbled on it in pencil are the words, 'Everything O.K. all know above named', and signed Corporal NF Sedgman, Pte NJ Forde, Pte JH Parker, Pte W Squires. All of them were from the Victorian 2/24 Battalion, veterans of Tobruk, Gruppignano and the rice farms of Vercelli.[15]

A plaintive letter from men hiding in an unknown place at an unrecorded time simply read:

John Peck,

We have been trying to find you all day but cannot. The cops are on us. So, we will have to piss off. Perhaps to-morrow or meet us to-night at the rail-way crossing.

Three Aussies.[16]

Another note said, more hopefully:

Dear Johnny,

Received your note, and see by same you are doing well. There are 13 of the boys here, at Vercelly [sic] camp, awaiting to go through without smokes, if you can get some where you are, come out with bearer and bring some … We don't think jerry will hold the line all winter, have you heard any word of Don Steele and Carlo, they were supposed to go through to Switzerland. There is nothing we want only smokes at present. A root is out of the ? at present.

Yours,
Ken O'Leary NX35892[17]

It was not just Australians who benefitted from Peck's help.

A South African by the name of LM Jarvis gave an account of his escape to Switzerland. After the Armistice he just kept working on a farm, at least until he was contacted by what he called 'the Johnny Peck organisation' on 12 October, and his escape to Switzerland was set in motion, guided through many, tortuous steps:

> I left Salero farm (near Constanzana-Vercelli) on 12.10.43 and went to a house belonging to the organisation at Monte Ferata where I remained until 15.10.43. On this date I walked with a guide to Trino and thence by bicycle to Vercelli where I remained in a poplar plantation until 23.10.43. I was fed by the organisation during this time. On 23.10.43 a guide took me by bus to Borgosesia. I stayed the night in a farm near Borgosesia and left the next morning with a guide on foot for Ceppo Morelli and crossed the frontier via the Monte Moro pass on 28.10.43.[18]

As his ambitions to help others grew, Peck's thinking became more imaginative. As time was in short supply, and the number of men in need was great, he contemplated having the men travel by train.[19] The idea was both simple and fraught. Peck himself was one of several guides who would accompany groups of men by train towards the border. At first he took just three or four, but in time he took larger groups of up to 12.[20] The men would be dressed in civilian clothing, would gather at a nominated railway station – typically a small one such as Olcenengo outside Vercelli – and then would travel to within a short distance of the Swiss border, to a place such as Domodossola, Luino or Ponte Tresa. In this way they would avoid inspections at border crossings and leave just a short yet inevitably arduous walk to freedom. For that final stage they would be met at their disembarkation point by a guide with local knowledge, who would walk with them to deposit them at the border. From there they would make their own way into Swiss territory, following their guide's instructions, until they were received by the Swiss.

All this was enabled by the small organisational masterpiece which Peck himself gave the grand title of 'liberation and resistance committee'.[21] The nature of its work demanded that its Vercelli core was expanded to include members in neighbouring provinces, and so the network grew, taking on members from such other places in Piedmont as Novara, Varese and Turin.[22] Most fatefully, at Luino, north of Vercelli on the shores of Lago Maggiore, Peck made a telling contact in Oreste Ferrari. The two men became very close, inventing fictional personas for themselves as respectable businessmen in the hope of avoiding suspicion. Donning a well-tailored suit and a pair of glasses – albeit without lenses – and speaking the language with a fluency gained over many months in Gruppignano and Vercelli, Johnny Peck appeared a pillar of Italian society.

In reality he and his committee were engaged in daily acts of subversion. To the tasks of collecting, feeding and accommodating POWs was added the surreptitious purchase of railway tickets. For that, money had to be raised and locals found to shepherd the men on and off the trains at the right place and time. A system of couriers, many of them women, provided invaluable information in the planning and execution of escapes. The names and addresses of trustworthy contacts were found along the routes to freedom running north and north-west of Vercelli, in places such as Luino, Como, Bellano, Domodossola and Pallanza. And with their help, Peck made deals and fixed prices with potential guides.[23] At the height of its operations, the Peck network was managing to bring about the liberation of 60 to 70 POWs a week.[24]

Soon Piedmont was too small for the network. With some help from collaborators in Turin, Peck spread his wings further, travelling to such far away locations as Rome, Venice, Trieste, Florence and Bologna, in each case trying to persuade the POWs hiding out in the area to place their trust in him and allow him to arrange their evacuation to Switzerland.[25]

In all of these places, as in Vercelli, Peck could rely on the cooperation of the local Committees of National Liberation, CLNs. These were groups of antifascists which had formed spontaneously in the wake of the Armistice. Though their composition might vary from place to place, typically the CLNs were a broad church, embracing political philosophies ranging from communism to conservative monarchism – it was an intense hate of fascism and the ignominy of German occupation that held them together. In northern Italy the largest and most influential of the CLNs was in Milan. By the time Johnny Peck contacted that CLN, it had already developed its own subcommittee to help Allied POWs on the run. This was the brainchild of Ferruccio Parri, a representative of the Action Party, and its formal title was Ufficio Assistenza Prigionieri di Guerra Alleati.[26] While at first it sought to help POWs on the run in Milan and surrounding districts of Lombardy, in time the Milan committee coordinated POW assistance throughout German-occupied Italy. To this end it came to comprise five members, from Milan, Turin, Genoa, Florence and Rome.[27] The areas with the highest concentrations of men on the run were, unsurprisingly, those near the sites of the big POW camps. By the CLN's own estimates, Piedmont had about 1800 men and Lombardy roughly double that number, while in the Veneto and the far north-east –

the site of PG 57 and numerous other camps – numbers were as high as 4500.[28]

While the originator of the Milan committee was Parri, the most active and effective of its members was a man by the name of Giuseppe Bacciagaluppi. Bacciagaluppi was the manager of a communications company in Milan. He spoke excellent English, largely as a result of marrying an Englishwoman, Audrey Smith, who became an important member of the network built through Lombardy. On a number of occasions she was known to have conveyed POWs to freedom in Switzerland by rowing them across the border that spanned Lago Maggiore.[29] Conveniently, she and her husband owned a house on the shores of Lago Maggiore, at Caldé, in easy reach of the Swiss border. In the same area, as Peck later recalled, there were two or three other English wives of Italian industrialists, one of whom, in a habitual act of defiance, wore a Union Jack wrapped around her bosom.[30]

Johnny Peck met Bacciagaluppi in Milan in early December 1943, and a close friendship developed. In the course of their work, their paths would cross again, as Peck's network was embedded into the operation directed from Milan. Though on a grander scale, the operations worked much as Peck's had from its early days in Vercelli. The first step was always to make discreet contact with the POWs in hiding. Those willing to risk the travel to Switzerland were provided with a full set of civilian clothing. That in itself was no easy task, since typically Australian and other Allied POWs were taller than Italian men. If their height alone did not attract attention, then an ill-fitting suit or pair of trousers could give the game away. Then the men were instructed to meet at a pre-arranged safe house. At the nominated time, organised in groups of anywhere between two and ten, they would assemble at a train station, where a guide would establish contact with them, give them tickets, furtively assist them onto the right train and travel the route with them. The first leg of the travel was commonly to Milan, the network's central point. After arrival in Milan the men went into hiding in empty trains or safe houses until they were able to take another train to a location north or north-west of Milan, usually with new guides.[31]

Having disembarked under the guide's supervision a stop or two short of the border, the group would be introduced to the person who would escort them there. Especially through the last weeks of 1943 and the first of the following year, this had to be someone who knew the local landscape intimately and possessed mountaineering skills. These guides knew the sheep and goat tracks, the crevices and ridges, and all the dangers posed by the Italian Alps in winter. In some cases they were men who were not necessarily motivated by altruism. Smugglers who habitually evaded the long arm of the law in taking goods across the border were well qualified for the task at hand, and they took it on in full expectation of monetary reward. When they had reached their destinations, the liberated men would sign a piece of paper to testify they had crossed the frontier. Back in Italy, the guide would claim his payment, funded by Bacciagaluppi's committee, on presentation of the signed declaration.[32]

On top of his involvement in assembling the Italy-wide network, Johnny Peck continued to play a front line role. That he could do so is some testament to the fluency he had gained in Italian by that time. It also attests to his courage. To be caught wearing civilian clothes while abetting POWs on the run was to invite catastrophe. One risk was that because of his youth – he performed these everyday lifesaving acts at the age of 21 – he might be thought to be an Italian draft dodger. In his demeanour he projected maturity and a worldly confidence. If required, he spun in flawless Italian a compelling narrative of his identity and the business to which he was attending. In reality, that story would vary from trip to trip, as would the identity papers he carried with him, some of them forged, some genuine but pilfered or extracted through some other dishonest means.

Unerringly modest though he was in his later accounts, written and oral, it is clear that his work brought him to the brink of disaster more than once. The Italian fascists and their German masters knew all too well that the border with Switzerland was leaking not just POWs on the run but refugees of many kinds, including Jews. They worked hard to plug the gaps, and would punish severely any offenders and their helpers.

On one occasion Peck's guiding task drove him to the point of utter exhaustion. It all began in the Piedmontese capital Turin. The long day's itinerary entailed guiding a group to a destination near Como, from where they would be escorted across the Swiss border. As Peck made a succession of stops – Vercelli, Novara, Milan – he picked up more men, probably too many. Milan proved a nightmare, because he had to herd a group of men, 20 or more, inside a sprawling, crowded station and steer them to the right train at the right time.[33]

Then the most implausible thing happened. As Peck's group was making its way through the station, a group of some 50 prisoners under German guard approached from the other direction. A member of Peck's group identified one of the 50 as a friend and, stupidly, made his way into the German column to express a hearty welcome. Standing alongside his mate, Peck's charge was mistaken by a German guard for a POW and hustled into the line, presumably to await transport to Germany. Peck had no way of retrieving him but acted quickly to protect his remaining protégés, ushering them into the station toilets, about six to a cubicle, where they stubbornly refused to open to all who came knocking.[34]

Finally it was time to board the train which would take them towards the Swiss border. Peck distributed the men through the carriages, imparting strict instructions on how to avoid attention. He then assumed his own seat in a different carriage. Overcome with weariness after a long and anxious day, he fell asleep. To his horror, he did not wake until the train was nearing the municipality of Mergozzo, some distance beyond the nominated disembarkation stop.[35] And as he frantically made his way through the carriages, he found that not one of the men was still on board.

He alighted in Mergozzo. As at all stations, there were German guards on the platform. He asked the station master when the next train would head back down the line, only to find it would not be until the following day. A German guard advised him to head off home, but Peck explained he did not live in Mergozzo, that he had missed his stop and wanted to go back. While one guard insisted he leave the station, another pointed out that the curfew had begun, and he might be shot if he did so.[36]

Peck faced an awful conundrum. The last train had gone, so he could not depart by rail. Neither, however, could he exit the station to seek accommodation for the night, because the curfew had begun, and the Germans would enforce it. It was a quandary the Germans shared, lumbered as they were with an unwanted station guest. Peck asked them what they proposed to do with him. 'Well, we'll shoot you', they joked. Then one of them suggested, 'Well, I'll tell you what, you can come down and you can sleep with us. We're in the hotel, we've commandeered the hotel, and the second floor is a dormitory for the German troops. Come down and sleep with us.'[37] Devoid of any alternative, Peck enjoyed a restful sleep in the midst of his enemies.

The next morning he knew it was pointless to return to the station where the men should have disembarked, so Peck made his way to the township of Intra on the shores of Lago Maggiore, and close to where some of his partisan friends were based. From them he hoped to learn news of the fate of his stray POWs.[38]

He received news earlier than hoped, because on the wharf at Intra he came across Audrey Bacciagaluppi, who was able to tell him that a couple of the local partisans, while returning from Milan by train, encountered small groups of passengers who, because of their size, appeared to be either English or German. In the end they decided that on the basis of their poor dress – short sleeves and trouser hems far above their boots – they were English. In any case, they decided to test a couple of them. 'We think you're English prisoners,' they told them, until the travellers conceded that they indeed were. And then they explained, 'We're waiting, because the man who is taking us to Switzerland, he's disappeared.' There were, they said, some 30 of them in this predicament.[39]

With great presence of mind the two partisans – in Peck's recollection they were Arca (in reality Armando Calzavara, commander of a group called Cesare Battisti) and Marco – rounded up all the men and escorted them from the train at the next stop, into their own territory in the pre-Alps and eventually across the border into Switzerland. Deeply relieved on hearing this news, Peck accompanied Audrey to her home at Caldé before returning to Piedmont and to his escape operations.[40]

On another occasion Peck's determination to establish an

impeccably Italian identity nearly brought about his undoing. Entering the council chambers in Vercelli, he claimed to be a refugee from southern Italy, by now under the control of the Allies, and requested that he be issued with a new identity card. His cunning was at first rewarded, and an appropriate identity card was issued to him, replete with photograph, and hugely beneficial as he went about his escape work. Some time later, however, the episode triggered an unfortunate sequel. After an absence from Vercelli he returned to town oblivious to the existence of posters displayed throughout the town, featuring him as a wanted fugitive. The authorities were onto his network, possibly through an act of betrayal, and he was being sought under the name he had provided for his identity card – and with the aid of the photo taken of him at that time and held in council files.[41] When he entered the railway station bar, the female bartender – his friend and accomplice Adele Maschietti – discreetly drew Peck's attention to the poster on the bar wall and encouraged a rapid but furtive withdrawal. 'Whatever you do,' she urged, 'go, go somewhere!'[42] Peck made a very speedy exit from Vercelli, his cover blown.

It was dangerous, but it was also thrilling, fulfilling work. The transformation in Peck's life, after spending so many fruitless months in captivity, was massive. He had found a new way to take on the Germans. By his own estimate, he himself guided over 200 men to safety in Switzerland.[43] As for the larger CLN networks of which he was part, and which he helped create, the CLN's figures suggest that in the period from October of 1943 through to March of the following year, 942 Allied ex-POWs were escorted into Switzerland with the help of the CLN networks, while a further 400 were able to make their own way south to cross the front line and join Allied forces there.[44] Some figures have it that the Bacciagaluppi network alone managed to aid 1843 men, all of whom were spared a stint in a German POW camp, and some of whom returned to the fray.[45]

In a quite different way, too, this period in Italy was deeply rewarding for Johnny Peck. Among the women who had treated him with exemplary kindness since his liberation from prison, who had not only helped him but helped him to help others, there was one by the name of Bianca Rossi. She was from a working-class family in Buronzo, a small municipality in the Vercelli region.[46] She and Peck travelled together quite a bit; it was she who introduced Peck to Oreste Ferrari in Luino.[47] It was reported that for a time they were living together in Vercelli.[48] At some point, it seems, she had become much more than a helper and travel companion, and that, too, was a reason for Johnny Peck not to head for Switzerland. At least, not yet.

12
PARTISANS

EVEN WITH THE BEST OF INTENTIONS, IT WAS IMPOSSIBLE TO arrange a passage to Switzerland for everyone. The occupying German forces collaborated with their fascist Italian acolytes to block the exits from Italy as best they could. At every opportunity they pounced on men on the run and despatched them to Germany and a lengthy stint in a Stalag. There was little that the Allies and the new Italian government in the south could do to stop the procession of captures and deportations. When winter set in, the crossings into Switzerland became hazardous; it was not for want of courage or effort that many failed in their bids for freedom.

Over half the British servicemen who left their camps at the time of the Armistice were able to remain safely hidden for months on end; only a third reached Allied lines or the Swiss frontier.[1]

The luckiest found brave and accommodating hosts who sheltered them through to the end of hostilities. It was no mean feat, though, to remain in hiding for that length of time, and the strenuous efforts to round up all those on the loose forced the evaders to remain on the move, hoping to keep one step ahead of their pursuers.

The rules that maximised the chances of avoiding capture were neatly summarised by a British soldier. The main points were never to be static and to trust no-one. As for the crucial task of locating a sympathetic host, a range of counsel was offered. As a general rule, the code suggested, the poorer the house, the safer it was likely to be – 'rich houses are invariably fascist'. Women working in the fields were usually reliable. Once a prisoner had stayed and eaten in a house, that house was very likely to be safe. The reasoning here was that such hosts would never betray a guest to the Germans, 'as their house would be burnt down for having kept you the one night'.[2]

The challenges were exacerbated by intense competition for places of refuge, and not just from other POWs on the run. Much more numerous were their erstwhile enemies, Italian soldiers. The armistice had filled Hitler with rage. The Italian betrayal, as he saw it, would not go unpunished, and in the forefront of those to feel the Nazi wrath were the Italian soldiers who had caved in to the pressure of the Allies and thrown in their lot with the former enemy. If these men were seized by German forces, they, like the Allied POWs, were rounded up and packed off to Germany, where they died in their thousands. Classified as 'military internees' rather than prisoners of war, they were denied the protections that the Geneva Convention might otherwise have given them.

If they managed to avoid the German net, typically these Italian soldiers abandoned their uniforms, returned to the regions from which they came, and looked to family and friends to shelter them. The best strategy was to head for the countryside, the more remote and sparsely populated the better. And there, in countless instances, they came across their former enemies, former Allied POWs with whom they shared the single, overriding goal which rendered their previous hostility redundant – they wished to avoid capture by the Germans and a long train ride north.

As time went by, that cohort of former soldiers was joined by another group of Italian men just as eager to avoid any contact with German occupying forces and their Italian fascist collaborators. They were a fresh generation, reaching an age where they might be conscripted into the new army which Hitler allowed Mussolini to raise. Of course, many did join the fighting forces of Mussolini's Italian Social Republic (RSI), and were sent to Germany for training. But others were war weary and dodged the draft by absconding into the countryside where they, too, shared a common purpose with Allied POWs on the run – to keep out of harm's way.

There were also untold numbers of Italians who were not content with sitting out the war. Driven by some combination of visceral antifascism and hatred of the German occupation, they formed a resistance movement which grew from strength to strength in the wake of the Armistice of September 1943. In part this was a political opposition of broad character, but it was soon evident that the Italian resistance was taking on a military character as well. Most prominent of all were the forces which began to gel in the last weeks of 1943. Although they commonly identified as partisans – *partigiani* – in reality, these opponents of the RSI and of the German occupation came from many different backgrounds and had a variety of views about Italy's future. That diversity attracted the attention of the author of an Allied military report, who observed 'an astonishing mixture' of oppositional elements from a great variety of social, regional and ethnic backgrounds:

> Italians who may be elderly lawyers, ex-army men, youths in search of adventure; Russians, Poles, Slavs, Alsatians who have deserted from the Germans; American airmen, British, Indian, Canadian, New Zealand and French officers and men who have escaped from Italian prison camps; and in the north-east tough Slovenes … Other hands are good militarily but also obsessed with political aims … Bands exist of every degree, down to gangs of thugs who don a partisan cloak of respectability to conceal the nakedness of their brigandage, and bands who bury their arms in their back gardens and only dig them up and festoon themselves in comic opera uniforms when the first Allied troops arrive.[3]

In all this variety, three groups stood out. In terms of age cohort, the military backbone of the partisan movement comprised the young men who eschewed enlistment in Mussolini's army; they would make up perhaps 80 per cent of the fighting forces of the Italian resistance.[4] Their average age was just 22.[5] In regional terms, the greatest strength of the Italian resistance was in the north. The topography alone of the Italian Alps and the pre-Alps favoured partisan warfare, just as the rugged, mountainous landscape of Crete was an advantage to the *andartes* there. Piedmont in the north-west was especially blessed with fighters, so that in time 35 partisan divisions of varying political colours collected there, more than double the number in neighbouring Lombardy.[6]

As for political persuasion, the partisan groups were every bit as piebald as the political parties in the CLNs. Some eschewed any overt political allegiance, most importantly the *Autonomi*, who maintained a sense of loyalty to the monarchy and the Italian tradition of a royal army.[7] Others, though, proudly flew the flag of one political party or another. Those who fought for the cause of the *Partito d'Azione* (Action Party) adopted the *Giustizia e Libertà* (Justice and Liberty) banner,[8] the socialists formed *Matteotti* brigades in honour of their martyred forebear, while Catholics threw their support behind the *Brigate Fiamme Verdi* (Green Flame Brigade) or the *Osoppo* brigades.[9]

In sheer weight of numbers, the most potent force, especially in Piedmont, were the communists. They had long despised fascism and stood in a tradition of armed struggle. In big cities like Turin the communists formed so-called *Gruppi d'Azione Patriottica*, Patriotic Action Groups, or GAPs.[10] In the countryside, too, they established military formations which cleverly appropriated the name of the Risorgimento hero Giuseppe Garibaldi. The military model they followed was provided by the Soviet Union, so that next to the military leadership there were also commissars who provided the ranks with ideological training and guidance.[11]

Among Piedmont's communists, one man stood head and shoulders above all others – Vincenzo Moscatelli, known by his *nome di battaglia*, Cino. Born into a working-class family in Novara in 1908, Moscatelli had experienced a standard communist apprenticeship, including two years in Moscow in the late 1920s. In the 1930s, like countless other Italian communists, he spent several years in a fascist jail. At around the time Mussolini was deposed in July 1943, Moscatelli was heavily involved in organising resistance activities in the Valsesia region, leading to his arrest in the town of Borgosesia in October. He was handed to the German command in Vercelli, but was liberated and, like so many partisans, took refuge in the hills.[12] It was exactly the kind of territory in which Australian former POWs were in hiding.

As a communist and partisan, Moscatelli was a marked man; frequent efforts to kill or capture him forced him to change headquarters many times. Nonetheless, the number of men joining his ranks continued to grow. In time the 'Garibaldini' under Moscatelli's command expanded into 12 brigades organised into four divisions, amounting overall to some 3000 men.[13] Among them were numbers of former POWs, who for one reason or another had not been able to cross into Switzerland. And of those there were at least a handful who had reached the conclusion that in fact they did not wish to leave Italy. Even if their first contact with partisans stemmed from a shared survival instinct, in the course of time they came to realise that with their combined resources they might turn the tables on their mutual enemy and strike back. In the most unlikely of circumstances, men who for months or years had believed their war over returned to battle.

Records suggest that there were more than 50 Australians who elected to serve in communist or other partisan formations.[14] The politics of the group they joined was much more likely a matter of circumstance than of ideological inclination. As there was such a strong Garibaldini presence in the area of northern Piedmont in which they found themselves, however, geography more than anything else dictated that many became involved with communist partisan formations, including those of the charismatic Cino Moscatelli.

For some of those Australians, contact with the partisans was fleeting. The unity of purpose in evading capture did not endure, and the Australians moved on, typically in the hope of crossing the Swiss border. Those willing to stay for a time and fight were often dismayed at the lack of military discipline and shortage of weapons in the partisan groups. Moreover, not all POWs had combat experience, and of those who did, not all wanted to repeat it. While grateful in their hour of need for the possibility of joining a kind of community of the hunted, the prospect of taking up the cudgels against a well-armed enemy filled them with a sense of dread. They, too, moved on.

But for those whose sense of common cause with the former enemy endured, life with partisans brought a return to military action of a kind they had never dreamed. Their war took on new meaning and stretched their martial talents and their powers of survival to the very limits.

Ian Sproule, a Tobruk and El Alamein veteran from Albury, was one of these men. Serendipity and force of circumstance delivered him and a number of other Australians to a communist group after the September 1943 Armistice. By his own admission Sproule and his mates were not happy about finding themselves among a group of 'Reds', but they accepted their fate philosophically: 'We felt the die had been cast. We had now joined a partisan group, even though it was politically the "wrong" group. With no alternative, we had to stay.'[15]

Edgar Triffett was another whose war was reignited through contact with partisans after the Armistice. The horse breaker from Queensland served in 2/15 Battalion, was captured at Derna in April 1941, sent to Gruppignano and then to one of the Vercelli work camps. Like Johnny Peck, Triffett had managed to abscond from his work camp in June of 1943, three months before the Armistice, reaching the village of Champoluc in the Aosta Valley, where he was hidden by a priest. When the Armistice was announced, he chose to make his way back to the rice fields of Vercelli to help those men who, he well knew, would be agonising over their next move.[16] Back at his work camp he contacted 139 men and guided 103 of them to a religious sanctuary, the Santuario d'Oropa, just north of Biella.[17] After a week in that refuge he presented the men with a stark choice – they could make for Switzerland, or they could remain in Italy and join the partisans. Most made the journey into Switzerland, but Triffett himself opted for the partisans. After guiding some 20 men across the border at St Bernard Pass, he joined a group of some 300 partisans and risked his life to liberate the people who had once been his captors.[18] He very soon became aware of how brutal the partisan war was. Captured fascists were brought up from the valleys for execution by the partisans. The method, as Triffett recalled later, 'was to shoot them in the fast flowing mountain stream which carried away the bodies'.[19]

Malcolm Webster's story parallels Johnny Peck's in a different way. Like Peck, he was a rare case of a POW in Italy who had been captured in the wake of the Battle for Crete. Webster and a small number of others fell into Italian hands when the destroyer *Hereward*, evacuating them from Heraklion on Crete's north coast, took a direct hit from a Stuka in the Kaso Strait. Webster passed out from sheer exhaustion as he swam towards the Cretan coast. Plucked unconscious from the sea by an Italian motor torpedo boat, he and other *Hereward* survivors were taken initially to the island of Scapanto, and from there, like Johnny Peck, to Rhodes, Gruppignano and Vercelli.[20] After the Armistice his efforts to reach

Switzerland proved futile. Eventually, with another Australian by the name of Bill Wrigglesworth, he joined a partisan unit, the Dellatezza Detachment of the Fontanella Brigade. Taking on the *nomi di battaglia* 'Sydney' and 'Melbourne', and eventually kitted out with a khaki-coloured uniform modelled on a British outfit, the two men, joined by several other Australians, served their adopted partisan command through to the end of hostilities.[21]

For a time one of Webster's partisan comrades-in-arms was Jack Rowe. One of the 490 captured at Ruin Ridge in Egypt in July 1942, Rowe had done stints at Gruppignano and Vercelli. After the Armistice he lived rough with a group of Australians and New Zealanders in the Vercelli countryside, presenting 'a villainous appearance', as he later recalled, 'unkempt, none clean-shaven. We wore an incongruous mixture of khaki uniform and civilian clothes, for the most part torn or patched. Instead of boots, a couple had peasant clogs. One wore sand-shoes through which a big toe protruded.'[22]

In time Rowe and a New Zealander, Frank Bowes,[23] paired off and joined a group of young Italians eager to avoid being drafted into Mussolini's army. In time the group was joined by other young Italians evading conscription, and by a couple more Australians in Bert Moore and Harry Herbert 'Mickey' Miller. For this group, as for so many others, the first priority was mere survival; their first actions took the form of a food raid, followed by a bank robbery. It was obvious to Rowe that the partisans had neither the structures nor the discipline of a potent force, so for a time he returned to the haven offered by a sympathetic farmer.[24] Later, when the partisans were more numerous and better equipped, he joined the ranks of a communist band in northern Piedmont, where he fought with several other Australians at his side.[25]

It was toward the hills above Biella that Stan Peebles and Keith Jones, both from 2/24 Battalion, made their way when they left their Vercelli camp on about 10 September 1943. In December the two men participated in the formation of a partisan group which was initially known as the 'Piave' group, later the 'Bandiera'.[26] Early the following year another Australian joined, the Scottish-born West Australian Dan Black of 2/28 Battalion. By August of 1944 Peebles and Black led a series of raids against German convoys and troop trains in the Biella area, particularly at Salussola. Reprisals against the group culminated in a fierce battle at Ronco Biellese over several days in September of 1944, ultimately forcing the two Australians to withdraw over the border into Switzerland.[27]

And it was in the area around Biella, just north-west of the town of Vercelli, that an Indigenous man from Western Australia, Harry Davis of 2/32 Battalion, joined a partisan band. After his capture in July 1942 he had served the usual time in Benghazi, Gruppignano and a Vercelli labour camp.[28] In seeking to stay clear of German patrols, he faced similar challenges to those of Reg Saunders in Crete, only to be met with the same hospitality Saunders found there. After the war he explained pithily, 'I escaped 10.9.43, stayed in the mountains until end of war, stayed with Partisans, but mostly in a village called Gaby [in the Aosta Valley] where the people kept me in food and clothes and lodging, especially a Russian woman.'[29]

No Australian became better known in the ranks of the partisans than the Queenslander Frank Jocumsen, who in time would acquire almost legendary status. A large and very powerfully built man, his nickname 'Butch' derived from his civilian profession. He joined partisans in the Valsesia area. Not only did he operate in an area where Moscatelli held sway, 'French' (an Italian approximation of Frank), became Moscatelli's bodyguard, driver and confidante, travelling with Cino through his large domain in northern Piedmont.[30] After the war, Moscatelli would pay tribute to the Queenslander, who during numerous partisan actions was almost inseparable from his Italian-manufactured Breda machine gun. While most infantrymen would operate the Breda on its tripod base, Jocumsen carried it with him on his shoulders.[31] The Italian resistance hero Edgardo Sogno, who accompanied Jocumsen on one of his treks into Switzerland, spoke highly of him. 'He was not a communist,' Sogno wrote after the war, 'but he thought that the partisans in Valsesia fought in a good way and it was right to help them.'[32]

From other sources, too, there is ample evidence of Jocumsen's heroism in partisan actions in Valsesia and beyond. George Evans, an English former POW who joined a partisan unit, witnessed Jocumsen using his gun to devastating effect in an engagement with fascist militia.[33] Another account places Jocumsen front and centre of a partisan ambush staged in Varallo on 12 December 1943. In the shootout Jocumsen ran into the middle of the piazza, 'face uncovered, and using his gun to spray a bar packed with Fascists'.[34]

On the surface, the contrast with the war Johnny Peck was fighting at the time is striking. Jocumsen craved direct engagement with the enemy, the action of a skirmish or firefight. He instinctively adopted classical guerrilla tactics, emerging without warning from hiding, striking the enemy with brutal speed, and then retreating to the refuge of harsh but familiar terrain. He risked a violent and sudden death in a hail of bullets or an exploding grenade. Johnny Peck, on the other hand, was an organiser, building a network of the like-minded, all of them dedicated to the task of rescuing men so that they might live to fight another day. He faced a different kind of risk, the kind of risk that brought capture, interrogation, imprisonment, torture and a slow death.

Yet by the end of 1943, the war Johnny Peck was fighting was becoming more like Frank Jocumsen's. Peck, too, was becoming a partisan.

13

GUEST OF THE GESTAPO

JOHNNY PECK'S PATH TO BECOMING A PARTISAN WAS unusual. Most of the Australians who fell in with partisans did so serendipitously in the wake of thwarted efforts to reach neutral territory or Allied lines. Peck, in contrast, had sought contact with oppositional elements in Vercelli from the moment of his release from jail. His motivation was to organise a helping hand for men who had little idea where to turn next, and whose initiative was blunted by long stretches as POWs. Without doubt that humanitarian impulse was shared by the Italian men and women who placed themselves at Peck's disposal and, through selfless acts of kindness, thumbed their noses at the new regime.

Other Italians sought less subtle ways of venting their opposition to the German occupation and the obscenity that was Mussolini's RSI. Resistance for them had to be much more than civil disobedience or passive defiance. In their view the reality of the post-Armistice order was that Italian antifascists had to take the war up to the enemy, fighting by whatever means available to secure Italy's liberation. As the weeks wore on, Johnny Peck met more people who thought in this way, and by the end of the year he was one of them.

The truth was also that the success of his operations to shift men across the border meant that fewer were asking for his help by December 1943. His contacts with oppositional elements already well established across Piedmont and Lombardy, other opportunities to insert thorns into the enemy's side presented themselves. Peck came to lead a kind of double life, not abandoning the POWs, but turning more of his attention to the military dimensions of resistance. As he himself put it, 'In December I started to interest myself in the underground fighting system and divided my time between the partisans and the POW. I began using our boys going up to the border as supply carriers for the partisans, each man carrying two or three kilos of rice or flour.'[1]

The base for his military activities with the partisans was Luino, on the Lombard shore of Lago Maggiore, north of Vercelli. In that area partisans were becoming bolder, more active and more numerous. Like other Australians joining partisan groups around this time, Peck decried the dearth of weapons and military competence, but he was heartened by the willingness to unsettle the enemy, even at great risk. To complement their courage, he recognised, a higher level of military savvy was required. A bloody partisan defeat by enemy forces at San Martino in the Lombard province of Varese in November 1943 highlighted in his mind the necessity to adopt the classic tactics of guerrilla warfare. That meant avoiding open confrontation with a better equipped opponent, and saving precious manpower and weaponry for strategic strikes designed to promote fear and uncertainty. Clandestine operations aimed above all at infrastructure should be followed by hurried retreats to well-hidden refuges.

The tough lessons of C Company's retreat across the rocky terrain of Crete had taught Johnny Peck the key principles of this kind of warfare. Now he was able to apply them to the tricky terrain of northern Piedmont. His response, then, to the fall of San Martino and the capture or dispersal of partisan forces in the area was, as he put it,

> to form another band, but with totally different tactics from the previous one. We acquired trucks and cars and as it was a fairly level area with plenty of roads I organised the men into flying squads. We made attacks and committed acts of sabotage all over the countryside, often making round trips of three hundred kilometres in a night. Our most notable successes were the blowing of the Asino and Luino tunnels [both of them on the railway line that ran from Switzerland down the eastern shore of Lago Maggiore to Luino], the derailing of two troop trains, and five goods trains, the blowing of railway and road bridges, the destruction of the German radio and telegraph station just out of Milan, the destruction of the parachute factory at Cremenaga, the attack on the CEMSA [Costruzioni Elettro Meccaniche di Saronno] armaments works at Saronno, the abduction of enemy agents and spies and the wiping out of enemy outposts.'[2]

It was the sort of activity that inevitably provoked a response from German and Italian fascist forces. Aiding POWs on the run was by comparison a minor inconvenience. Partisan military activity and sabotage on this scale seriously degraded the German war effort, and it could not remain unaddressed.

There was little ambiguity in German-occupied Italy as to where the responsibility for the conduct of the war lay. It was with General Field Marshal Albert Kesselring, whose primary focus at that time was the south of Italy, where his Wehrmacht forces were engaged in a vicious battle to stop the northward advance of the British Eighth and the US Fifth Armies. As a matter of necessity, the task of dealing with partisan activities in northern Italy fell not to the regular Wehrmacht units but primarily to an array of security forces operating behind the front line. While Kesselring in principle maintained overall command of the war effort, the key figure in the vicious partisan war developing in the north was the SS General Karl Wolff, a former chief of staff to Heinrich Himmler and SS liaison officer to Hitler.[3]

Having gathered first-hand experience of the harsh German occupation practices in eastern Europe, Wolff occupied the position of Supreme SS and Police Leader in Italy, setting up his headquarters in Monza. In exerting German control he drew on a wide range of German forces, ranging from elite SS units down to humble policemen. Though it was not his only task, combatting partisan operations became an increasingly important part of his work and, like Wolff, many of the men at his disposal could draw on their experiences in occupied eastern Europe. As the extent of partisan activity grew in northern Italy, so too did the array of forces he committed to suppressing it and the ferocity with which they pursued their task.

These were not just German forces. Whatever reservations Hitler had about Italy's treachery, he could not do without Musso- lini, with the result that the RSI's manpower, too, stood at Wolff's disposal. Like their German counterparts, there was a great vari- ety among them. At the lowest level they comprised police forces, the *carabinieri*, left over from the days when Mussolini reigned supreme. Not all of them participated with great enthusiasm, but through weight of numbers they became a mainstay of the RSI's contribution to the war on partisans.[4] In contrast, there were some units of the RSI's military who were more than eager to prosecute the war, driven by an ideological passion matching that of their German counterparts. This was true of the National Republican Guard, the GNR, who remained loyal to Mussolini through the Armistice and beyond and drew on a tradition of political thuggery dating back at least as far as 1919. In time, as Hitler out of necessity allowed Mussolini to boost the RSI's forces, most German-trained Italians found themselves not battling the Allies in the south but pitted against their antifascist countrymen in the north.[5] Of the newest breed of fascists, the most feared were the *Brigate Nere*, the Black Brigades. In their origins a paramilitary offshoot of the fascist party, what they lacked in military competence they made up for in ruthlessness.[6] Together with a slew of other paramilitary units, they stalked partisans unremittingly through the last, des- perate year of hostilities.[7]

Working together under German command, these Italian and German forces engaged in a war which, for its intensity and vio- lence, was the equal of all the horrors of the anti-partisan cam- paigns waged elsewhere in Europe. From the end of 1943, the conflict in Italy was not just a conventional war fought against a conventional, uniformed army. In Italy's north it had erupted into a civil war fought through irregular means, and often with a cold disregard for the ethics of traditional warfare. At the very top of the chain of command, Kesselring made it clear that he shared Hitler's utter contempt for partisans, who in his view did not warrant treatment according to the Geneva Convention. He told his commanding officers, 'I will protect any commander who exceeds our usual restraint in the choice of severity of the methods he adopts.'[8]

What the Germans wanted, by whatever means necessary, was nothing less than the total destruction of partisan resistance.[9] The favoured tactic was to send available manpower into areas thought to harbour partisans so as to undertake *rastrellamenti* – literally 'rakings'. Using the element of surprise, they entailed rapid, thorough searches of civilian populations and even sparsely populated areas in the hope of flushing out partisans, along with any other miscreant elements such as former soldiers, draft dodgers and POWs on the run. They were conducted with particular intensity in the mountains and valleys of Piedmont, initially under German supervision, later under Italian. On one occasion an entire division was committed to the task and blocked off entire valleys in the hope of destroying or at least scattering the partisans in the area.[10]

One of the Australian partisans, Bert Wainewright, recalled the panic that the sudden commencement of a *rastrellamento* unleashed:

> The Jerries, they used to give us a hammering, week after week they'd come up. But you couldn't do anything, we never had the fire power or nothing. They used to come up, they'd come up with mortars and … artillery once, they did. I can remember they busted us up, and they burnt down seventeen of the peasants' huts – haystacks and mudhouses, seventeen,

right up through the mountains, you could count them.

Of course we'd slip through their lines and lay low.

There's hundreds of episodes like that occurred.[11]

By the end of the 1943 the Germans and their local fascist collaborators were closing in on Johnny Peck and his network. A message sent from a local police station in Piedmont to German security headquarters in Monza on 23 December made mention that Peck had recently participated in a meeting of partisan leaders. Here he is referred to as 'the Australian lieutenant John Ech (escaped prisoner)'. The report expressed concern that Peck was involved in discussions with other partisan leaders, with the aim of creating a more unified partisan movement.[12]

Then in January 1944 Peck's Vercelli escape network was busted open. At one point Peck himself was almost arrested, and under quite unusual circumstances. One night some policemen came knocking on the door of the house where he was staying in Vercelli, in search of a stolen bicycle. He was questioned, affably enough at first, but then his interlocutors' tone hardened. Peck asked the young men why their attitude had changed. They replied that they had become suspicious he was not the Italian he claimed to be because of the way he knocked the ash from his cigarette. It was not, it seems, in the Italian way, but by flicking the top of the cigarette with his forefinger as it was poised over an ashtray. Peck was able to restore an atmosphere of conviviality, and while the policemen were convinced that Peck was the man they sought, they did not know what to do with him. They might well have been aware that if they moved on Peck, he would kill them. Detecting their indecisiveness, Peck steered the discussion in a new direction, proposing that they might consider changing sides to the antifascists. It was not an unattractive offer, but they said they would need to discuss it with their Chief of Police. In time that Chief of Police came to the same renegade views as his men, so that he, too, was persuaded to throw in his lot with Peck's network.[13]

Others in Vercelli were not so lucky, and in January a number of arrests were made, including that of Peck's close associate in Vercelli, the café owner Oreste Barbero. It seems he had been denounced by an unnamed female source as a helper of escaped POWs, with the result that security forces moved on his café on 19 January. At the time of his arrest Barbero was carrying letters from 'Nino' and 'Gianni' concerning arrangements for moving POWs to Switzerland via Luino.[14] The life of Nino – that is, Filippo Bonardo, a member of the escape committee – was now at risk, but with a tip-off from Oreste's wife he was able to avoid capture and apprise Gianni – Johnny Peck – as well as Freddie Muller of the trap.[15] Both men steered clear of danger, Freddie Muller choosing at that point to make his way to the safety of Switzerland,[16] while Peck used his partisan contacts to seek refuge outside Vercelli.

Further arrests soon followed, including those of Peck's associates Luigi Mastroviti, Anna Marengo, Pina Gamba and his girlfriend Bianca Rossi.[17] Before long a tribunal was staged to investigate their roles in aiding POWs to elude authorities. At its conclusion in February 1944 it came down most harshly on Oreste Barbero, who escaped the death penalty but received a hefty prison sentence of 27 years, 7 months and 14 days.[18] Mastroviti, also charged with lending assistance to escaped POWs, received 15 years. In Peck's case, the absent defendant was given just two years, largely because he was not an Italian national and so the charge of aiding POWs on the run could not stick. His guilt stemmed from the relatively minor infraction of the fraudulent use of an identity document.[19] Fortunately none of the three women arrested – Marengo, Gamba and Rossi – received a jail sentence. Rossi seems to have done best to preserve her dignity, confessing that she knew Peck to be an escaped POW, but arguing that she had not betrayed him because 'spying is a contemptible thing to do'.[20]

What Peck's pursuers do not appear to have appreciated at this time was that Peck's crimes extended far beyond helping POWs on their way to Switzerland. By early 1944 he was already up to his neck in sabotage activities pursued from his base in Luino. In these activities he was operating hand-in-glove with Italian partisans and was probably also – as he implied many years later – responding to active but clandestine encouragement provided by Allied sources across the Swiss border.[21] It was just a matter of time now until Peck's hunters became aware that there were some compelling reasons to capture him, in which case the punishment would be far more severe than the paltry two years handed down in Turin in his absence.

The unwitting architect of the disaster about to unfold was one of Peck's fellow partisans, a man by the name of Lupano. Attending the theatre one evening, and within earshot of fascist sympathisers or perhaps German spies, Lupano had spoken boastfully to a female companion of his partisan exploits. Thereafter he was followed, arrested in the middle of the night, and interrogated.[22]

When Peck learned of Lupano's arrest, his concern was not so much that the Italian would cave in to pressure under questioning and spill the beans, because Lupano was a trusted member of his partisan group. Rather, the worry was that the arrest signalled a fresh wave of anti-partisan activity, so Peck made his way back from Milan to Luino, where he expected to spend a long night preparing for an onslaught on his partisan network.[23]

What he had not reckoned with were the Germans' powers of persuasion and Lupano's susceptibility to them. It was revealed later that Lupano's interrogators identified Lupano's weakness by inviting both his parents to the interrogation and making it plain that any silence or evasiveness on Lupano's part would cost his parents their lives. Under those conditions, he crumbled and divulged vital details of his band's activities, along with the identity of Johnny Peck and his likely place of hiding.[24]

When he arrived in Luino, Peck had no idea of the dangers that lurked there. Even in the face of heightened German attention, his aim was to continue his sabotage operations, and in particular to make a second attempt at blowing a railway tunnel on the main line to Switzerland outside Luino. Peck was met at the Luino station by Oreste Ferrari and a man by the name of Lazzarini. He learned further details of Lupano's arrest and the need to brace for a fresh round of anti-partisan activity. As it was already late, they resolved to do no more that evening; instead, they would await news on what the Germans planned to do with Lupano so that they might stage a rescue. Such were the relations between Peck's band and the Italian authorities holding Lupano that a note was smuggled into Lupano's cell, advising him not to worry, but to hold himself in readiness for a rescue mission.[25]

It was decided to spend the night at Oreste Ferrari's residence in Luino rather than make a testing late-night trek to the safety of their headquarters in the hills. Ferrari was dubious about taking the risk, but in the end he concurred. Then in the middle of the night there was a banging at Ferrari's door, accompanied by a raucous voice shouting 'German police! Open up! German police!' There followed a crunching of gravel around the house, followed by further banging at doors and windows. Startled into action, Peck jumped up, pulled on trousers and a coat, shoved two pistols into his pockets and grabbed four hand grenades from under the bed. Ferrari's wife Ines reported that she could see a group of armed men gathered at the back of the house, while others formed a cordon around the area. Peck, Oreste and Ines prepared to dash for the stairs in the hope of making an exit via the cellar, but as they opened the door to the stairs a volley of shots crashed into the house. When a momentary silence returned, Peck and Oreste, still uninjured, headed up the staircase, just as the front door was being smashed in. A spray from Peck's automatic gun pushed open a door to the escape route, but the Germans were already behind it. Peck lashed out blindly with a Luger in his right hand and heard someone fall to the ground, but there could be no exit in that direction. The final, slender hope was the front door, by now almost beaten in. As Peck approached it, it gave way, and three Germans stepped through, shouting 'Raus, raus!' The Australian opened fire on them, forcing a rapid retreat, and Ferrari followed suit with his Browning, his wife downstairs crouching out of harm's way. Both men made their way down to her and resolved to renew their plan to shoot their way through the now open front door and dash down the road to the nearby gorge.[26]

Peck went first, shooting as he went, but as he passed through the door a pair of strong hands grasped him round the throat and then sent him sprawling across the ground. As he fell he saw a circle of some ten men, while others were still forcing their way into the house. A boot struck the side of his face as he hit the ground, forcing a cry of pain. The pummelling that followed caused him to black out; when he came to, lying on his back, two assailants stood on his outstretched arms, while another sat on his legs. Two others were rifling through his clothes and turning the contents of his jacket onto the ground. Suddenly he was dragged to his feet again and punched in the mouth with a heavy fist.[27]

So began the greatest punishment and pain he had ever experienced in his life. Years later he wrote:

> Blows were rained on me from all sides, especially on my
> face and head and I was screaming again, shrieking at the
> top of my voice until the breath was battered out of me, and
> I could only make hoarse little grunts like a sow in labour. I
> couldn't fall down, the ring being too tight, and I was bashed
> backwards and forwards and round and round until I ceased
> to feel pain and a velvety blackness descended over me like a
> shroud.[28]

When he regained consciousness, he became aware that half his teeth were smashed in, his lips crushed and his face and body covered with cuts and wounds. Blood was dripping from his chin and running down his neck. Hauled once more to his feet, he used what strength he could still summon to remain upright, pressed against a wall, keeping his hands in the air.[29]

By now Peck assumed that his fate would be execution. The Germans were well aware who it was they had in their grasp; moreover, it did not augur well that he had been wearing a German officer's jacket and resisted arrest. So why prolong the torture of this endurance test in the light of his impending demise? All he needed to do, he reasoned, was to drop his arms and be shot where he stood. But with the faintest flicker of hope still alive, he maintained his tortured pose. For their part, his German captors must have reasoned that it would be worth extracting intelligence from him before delivering the coup de grace. And perhaps for the same reason, both Oreste and Ines were lined beside him against the wall, awaiting their assailants' next step.[30]

The first stage of Peck's interrogation began then and there. Asked if he was an '*Engländer*', Peck replied in the positive, and was then struck in the face and called a spy and a dog. A tirade ensued in which Peck was accused – with good justification – of committing numerous acts of sabotage. Answers delivered, the Germans appeared to prepare his execution, assembling a firing squad at a few paces, guns raised to their shoulders. At that point a German officer emerged from the house carrying an attaché case which, Peck well knew, contained sensitive information. Its contents would require further explanation, and when Peck identified himself as its owner, a stay of execution was achieved.[31]

14

ESCAPE FROM SAN VITTORE

IT IS A SIGN OF THE PLACE THAT MILAN'S SAN VITTORE PRISON occupied in Johnny Peck's life that he would one day give this name to his home. It was an action laden with irony, because the San Vittore Peck became acquainted with in early 1944 was a far cry from the green and pleasant pastures of postwar England. That first San Vittore, which exists to this day in Milan, was in 1944 used as a Gestapo prison. Peck had stared death in the face many times since he was first thrown into battle at Bardia, but he was never so close to death as he was in San Vittore.

After his arrest the path to Milan led via German Headquarters in Luino. There, he reported later, 'I was tortured, with others of my band, for three days and nights, but finally they sent me to Varese.'[1] From Varese he was taken to Como in northern Lombardy, where he faced a court-martial. 'The trial,' he later said, 'was the biggest farce I have ever witnessed, and throughout I hardly spoke a word.'[2] The sentence, predictably, was death. To await execution he was taken to San Vittore prison. The rules of international law dictated, so he was told, that a period of three months needed to elapse before the sentence could be carried out.[3]

The name 'San Vittore' conjured an image entirely appropriate for the institution in which he found himself. The particular Saint Victor who had been accorded the dubious honour of giving his name to a prison had been 'martyred' in Milan back in ancient Roman times. A member of the Roman Praetorian Guard, he took his Christianity sufficiently seriously to set about destroying pagan altars, prompting his arrest. His hagiography has it that he was dragged through the streets, tortured and imprisoned, yet still managed to convert three of his prison guards to Christianity. That did nothing to endear either him or his proselyte guards to the authorities, with the result that the guards were beheaded and Victor subjected to further torture. When he refused to offer incense to Jupiter, he was crushed in a millstone and beheaded.[4]

None of this augured well for Peck, who had already been arrested, tortured and sentenced to death. He would have little reason to expect mercy from Karl Wolff's SS representative in Milan, Theo Saevecke, who was well on the way to earning the epithet 'The Hangman of Milan'. He had been appointed head of the Gestapo there on 13 September 1943, just a few days after the

Armistice, and went on to distinguish himself above all in deporting Italian Jews to extermination camps and in waging a bitter, dirty war against partisans.[5] Just a few weeks after Peck's arrest, in March of 1944, Saevecke earned the praise of Wolff, who gushed that Saeveke had behaved in an exemplary fashion, 'in particular in combatting partisans in Lombardy and in standing in the front line of almost all operations'.[6]

A wing of San Vittore prison was made over to Saevecke and his minions. A report from the time indicates that within that part of the prison the Germans had free rein to deal with their captives as they wished.[7] In time, American Intelligence gained some insight into what exactly what was happening inside the jail's imposing stone walls, gleaned from a captured German who had himself spent some time there:

> Conditions in this prison were described as barbarous. It was run by an SS Oberscharführer and his assistant, an SS Scharführer, and held civilian and military prisoners. The worst treatment was meted out to the Jews, who represented a large proportion of the inmates. Jews were stripped naked and given leather lashes with which they had to beat each other. If they did not hit hard enough, the two SS men would beat the 'slackers' with horse whips. The Scharführer's hobby was to put two or three Jews into a cell, their hands tied behind their backs, then pour water on the floor for them to lick up.[8]

Atrocities were not confined to Jews. Other inmates too, the Americans learned, were stripped of their boots, shirts and valuables when they were admitted to the jail. 'Beatings and floggings — even of women — were part of the daily routine in this prison.'[9]

That accords entirely with Johnny Peck's experience of San Vittore. For the greatest part of the time he spent there he vegetated in solitary confinement. He was given the number 1310 and locked in cell 48 in the 6th bay, where he was held under special guard for – by his calculation – 75 days.[10]

Though his contact with others was strictly limited, he was in good company. It seems that German and fascist intelligence networks had done a great job in penetrating the resistance in early 1944; Johnny Peck's was part of a wave of arrests that enveloped Lombardy and Piedmont at that time.[11] A little later, in April, Giuseppe Bacciagaluppi too was caught, further eroding the capacity of the escape networks to do their job. Then there was another 'British' inmate in George Paterson, a Canadian whose story closely resembled that of Johnny Peck.[12] He had been captured in Calabria during an airborne commando operation and spent more than two years as a POW. He would have been among those sent to Germany after the Italian Armistice, except that he managed to escape from his railway car en route and crossed into Switzerland. Then, like Peck, he had crossed back into Italy to help other POWs escape, only to be recaptured and spend time as a guest of the Gestapo in San Vittore.[13]

As the date of Johnny Peck's execution approached, his jailers unwittingly extended him a lifeline. By this period of the war, Milan was coming under increasingly heavy Allied bombing raids. The local authorities needed a workforce to tackle the proliferation of unexploded ordnance. It was exceedingly dangerous work, so not surprisingly it was delegated to men like Johnny Peck, who were in any case on death row in San Vittore.

In May Peck was detailed to a UXB (unexploded bomb) disposal squad comprising a group of prisoners. On one particular day, after exiting the prison, they were escorted to the railway yards in the Lambrate district of Milan, a few kilometres north-east of the city centre.[14] As they were working, a daytime bombing raid took place. Peck himself best describes what happened next: 'The guards ran and so did I – in the opposition direction. I crossed the marshalling yards under the bombing, walked towards Milan until the All Clear and then hid until evening. I then caught the train to Milan Central Station.'[15] Peck knew the station well, having guided former POWs through it, but by this time security was tight. He asked an elderly woman to get him a ticket to Novara – he needed to visit his sick daughter, he explained. Ticket acquired, he hid in a restroom, where he managed to wash, shave and spruce up his clothing. To complete his spontaneous reinvention, he bought himself a newspaper. There still remained, however, the challenge of passing through a security barrier before boarding the Novara train. Spotting a young woman with a baby and too much luggage, he 'helped her' and solved his own problem at the same time.[16]

Having boarded the train, he found himself seated next to a Blackshirt, an Italian fascist. The satisfaction at reaching Novara without incident was soon spoiled when he realised that none of his partisan contacts was at hand – they had either been arrested or had fled. To avoid local security patrols he took to the country-side, sleeping in rice fields and rolling into the water when danger threatened. The next day he returned to the Novara station and managed to catch a train to Laveno. From there, on 15 May, Peck took the steamer across Lago Maggiore to Intra on the western, Piedmontese, shore and called on a partisan contact there. Peck was then able to make his way to 'Arca's' (that is, Armando Calza-vara's) partisans, remaining with them for nearly a week at their headquarters near Monte Vadà to recuperate. The partisans then guided him to Switzerland, crossing the border at Monte Limidario above Brissago on 22 May 1944.[17]

Across the border Peck slept in a forest then walked on to Locarno unchallenged. Yet his arrival in Locarno was not unannounced. The Italian partisans who had guided him across the border had communicated with the British consulate in Lugano. One of the consular staff, Major John Birkbeck, himself a former POW, collected Peck from Locarno and listened to his story with great interest. Birkbeck took Peck to the Swiss capital Berne, where the British Embassy was located, and here, too, the story of his escape received much attention, especially from a man by the name of Jock McCaffery, Birkbeck's superior.

From that time Peck was treated much like the men whom he himself had helped across the border in the preceding months. After the Italian Armistice, and with the realisation that thousands of former POWs were heading for the Swiss border, the British and Swiss governments rapidly arranged discussions on what to do with them. At that time Switzerland was surrounded by territory that was either German or friendly to Germany, so there could be no ready exit from Switzerland to the UK. In international law, Switzerland was not permitted to detain escaped prisoners of war. In the circumstances, though, it seemed sensible to all interested parties to gather together the men converging on the border. Initially the dilemma was resolved in the English manner, with a 'gentleman's agreement' proposed by the British legation in Berne and agreed to by the Swiss government, to the effect that Switzerland would immediately admit all the 'British' escapers on the understanding that they would be subjected to 'a measure of Swiss military control'.[18] The British authorities duly passed on the news of these arrangements to Canberra, with the firm assertion that the best course of action was for Switzerland to 'exercise some restraint over the freedom of these men, greater than merely assigning them a residence'.[19]

What had followed then was that the Swiss established a series of internment camps for escaping POWs, all of them subject to Swiss military control. Labelled '*évadés*', the men would not be required to work but would be adequately fed and looked after. Most of the Australians found themselves in the Wil area in the Canton of St Gallen, far from the Italian border, and most would serve out their time in Swiss camps until October 1944. By then the liberation of France enabled their safe transfer to England and, for the 400 or so Australians among them, on to Australia. Altogether they were much better off than sitting in an Italian or German POW camp. Life would be safe, but it would also be dull, since in effect their war was over. While for many that was an entirely attractive proposition, for others it was anathema.

His discussions with Birkbeck and McCaffery concluded, Peck was sent to the already well-established internment camp at Wil, where he was given a medical and dental check.[20] After an exhausting life on the run in Italy, followed by three months on death row in San Vittore, and then a daring break over the border, he desperately needed to recuperate. That the rest and the attention did him the world of good was evident in a letter he wrote home from the camp: 'Well, people, at last I'm a free man again having arrived in this free country about a month ago after being through hell and high-water in Italy since the Armistice.'[21] His buoyant mood jumped from the page of a letter he penned a month later. The easy Swiss life, he told his parents, meant that he was putting on weight 'like a prize porker entered for the Melbourne Show. I came into this country weighing 61 kilos and now I'm just touching the 78 mark. Not a bad effort for a young fellow, is it?'[22]

Back at Crib Point, Johnny Peck's family could have no idea of just how lucky he had been. Had they known the fate of a number of other Australians who had offered their services to Italy's partisans, a shudder would have run down their spines.

One of the unfortunates was Harry 'Mickey' Miller, who, with his friend Jack Rowe and other former POWs, had joined a partisan band in northern Piedmont. In February 1944, the month of Johnny Peck's capture in Luino, the Italian and German security forces were conducting *rastrellamenti* in Piedmont to flush out partisans. When they stumbled upon Miller's detachment, seven partisans were caught, among them Miller and the New Zealander Frank Bowes. They were held overnight as their fate was decided. The next day they were subjected to summary judgement and executed at the cemetery wall in the township of Mosso Santa Maria. The executions were carried out by members of the notorious fascist Tagliamento Legion of the 63rd Battalion.[23]

Another was Les Parker, a close mate of Tobruk and El Alamein veteran Ian Sproule. During a fascist raid the two men were caught on an open mountainside and exposed to acute mortar fire. Parker was wounded, scooped onto a stretcher and carried by a tortuous series of trails to a place where he could receive medical attention, but he eventually succumbed to his wounds.[24]

Altogether 39 Australians were recorded as 'killed in action and presumed dead whilst prisoners of war' in Italy.[25] Not in all cases, though, had the dead been serving with partisans, or indeed even bearing arms, when they were murdered. Douglas Smedley from Corryong in north-eastern Victoria and two New Zealanders, JT Clark and Leslie George Batt, were neither carrying guns nor engaged in partisan activities when they were arrested. They were holed up in a farmhouse in the village of Andorno Micca with four other men when a unit of the 115th Montebello Battalion of the GNR turned up to trap them. Smedley, Clark and Batt, so a postwar investigation concluded, tried to escape through the front door, only to be gunned down the moment they emerged. Whether it was a bullet that killed Smedley was not clear. His skull had been bashed in, and he had a wound to his lower jaw, leading to suspicions that after the burst of gunfire that brought him down there was a flurry of beatings with rifle butts or bayonets.[26]

Five Australians and one Englishman were captured on the Sessera River in the Biella Province on 5 May 1944. They, too, were unarmed, and were not members of a partisan unit, but they ran great risks by wearing civilian clothing. In all likelihood their fate, like that of many others, was sealed by the loose lips of a fascist spy. After their capture and execution by members of the Tagliamento Battalion, locals buried their bodies. The name of the Englishman was never established, but the Australians were Harry Blain (2/24 Battalion), Bill Harvey (2/32 Battalion), Clive Liddell (Australian Army Service Corps), Jack 'Tricker' Nicholls (2/28 Battalion) and Ernie Wolfe (2/32 Battalion).[27]

For pathos, though, it is hard to beat the case of the Australian Private James McCracken. On 9 April 1944 he and two British POWs were caught at Varallo, north-east of Milan. Once more their nemeses were members of the Tagliamento Battalion, who held them along with a number of Italians for several days in the village school. According to a priest who witnessed the events that unfolded, a rumour spread through the village on the morning of 15 April that some of the men were to be executed. Later that morning nine men, including the three former POWs, were taken to the local cemetery, their hands bound behind their backs. As they stood facing the cemetery wall, a firing squad of 18 men was assembled, and a fascist officer gave the prisoners the opportunity of joining the fascist armed forces. All refused. McCracken and the two Englishmen were thereupon stood against the wall of the Varallo cemetery and shot in the back. All the men dropped to the ground as a fascist officer went to each to deliver the final coup de grâce to the back of the head with his revolver.[28]

Before his execution, McCracken was allowed to write to his family in Bendigo. The full letter reads:

My Dear Pop,

Just a line to tell you that I will not see you again as I am going to be shot by the Fascists in Varallo this morning. Would you let Mrs Beggs know what has happened to me please also I left my alloppo [i.e. allotment] with Phyllis at Ballarat so you can do what you like with it now. I hope you are all well just at present so give my love to all the Beggs also Gwen and my girl friend Phylis and hoping she will be happy without me being there with her. I am with two English boys and they are going with me. I hope you got that letter that I wrote to you a fair while ago. How is Melbourne I suppose it is just as bad as ever.

Lots of love to all from your loving Brother

Goodbye[29]

15

THE SOE
IN ITALY

WHEN JOHNNY PECK WROTE TO HIS FAMILY FROM SWITZER-
land, he maintained a strict silence on his Italian escapades. On
one other point, too, he had necessarily been economical with the
truth. Before landing in Wil, his contacts with British officials in
Switzerland were neither innocent nor without consequences. In
his letter home, he could only hint at what those consequences
might be. The other fighting men in the family, he noted, including his father, had been promoted. 'But even I,' he added, 'scoun-
drel though I may be, will surprise you all very shortly.' The most
he could reveal was the name of the man with whom he would
share that surprise. It was his Wil room-mate, the South African

Freddie Muller, who Peck knew from his days helping POWs in Vercelli.[1]

After crossing into Switzerland, Peck's travels to Lugano and Berne had not been for the purpose of the standard diplomatic or administrative formalities required of an *évadé*. The former POW, Major John Birkbeck, formally attached to the British consulate in Lugano, was in reality a representative of the Special Operations Executive, the SOE.[2] In Berne, a hive of espionage activity at this time, Jock McCaffery was the SOE's 'man in Switzerland'. And among those with whom Peck met in the Swiss capital was Allen Dulles. Later in his career Dulles would become the first civilian Director of Central Intelligence in the United States. When Johnny Peck made his acquaintance in 1944, Dulles led the Swiss operation of the Office of Strategic Services, the OSS – forerunner of the Central Intelligence Agency – and was intensely interested in what was going on in neighbouring Italy.

It was the SOE that had the first claim on the Australian Johnny Peck and determined what would happen next. His fate was largely in the hands of the Glasgow-born Irishman Jock McCaffery, whose fluent Italian had been acquired over several years in a Rome seminary and then at the British Council in Genoa.[3] Aged 35 when he joined the SOE in mid-1940, in March of the following year McCaffery was infiltrated into the British legation in Berne via Lisbon, Spain and Vichy France – a journey open to officials with diplomatic status.[4] Formally McCaffery was accredited as assistant press attaché in the British legation, while his clandestine SOE brief was to run lines into every state surrounding Switzerland, including Nazi Germany and fascist Italy.[5] As for Switzerland itself, McCaffery did what he could to assist acts of sabotage conducted against German trains running between Germany and Italy.[6] As he later described it, McCaffery's mission was to make out of the Swiss base 'an advanced HQ as near to enemy territory as possible, with as many and as smooth channels of communication with all parts of Europe as were relevant, not only for the passage of messages and funds, but for the provision of weapons and sabotage material, for a two-way traffic of couriers and agents, and when necessary, for a haven or escape-route'.[7]

The other SOE base which could be used for operations into Italy was code-named 'Massingham', and it was located on the outskirts of Algiers. But like McCaffery in Berne, Massingham had little success in Italy before the Armistice. A low point in its operations was reached when it sought to infiltrate an agent, Dick Mallaby, into northern Italy on the night of 13–14 August 1943.[8] Mallaby parachuted onto Lake Como as planned, but on a clear, moonlit night he was picked up immediately by Italian security forces. His parachute reportedly 'floated down to the water before a large and fascinated audience'.[9] In fluent Italian he attempted to convince his captors that he was an Italian fighter pilot who had bailed out, but an abundance of evidence told another story.[10] He was duly interrogated and beaten up in Como's San Donnino prison.[11]

Both the scale and the success of SOE activity in Italy would change dramatically just a month later with the Italian Armistice. By coincidence, when Allied armies staged their landings in southern Italy in September 1943, in London a new head was appointed to the SOE, and a new era in its operations was about to commence. The Tokyo-born, multilingual Major-General Colin Gubbins was a veteran of the British forces that had intervened in the Russian civil war to depose the Bolsheviks.[12] It was soon clear that Gubbins was to raise the concept of close coordination between the SOE and regular military forces to a golden rule.[13] In time, it also meant that SOE operatives would be charged with bolstering the fighting capacity of Italian resistance forces in the northern part of Italy.[14]

Under Gubbins the SOE moved rapidly to take advantage of the new circumstances in Italy. A new base, Maryland, was set up on the Italian mainland, initially at Brindisi and then at Monopoli, and was tasked with providing whatever assistance it could to the regular army units battling German defences in the south. Meanwhile, from Berne, McCaffery would do whatever he could to unsettle the German occupying forces and their Italian collaborators in the north. In this he was aided by the establishment of a second Swiss base in Lugano, where the British consulate gave Birkbeck suitable cover for his work.[15] Whether from Switzerland in the north or from the southern mainland, the SOE's clandestine interventions in Italy went under the banner of 'No. 1 Special Force'.

SOE did not, however, have the field of 'irregular' warfare to itself. The Americans, too, through the OSS, wanted a piece of the action in Italy. Between them, the SOE and the OSS reached an understanding that in the case of Italy they would operate on roughly equal terms.[16] Strategically, the two services were not always of the same mind. While the Americans were wary of the British policy of supporting monarchies, SOE for its part worried that the main beneficiary of the OSS infiltration of Italian-speaking Americans might be the Mafia.[17] But at the level of practical cooperation, relations between McCaffery and Dulles in Berne were good, with the result that much intelligence was shared, and generally their operations in Italy complemented each other well.[18]

A much more challenging relationship for the SOE to cultivate and maintain was with the Italian resistance. McCaffery had laid a foundation before the Armistice, as resistance organisations sent intermediaries back and forth across the porous Swiss–Italian border.[19] After the Armistice, and as the multi-party CLNs formed throughout German-occupied Italy, McCaffery soon found that ever more Italians were beating a path to his door in Berne. The most influential of them were delegated from the CLN established in Milan, the largest of the Italian cities in the German-occupied north. Milan's became a kind of umbrella CLN and adopted the title CLNAI (*Comitato di Liberazione Nazionale Alta Italia*; Committee of National Liberation in Northern Italy). Unofficially, it was at first a kind of shadow Italian government in occupied territory, until in August of 1944 it was recognised by the government in the Allied-controlled south as the body controlling resistance behind German lines.[20]

By the end of 1943 the trickle of visitors to McCaffery was growing to a stream. On 2 November Leo Valiani and Ferruccio Parri, key figures in the *Partito d'Azione* (Action Party), slipped across the Swiss border to meet with both Dulles and McCaffery.[21] The outcome of these discussions was the clandestine provision of money and weapons for the partisan movement.[22] In addition, there was an agreement to send into occupied Italy Allied liaison officers, who, in the case of those despatched by McCaffery, were known as British Liaison Officers (BLOs) and entrusted with collaborating closely with resistance groups. In this way a relationship commenced which, though sometimes fraught, was generally productive and lasted to the end of the war.[23]

No matter which part of the political spectrum the representatives of the Italian resistance were from, their goal was always to garner whatever material or financial support they could in undermining the German occupation regime and the RSI. So numerous were McCaffery's visitors that by March of 1944 he acquired a commodious house on the fringe of town called Casa Rossi – the label stemming from his own code name of 'Rossi'. On the staff there he kept a small number of hand-picked ex-POWs.[24] They helped him host a vast range of visitors: 'delegates from Milan, from Turin, from Lugano; our own agents and BLOs; emissaries of separate bands such as Moscatelli's, the Green Flames, etc.; the Franchi organisation were seldom without representation there.' The traffic passing through Casa Rossi, as McCaffery later recalled, was 'unremitting and intense'.[25]

It was not just the volume of work this entailed but its political delicacy that made McCaffery's life difficult. Confronted with demands from groups ranging across the political spectrum, he could not be seen to be favouring any of them. In Berne, as in Italy, the antifascist coalition had to be kept together, not just for the sake of winning the war but for the creation of a viable postwar political order as well. It was a grim and neverending challenge to hold the various groups together and to dispel any suspicion that, through their allocation of precious resources, the British or Americans were seeking to privilege one group over others. Under the surface of what appeared a common fight, McCaffery later lamented, another battle was being waged:

> There was constant jockeying for position; and Dulles and I had the job of trying to hold together these opposing factions. We strongly supported the politicians behind their backs to our own people and scolded them vigorously to their faces. In one somewhat heated meeting with Party representatives

in Lugano I told them that Allen and I were the only two Italians in the room, because we were the only ones who were not motivated by sectional interests and who saw Italy as one sole piece on the international checker-board.[26]

By the middle of 1944, when Johnny Peck was visiting McCaffery, Dulles and Birkbeck in Switzerland, the SOE's work with the Italian resistance was taking on a distinctly military character. Partisan groups of all political colours were gaining in numbers and strength, even as the Germans redoubled their efforts to crush them. The Allies could see the military benefits to be gained from encouraging and supporting partisan activity in northern Italy. Any pressure exerted there that required the diversion of German and RSI forces would inevitably facilitate the painfully slow Allied advance in the south.

The SOE moved to press home the advantage, sending No. 1 Special Force missions into northern Italy to coordinate and participate in the activities of Italian partisan groups.[27] As in the political realm, the military collaboration with the Italian resistance was a herculean task, and it did not always run smoothly. As the Allies had to ration their scarce human and materiel resources across several countries, the Italians commonly thought themselves deprived of the level of support they deserved and questioned the Allies' commitment to their cause. Worse than that, even as their ranks swelled, the partisans lacked discipline and cohesion. The risk was that each political group would fight in its own way and for its own ends.

The SOE accordingly did its bit to provide a unified command for Italy's disparate groups. It supported the formation in June 1944 of the *Gruppo Volontari per la Libertà* (Corps of the

Volunteers for Freedom, or CVL). The CVL gathered under its umbrella all partisan groups operating north of the German defensive line. Then in August, and on behalf of the CLNAI, the SOE parachuted an Italian general, Raffaelle Cadorna, into occupied Lombardy.[28] Cadorna boasted useful political and military credentials, since he had commanded the only Italian division to oppose the German occupation of Italy at the Armistice, fighting the Wehrmacht until his ammunition ran out.[29] After his infiltration, made with an SOE British Liaison Officer and a wireless operator, his brief was to coordinate partisan activities on behalf of the CLNAI.[30] His own conservative political inclinations were balanced on the CVL by the presence of Ferrucio Parri of the Action Party – closely associated with the *Giustizia e Libertà* partisan brigades – and, crucially, Luigi Longo, also known as Gallo, and a prominent communist.[31]

In the summer of 1944 the war was going well for the Allies. D-Day landings in France demanded the rapid and massive commitment of German forces to the western front, while in the east the Red Army was notching up one success after the other. In Italy, too, everything was running in the Allies' favour. In the south, the Germans had been forced to abandon Kesselring's Gustav Line. Combined Allied forces staged a massive assault on the line from 11 May; a week later, the line was broken, Polish troops managed to eject German defenders from the Benedictine abbey of Monte Cassino. Those ejected German forces scurried back to defensive lines further north, but such was the momentum of the Allied advance that it could not be halted short of Rome. Rather than attempt to defend Rome, German forces retreated to positions further north, so that Rome became an 'open city'. The Americans moved in on 4 June, while the Germans hung a new defensive line – the Gothic Line – across the Italian peninsula, stretching from the western coast just north of Pisa to the eastern coast just south of Rimini.

North of the Gothic Line, too, all the developments were in favour of the Allies and their partisan collaborators. With the interventions of the SOE and Cadorna, the partisans were a constant and painful thorn in the Germans' side. News of the Allied victories in the south only strengthened their resolve and filled their ranks. While Kesselring committed whatever forces he had available to combatting the partisans, he could not eliminate them. Slowly but surely, desperation grew among the Germans, who could scarcely avoid the sense that they were living in a permanent state of siege. As their anxiety grew, so too did their determination to lash out at their enemies, real and perceived. The war was entering its final and nastiest phase.

For Jock McCaffery and the SOE, the developments through the summer of 1944 were a source of much satisfaction. The antifascist front appeared to be holding firm in the face of its common enemy. Yet there was also a downside to this favourable turn of the tide. With the scent of victory in the air, the partisans' claims for support knew no bounds, while the Allies were obliged to commit the largest portion of their limited resources to other theatres such as France and Yugoslavia. Without the human and material resources to meet the partisans' demands, the risk was that the military front in Italy would fray and play into the Germans' hands. As an official SOE report put it:

> Liaison officers, W/T operators, and couriers had to be
> found and trained in large numbers. Volunteers were now
> abundant but it was a large task to select and train those

who were suitable as agents. Nor could SOE obtain the quantities of arms and supplies for which the partisans repeatedly asked: and, if it had been able to obtain them, the RAF and USAAF Commands in the Mediterranean, with similar heavy commitments in Yugoslavia, Greece and Poland, could not allot sufficient aircraft to drop them. The Italians, with more courage than prudence, left the towns and concentrated their forces in mountainous areas. There they engaged enemy troops in open warfare which, owing to the inadequacy of their arms and ammunition, was often costly.[32]

In those circumstances it is little wonder, then, that Birkbeck and McCaffery would have licked their lips when Johnny Peck turned up on their doorstep on the eve of summer 1944. His usefulness extended far beyond the intelligence he was able to deliver about the partisan groups with which he was familiar. By that time he ticked all the boxes for the role of British Liaison Officer. He had travelled widely in Italy, knew the conditions there intimately, had military training and combat experience, spoke Italian fluently and was very well connected in the Italian resistance. SOE badly needed people like him, and sure enough a new opportunity to engage the enemy was dangled before him.

It is very difficult to gauge to what extent he was surprised, perhaps even flattered, by the offer that he be recruited as a BLO. If accepted, it was a job which would expose him to dangers from which he had only just managed to extract himself by the skin of his teeth. If rejected, his decision would have entitled him to rest on his already very considerable laurels in a Swiss internment camp until the war was decided.

It is unlikely that Peck's enthusiastic response to the proposal was founded in youthful naivety. True, he was still just 22 years of age, but he had spent months in Italy since the Armistice, and he had no shortage of first-hand experience of how vicious the war had become there. Moreover, in all likelihood he already had a good idea of how, since the Armistice, SOE had managed to spread its tentacles down from the Swiss border into Piedmont and Lombardy, heartily aided by partisans of many political persuasions. If Peck had not himself met with SOE officers when in Italy, his own partisan activities through the final weeks of 1943 and the first of the new year had probably given him some insight into SOE's covert operations. The partisans with whom Peck mixed back then knew that it was more than just moral support that was being both offered from Berne and gratefully accepted in Italy. In time, Allied goodwill towards the partisans was taking the form of men and arms infiltrated into the German-occupied north from Switzerland and the Allied-occupied south.

Apart from the much-needed recuperation in the Swiss Alps, there is precious little information on how Peck was prepared for his new role. A photograph from the time, taken in the Swiss town of Wil with Peck dressed in civilian clothing, shows his hair returning to normal length after having been shaved to the scalp in San Vittore. One postwar source has it that during these weeks in Switzerland Peck 'volunteered for training as a sabotage instructor'.[33] Certainly SOE was keen to use its collaboration with partisan groups to target the enemy's infrastructure; Peck and BLOs like him would have been expected to engage in acts of sabotage, but also to teach others how to do such work.

At the end of their preparation, BLOs like Peck had to be ready to perform a number of duties after their infiltration into enemy territory, and they needed to be able to adapt from one to the other at lightning speed. The historian Charles Delzell summarises the gamut of a BLO's work like this:

> As soon as he reached his destination, the mission head (usually attired in standard uniform) became liaison officer with the Resistance and sought: (1) to assure regular contact between the patriot organization and the base, (2) to interpret Allied decisions to the patriots and convey their needs and ideas to the Allies; and (3) to take the necessary steps to arrange for delivery of supplies and their proper distribution. Such tasks demanded much of the liaison officers, whose experiences were often more harrowing than those of soldiers at the front. The anonymous agents (usually young volunteers) had to be willing to forego for months at a time the morale-sustaining effects of association with fellow nationals. Playing a constant cat-and-mouse game with a foe who would probably show them very little mercy if he caught them, they had to rely almost entirely upon their own judgment and resources.[34]

Johnny Peck was not the only Australian entrusted with this crucial, secret work. In July 1944, a couple of months after Peck, the sapper Frank Jocumsen, who had become remarkably close to the communist partisan leader Cino Moscatelli, trekked over the Alps to meet with McCaffery in Berne. In his group was the liberal antifascist Edgardo Sogno, the leading figure of the Franchi resistance movement, once praised by McCaffery as 'the most care-free, dare-devil, likeable bunch of youths one could have wished to know'.[35] Sogno and his comrades would go on to perform countless acts of valour, including the rescue of hundreds of Italian Jews. As for Jocumsen, what McCaffery had in mind for him, as for Johnny Peck, was that he return to what was in effect the guerrilla war being waged in Piedmont.

The powerful Queenslander clearly made a lasting impression on McCaffery, who later wrote of Jocumsen:

> There was nothing of the maverick about Frank Jocumsen. Colourful, yes: for he wore and went into action with an Anzac hat, and when I met him first (though he removed it in Switzerland), it had two bullet-holes through it. But he was not just courageous: he was far-sighted and astute, and on one occasion, on a half-hunch, he saved several hundred men from being surrounded and wiped out by enforcing and directing a stealthy, rapid evacuation during the night.

> Frank knew nothing and cared less about Italian political in-fighting. It so happened that the band he had joined was Communist, but like ourselves who supplied them his preoccupation at the moment was to help make them the most efficient harassing weapon possible, and Cino Moscatelli, their leader, would, I know, have been most willing to recognize the immense amount he owed to Frank for the fact that his formation became the best Garibaldi Brigade in the country, and that in Italian Resistance annals some of their exploits became famous.[36]

George Paterson, the Canadian former POW whom Peck had met in San Vittore, and who also managed to escape from the prison, also became a BLO. His own escape from San Vittore was less dramatic than Peck's, but no less cunning – he had bribed a guard to get a key cut. After his escape he had made his way once more to Berne, where McCaffery was keen to recruit him and send him back into Italy.[37]

By August 1944, with several weeks of recuperation and preparation behind him, Johnny Peck was ready for re-infiltration into Italy. He was given a uniform and a promotion in the field. In the case of capture by the enemy, the first might help him avoid summary execution as a partisan. The promotion was a tacit acknowledgment of his senior status as a BLO, but it would also strengthen his hand in the dealings with partisans which lay ahead.

Peck's orders, as he summarised them later,

> were to carry on as before, ie. Sabotage, espionage, organising and fighting. As my own name was known to the Germans and Fascists who had published it with my photograph, I was given the name and paybook as Captain Fishlock to go back with. This didn't work as I was too well-known to the Italian resistance under my old name, so I dropped it and carried on as Major Peck.[38]

Peck's mission comprised four men. Two of them, by the names of Forth and Waler, were radio operators, but when it was clear there was little need for them, they returned to Switzerland. The other man was Freddie Muller. On 5 August 1944 they crossed back into Italy. For Johnny Peck, the final and most exciting phase of his war was about to begin.

16

THE DOOMED REPUBLIC

WHEN JOHNNY PECK AND FREDDIE MULLER WERE INFIL-
trated back into Italy as British Liaison Officers to the partisans in
early August 1944, they were entering extremely dangerous territory. German anger at partisan activity was reaching an apogee;
even if it meant the mass murders of innocent civilians, the Germans would do whatever necessary to assert their authority.

As overall commander of German forces in Italy, Albert Kesselring had long shared with Hitler the view that partisan warfare was a degenerate form of war.[1] As the war heated up in the
summer of 1944, he ordered that hostages were to be taken in areas
where there was evidence of a strong partisan presence. If German

troops were fired on from a village, that village was to be burnt to the ground, and the perpetrators and ringleaders burnt in public.[2] By September Kesselring was ordering that operations against partisans 'should be conducted with all means available', noting that 'innocent elements sometimes are made to suffer'.[3]

In north-western Italy, where Johnny Peck would operate as a BLO, Kesselring installed SS-Brigadeführer Willi Tensfeld as commander of security forces ('SS and Police Leader North-west Italy'), with headquarters in Bologna, later Desenzano. His immediate superior was Karl Wolff in Monza. Tensfeld had gathered vast experience in the brutal suppression of partisans in the occupied Soviet Union, and it was soon clear that he would apply his eastern front experience to Italy.

None of this would have surprised Johnny Peck, already well acquainted with German occupation strategies, but neither did it deter him. Following McCaffery's instructions, he and Muller made their way to the area of Valsesia in north-eastern Piedmont. Though not large geographically, its mountainous terrain made rapid travel and communication difficult and favoured the presence of multiple pockets of relatively independent partisan groups. Divided between the provinces of Vercelli and Novara, it is located north of Biella and west of Lago Maggiore. Its distinguishing features are the deep valleys that run through it, including the Anzasca, a valley through which many Australian POWs had hiked on their way to the Monte Moro Pass and Switzerland.

Though not exclusively so, the Valsesia was Moscatelli territory; Cino Moscatelli and his communist Garibaldi brigades were the dominant partisan force. According to Peck's report, Peck made contact with Frank Jocumsen, the Australian who had established himself as a trusted member of Moscatelli's inner circle. By this time Jocumsen himself had spent some time in Switzerland before returning to Moscatelli's side; well aware of the nature of Peck and Muller's SOE brief, Jocumsen took them to meet his leader.[4] As a sweetener, it seems, the arrival of the new men was accompanied by the provision of 100 000 lire, which Jocumsen had brought with him from Switzerland, with instructions from McCaffery that the money was for the 'maintenance' of the British ex-POWs in Moscatelli's ranks.[5]

According to Peck, Moscatelli wanted Peck and Muller to play a military role with his Garibaldi divisions in the area. Italian sources indicate that Peck at this time joined the 2nd Garibaldi Division,[6] and in Peck's recollection, Moscatelli 'wanted us to take over the organising and fighting direction of his two divisions, as he had been asking Berne to send British officers to help him out'.[7]

Peck accepted the challenge, so that he and Muller carried out, in Peck's words, 'many successful actions, including much sabotage'.[8] Just how successful Peck and people like him were at this crucial phase in the war in Italy is revealed by a telegram sent by Kesselring to Karl Wolff on 21 August 1944:

> Destruction of railway bridges by partisan bands, particularly in the north-west and north-east, has increased so much recently that the reconstruction of stretches which are important for the prosecution of the war is now impossible in the foreseeable future. The attacks in question are carried out by fairly strong groups after lengthy preparation. For example, on a bridge between Turin and Milan, partisans built in charges of several hundred kilogrammes of explosives.[9]

Then, however, an incident occurred which poisoned Peck's relationship with Moscatelli irretrievably. Johnny Peck was by no means a political animal, though instinctively his attitude to communism was at best reserved. His view on Moscatelli as expressed to his superiors was, 'I have never had any row personally with Moscatelli, my differences being with some of his officers on questions of mixing politics with the partisans' military sins.'[10] By Peck's own account, Moscatelli's politics did not concern him. Rather, in this instance, the issue was money or, to be more precise, gold.

At the village of Pestarena in the Anzasca Valley there was a privately-owned gold mine which employed upwards of 600 men. In July of 1944 the valley was taken over by partisans, who also took control of the mine. The new manager installed to run the mine found a large quantity of gold stored there, and for safety's sake arranged for it to be hidden in the mountains. Both the British and the CLNAI in Milan were informed of the existence of the gold; instructions were given that it was to be placed at the disposal of the CLNAI, who in turn asked that it remain hidden until it could be safely transported to Milan. Under the circumstances of the time, that would prove extremely difficult, with the result that the gold was left in its hiding place, known only to the engineer in charge of the mine, his two assistants and Johnny Peck.[11]

That was fine until Moscatelli's Garibaldini were extending their authority into the Anzasca Valley, forcing non-communists out of the area. Peck got wind that Moscatelli had his eyes on the gold. He came upon a letter to Moscatelli from a party agent in Milan, advising Moscatelli to seize the gold and transfer it to a new hiding place, sending only a small part of it on to the CLNAI in Milan to keep them quiet.[12] Sure enough, Moscatelli sent a group of his men up the Val Anzasca to take control of the mine. Their discontent, it seems, stemmed at least in part from the failure of the CLNAI to keep up with its promised payments for the upkeep of the mine and the wages of its workers.[13]

Peck felt he had to respond to the impending threat, since he considered the mine one of his responsibilities. Moreover, he knew that the proposed seizure of the mine would cause trouble in the valley, where most of the partisans were anti-communist. As it happened, he was able at the moment of looming crisis to call on the help of Frank Jocumsen, who coincidentally was passing through the valley on a trek into Switzerland.[14]

When Moscatelli's delegation arrived at the mine, trouble broke out immediately. Freddie Muller did his best to control it. In response, Moscatelli's men turned on him and on other British men in the valley, saying that the British were there to steal the gold. In Johnny Peck's reading of events, this was merely a ruse to cover up their own actions, readily seen through by the miners and the local partisans.[15]

As a compromise the engineer in charge of the mine offered to travel down the valley to consult with Moscatelli personally, only to be told by Moscatelli's followers that he would never reach his goal. Any party attempting to exit the valley would be ambushed along the way. When plans for such an ambush were laid that evening, Jocumsen and Muller overheard them, disarmed the conspirators and placed them under arrest.[16]

The story had a sequel some days later, when Jocumsen was back in the Valsesia with Moscatelli, who firmly denied sending his men to seize the mine. He offered to have the two ringleaders shot the next day. Johnny Peck refused to believe that the men sent to the mine were not acting under Moscatelli's express orders;

his deep distrust of Cino from that time was never allayed.[17] The feeling may well have been mutual. Peck soon noticed that Moscatelli 'no longer gave us the full support and co-operation which he had promised and had given at first. I asked him about this many times, but he always confirmed his first avowals and denied any underhand work.'[18]

There is another record of the deterioration of relations between Moscatelli and Johnny Peck, though it identifies a different reason for it. That record is provided by Frank Jocumsen, who had introduced Peck and Freddie Muller to Moscatelli after their infiltration as BLOs, and it suggests that Peck and Muller might have acted to curb the communist influence in the area. Some time later Jocumsen reported on his relations with Moscatelli and recalled that after the arrival of new BLOs – possibly Peck and Muller – 'it became obvious that their presence in the band would be disastrous. They began issuing orders to the partisans to remove their Communist badges and red scarves, and worse still commenced to sell their stores to the highest bidders.'[19]

There might also have been more plainly military reasons why Johnny Peck was inclined to sever ties with Moscatelli and his divisions. Battles with German and fascist forces, while fought courageously, were in Peck's view lost unnecessarily because of poor organisation and support. The final straw seems to have been the failure by communist-led partisan units to take the township of Gravellona Toce after a poorly coordinated attack. The waste of human life hit home as Peck helped bury the dead, among them an Englishman:

I was so damn mad that our boys who were willing to fight were being thrown away like that for nothing, that I pulled all our English fellows out of the Garibaldi Division and sent them home to England, via Switzerland. I know that they reached England safely as I heard the special message over the London Radio I had given them to send when they arrived in London (*Londra è bella*). They were all quite willing to go, as they had had enough of partisan fighting.'[20]

So it was that after about a month back in Piedmont, during which time he had frequent dealings with Moscatelli and his men, Peck moved on. His precise movements are unclear, though one official source insists that after a period of sabotage work Peck himself returned to Switzerland for instructions.[21] The same source has it that he then returned to Italy to command a 'Patriot Battalion',[22] and on this point Peck himself was quite specific – he took command of a non-communist unit, the 'Lombardy' Brigade, in the Valdossola (or Val d'Ossola) Division.[23] Though inter-partisan rivalries would not disappear, his new role dictated that from this point he would play a more directly military role with the real enemy, the Germans.

In September 1944 an already heated partisan war in northern Piedmont was about to escalate. Their confidence growing, and a number of isolated enemy garrisons in northern Piedmont already overrun, the partisans in the Ossola Valley decided that it was time to proclaim independence from both the German administration and its RSI partners. On 8 September coordinated partisan attacks targeted a series of fascist strong points and frontier posts. The next day the major town in the area, Domodossola, was isolated and surrounded by 3000 partisans. They had at their disposal a score of mortars, some 50 heavy machine guns, fewer than 100 light machine-guns, about 200 sten submachine guns, 50 automatic rifles and an unknown quantity of carbines and grenades.[24] The garrison of 500 German and Italian troops was disarmed and allowed to leave. At dawn on 10 September, the partisans entered the town, to the joy of many of its citizens, and a proclamation was made to the gathered crowd of the birth of the Free Zone of Ossola.[25]

It was easy to see why the partisans had targetted Domodossola. An ancient and picturesque town on the banks of the Toce River, Domodossola was the largest population centre in a region by now bristling with an assortment of resistance groups. While fully aware of the capacity of the fascists and German forces to retaliate strongly, the partisans were nonetheless emboldened by the seemingly irreversible gains of Allied forces in Italy and beyond. Strategically, too, Domodossola was a treasured prize. Located on the main railway line connecting Milan with Switzerland, it was the largest major stop before the Simplon tunnel and, with it, the Swiss border. Should the partisans' daring actions prove premature, then the mountains in which Domodossola nestled, and the Swiss border which ran through them, offered some hope of refuge.

The Free Republic of Ossola, as it soon became known, covered an area of some 1600 square kilometres and had a population of some 82 000; at its heart, beautiful Domodossola, with its 14 000 citizens, was declared the capital of an ambitious experiment in democracy.[26] There and throughout the Ossola Valley, stretching as far as Mergozzo and Ornavasso, fascist mayors and officials were removed from office, and new laws were passed to mark the commencement of a radically new order. Head of the new government was the socialist Ettore Tibaldi, recalled into Italy from Swiss exile for this very purpose. A special train bore him from

Berne and through the Simplon tunnel so that he could take up the reins of power. To assist him in the imposition of the new state, a number of ministers were appointed. All colours of the antifascist alliance were represented in the government, which worked hard to impress on its citizens that it ruled in the interests of all antifascists. Outwardly, too, the nascent Republic worked hard to win support, managing even to persuade a sympathetic Swiss government to extend formal diplomatic recognition.[27]

These developments were observed intently from Berne. While there was much to admire about the partisans' actions, this was the kind of bravery about which the SOE and the OSS felt deeply ambivalent. Even if the partisans managed to assert authority over Domodossola and establish a functioning, popular government, it was inevitable that the Germans would not only hit back, but hit back hard. In those circumstances, and with limited resources at their disposal, there was little that the Allies would be able to do to prevent a catastrophe. A troubled Jock McCaffery wrote,

> I realised that there was no way of stopping it, we enlisted the aid of Allen Dulles and we lobbied for all we were worth to have the operation backed. We actually half-indulged in blackmail by speaking of the extremely negative reaction it would have upon all of the Italian Resistance and upon the country in its entirety if we did not do all we could to help. After all, these men were our friends and collaborators and whether or not they were mistaken, we now had to stand by them.[28]

Fearing the worst, McCaffery sent George Paterson across the border as an 'observer–adviser' to the partisans.[29] In advance of his infiltration, McCaffery raised two key issues with the Canadian. If the partisan uprising in Piedmont succeeded at all, it might well need airdrops to keep the Germans at bay, and Paterson might help coordinate them. Secondly, McCaffery was keen to monitor the politics of this new Italian experiment in self-government. How would the various groups cooperate in establishing their cherished free zone? Would the unity forged in the face of a common enemy disappear when victory seemed in sight? McCaffery, it seems, saw the uprising in the Ossola as a microcosm of what a new, post-fascist Italy might look like. If it succeeded, even for a short time, it might give some hint as to which political colours would prevail when the larger war was won.[30]

As McCaffery feared, the sweeping political ambitions of the new republic soon gave way to urgent military concerns. The Germans and their fascist allies had licked their wounds and were now preparing a counter-attack – the self-proclaimed republic was an affront to the fascist order and could not be allowed to survive. Paterson met with the leaders of all the key resistance groups in the area, including Moscatelli, and was involved in the efforts to establish a unified command structure.[31] On the one hand, Paterson was impressed with Moscatelli's energy and commitment; on the other, he observed that he had 'an evil reputation for solving political differences with a bullet', and that little love was lost between the communists and the other groups.[32] That did not augur well.

Paterson knew Johnny Peck from their San Vittore days, and of course McCaffery and Birkbeck would have informed him of Peck's presence in the region as a BLO. It is not recorded, but it is conceivable that Paterson might have pressed for the inclusion of

Peck in the preparation of the republic's defence. In any case, Peck later reported,

> About the middle of September I received a message from the United Command in Domodossola to go and have a talk with them. I went and they explained to me that they wanted an experienced officer to take over the command of the Central sector of the front to build defence lines there, as it was the most exposed and weakest part in the Val D'Ossola defence. They said they had heard about me and offered me the job. I accepted and was given command of the 'Lombardy' Brigade and two battalions of the 'Matteotti' Brigade and the artillery of the 'Val D'Ossola' division.[33]

Overall command of the Valdossola Division to which Peck was attached was in the hands of Dionigi Superti. Altogether, some 700 men served under him, disposed along the left bank of the Toce River between Mergozzo and Domodossola.[34] A former air force officer and, more recently, director of a logging firm, Superti proclaimed no particular politics, though he was instinctively anti-communist and distrustful of Moscatelli. This would have been well known to Jock McCaffery and Allen Dulles, because Superti spent some time in Switzerland in 1944 making contact with both SOE and OSS.[35] It was an attitude which might well have engendered a level of mutual respect between him and Johnny Peck, and perhaps played some part in Superti's men benefitting from airdrops of weapons and supplies from the Allies.[36] After the war Superti would pay tribute to the role played by the Australian as a major serving under Superti's command.[37]

Partisan units did not have the strength of conventional army units, yet by his own calculations Peck had some 450 men and 30 officers under his command as he set about preparing defences at the south-eastern entrance to the Ossola Valley. Able to draw on military experience which many other members of his division lacked, Peck took control of the central part of the front formed by the Valdossola Division in the vicinity of Mergozzo.[38] Early in the campaign there were regular skirmishes with enemy forces, especially at Fondo Toce and Gravellona, in the area where the Toce River flowed past Lago Mergozzo and into Lago Maggiore. It was strategically vital territory, on the major route from Milan to Switzerland, with three roads and a railway line running through it. All of these were blocked and fortified to form a first line of resistance. Then a main line of defence was built on the bank of the Toce at a place called the 'Battala'. Here, as Peck explained, were

> walls of rock dropping a thousand feet, and on the top and sides of this we built machine gun emplacements. We blocked and fortified the railway tunnel above the road and dug a tank trap from the side of the tunnel down to the river. We mined the railway bridge over the road, and mined the road and tracks.[39]

All of this work was completed by early October, by which time their spies on the enemy side were telling them that their enemies were mounting a large-scale offensive to reclaim the Ossola.[40]

They were right. At the beginning of October the Germans were preparing to smash the partisans, and not just in Piedmont. On 1 October Kesselring sent a telegram to all important army and police authorities ordering the execution of an 'Anti-Partisan

Week' from 8 to 14 October. This week, he declared ominously, 'must make finally clear to the partisan bands the extent of our power, and the fight against these bands must be carried out with the utmost severity in accordance with my directive'.[41]

Willi Tensfeld was charged with reorganising the German and fascist forces at his disposal to expel the usurpers from Domodossola, and by early October his gathered forces were ready for action. With the aid of his spies Peck anticipated a first attack on 10 October, and he braced for it by sending two companies to stage an ambush on the southern shore of Lago di Mergozzo with heavy machine guns and mortars. Sure enough, the Germans and fascists launched their 'Operation Avanti' and walked right into the partisans' ambush when they crossed the Toce River at Gravellona; after an hour's vicious fighting they were forced back across the river, but not before some 40 of their number had lost their lives.[42]

Peck formed a new defensive line along a road and railway line in preparation for a renewed enemy assault. This time they were pushed back until digging in, then withdrawing to safety under cover of darkness. As they withdrew, Peck had road and rail bridges blown and compression mines set on areas the enemy was likely to traverse. They were, as was later established, devastatingly effective.[43]

At dawn the following morning the enemy attacked in full strength, deploying tanks and infantry, and repeatedly assaulting fortified positions, but they were repelled on every occasion. The pattern was repeated the following two days, until Peck and his men could see the enemy's dead littering the countryside. The prisoners they captured during nocturnal counter-attacks had reached the limits of exhaustion.[44]

On the morning of 14 October the enemy's attacks increased in both number and in fury, but among Peck's defenders not a man abandoned his position. The mid-morning word was delivered from the Val Toce Division defending the other, western, side of the Toce Valley that the enemy had broken through there. Peck asked the Val Toce Division to hold its position for at least five hours so that his men could make their way north to avoid being outflanked by the enemy. When word arrived after midday that the Val Toce had been forced to pull back to another defensive line, Peck ordered an immediate withdrawal of his own forces as well. That meant moving north at pace along the eastern bank of the Toce toward the town of Domodossola, and, as Peck later described it, 'under a withering fire from machine guns, mortars and cannons'.[45] In that withdrawal some 60 men were killed, but there had been no panic, and he was proud of the behaviour of the men with whom he fought.[46]

So thinly spread were the defences by this point that the withdrawal proceeded north-west to Domodossola itself, the capital of the Free Republic, following the Toce upstream. As in Crete some three years earlier, Peck was fighting delaying actions to slow the enemy advance. As in Crete, the Germans were not to be halted, as they exerted pressure on both flanks of Peck's force, threatening to isolate them. When the opposition's momentum became irresistible and other partisan groups yielded to the inevitable, Domodossola had to be abandoned, as Peck and the remaining elements of the resistance sought refuge in valleys further north.

Retreating with Peck to the north of Domodossola were his commanding officer, Dionigi Superti, and the other surviving members of the Valdossola Division. Superti's men had also been fighting a vicious defensive action up the valley of the Toce, and they too had been forced northward until they combined with Peck's men in following the Toce. The rugged Val Formazza offered a line of retreat as far as the Swiss border. Fighting as they went, Superti took command in the right half of the valley, Peck in the left. By 16 October the situation was hopeless; two days later, Superti and 50 of his men crossed over into Switzerland to escape capture, while another 200 were either killed or captured.[47]

Peck himself, though, was not quite done. He and his remaining men continued to hold the left side of the valley, even under sustained artillery fire. On 20 October there was even one last opportunity to hit back, as his men staged what he called 'a beautiful ambush', killing over 70 and capturing 23 prisoners, including a young woman of 24 armed with a tommy gun and pistol.[48] But by now the defenders had almost run out of ammunition, and they were aware of being surrounded by enemy troops. The Italians on their heels were from the Monte Rosa Division, while in an eerie echo of the rearguard actions fought in Greece and Crete, the Germans were Alpine troops.[49]

Their situation hopeless, Peck and his men climbed to the head of the Val Formazza, and with it the Swiss border, trudging through 3 to 4 feet (0.9 to 1.2 metres) of snow. Devoid of winter equipment, and just about dead on their feet, there was no other way to escape the fascist forces closing in on them. Hiding the last of their weapons before stepping to safety, Peck's remaining men crossed into Switzerland by dawn on 23 October. With four other officers Peck, too, went through. They were the last to leave.[50]

One other member of the Valdossola Division who made it to Switzerland through the San Giacomo Pass near the head of the Val Formazza was Claudio Perazzi. His *nome di battaglia* was 'Nebbia' – fog – in recognition of his capacity to disappear into his surroundings with silent efficiency. He recalls that along with 'Maggiore Peck' and others he was collected at Bellinzona, the capital of the Swiss canton of Ticino and a safe distance from the border. It was there that Peck parted ways with his Italian comrades. Perazzi remembers that Peck made a phone call from Bellinzona, 'and after a couple of hours a long and big car picked him up. It was the last time I saw him. Two men got off the car and saluted him. Before leaving, he greeted us very warmly. He hugged me.'[51] Almost certainly, the car had arrived from Lugano and one of the men was Major John Birkbeck, no doubt happy to find that Peck had once more cheated death.

After 40 days of freedom, the bold experiment that was the Free Republic of Ossola was indeed no more, just as Jock McCaffery had feared. For the partisans who did not get to safety, the consequences were disastrous. An American journalist reported that 23 captured partisans were hung up on meat hooks in Domodossola; they writhed and screamed until a comrade entered the town in the dead of night and ended their misery by shooting them.[52] Fearing a similar fate, thousands of citizens of the Republic retreated across the border into Switzerland.

When Johnny Peck made his way to Berne, he was debriefed on the stages of the disaster as it had unfolded. At the end of it, McCaffery decided that Peck would not be sent back into enemy territory. That crossing of the border on 23 October, Germans and fascists snapping at his heels, had been his last escape.

George Paterson was not so fortunate. Attached to Marco Di Dio's Val Toce Division, he was caught in an ambush just west of Lago Maggiore. Di Dio was killed and Paterson captured. After several weeks in a Novara jail he was returned to the San Vittore prison in Milan, where he would vegetate until the end of the war.

For all the courage displayed by the men who had defended it, his assessment of the Free Republic of Ossola was not rosy. It was an experiment doomed from the start by toxic partisan politics; the Allies had been right to limit the resources they committed to it. On the other hand, he concluded, it would have been better from the beginning to be absolutely clear to the partisans that they could have no expectation of substantial Allied aid. To issue half-promises of supply drops and fighter bomber support that never came had been helpful to no-one.[53]

Back in Baker Street, SOE's London Headquarters, the assessment of the sudden rise and fall of the Republic was more damning:

> Our plans were overthrown by the precipitate action of people driven by political ambition. The sequel is well known. We were called in to repair the harm done by others … But the business was hopeless from the word go. The best that can be said of it is that it was liquidated in orderly fashion and with a minimum of bloodshed.[54]

17
VICTORY

THOSE LAST, EXHAUSTED STEPS INTO SWITZERLAND ENDED Johnny Peck's war. With no plan to redeploy him in Italy, and with Allied control over France, there was no need to keep him in Switzerland. So he was sent via Lyon and Paris to London, where he could observe the course of the war from afar.[1]

By this time the Third Reich's defeat seemed assured. Hitler's armies were being squeezed from the east by the Soviets and from the west by combined Allied forces. Yet no one yet knew just how long the death throes would last or how many more millions would lose their lives in the process.

In Italy the battle for the Free Republic of Ossola had re-enforced a valuable lesson – there was little to be gained from supporting open partisan warfare against the German army. Fatally wounded though it surely was, the Wehrmacht would lash out at every available opportunity, and was still sufficiently potent to cause massive grief. What was required, then, was patience. Given time, the relentless pressure on German territory from all sides would eventually demand the recall of all German forces into the heart of the Reich. Sooner or later, all of Italy would fall into Allied hands.

After the reassertion of German control in the Ossola, and with doubts expressed in some quarters about Allied commitment to the partisan cause in Italy, efforts were made to smooth relations between the partisans and Allies. In early December members of the CLNAI in Milan were secretly flown to Rome for discussions on how the war would proceed in the months ahead. The Italians agreed that the overall war effort through to final victory would be led by the Allies, whose military instructions they would follow and whose military government they would accept when the German defeat was achieved. In return, the Allies promised support for partisan efforts in northern Italy, albeit on the understanding that the primary tasks were not open engagement with the enemy but sabotage and the disruption of the enemy's lines of supply and communication. In a symbolically important concession, the Allies accepted that the CLNAI was in effect the shadow government of the German-occupied north.

On this foundation the SOE maintained its involvement in the war in Italy. There was no longer a role for Johnny Peck, but BLOs and military missions were infiltrated into the German-occupied north to take up contact with partisans and coordinate the resistance. As far as possible, too, the SOE's brief was to insist on the primacy of Allied military authority, while also performing the task of holding together the delicate coalition of antifascist forces.

As victory approached, that delicate political task received an ever-higher level of priority.

In his memoirs Jock McCaffery makes no explicit mention of Johnny Peck or of why he might have chosen not to send him back into Italy. His thinking, perhaps, was that after the Ossola disaster Johnny Peck was no longer the kind of man needed for the job at hand. True, he had distinguished himself on the field of battle, but what was required now was a diplomat as much as a warrior. Peck's relations with Moscatelli and the Garibaldini had soured to such an extent that to reinfiltrate him might have ruffled too many feathers at a sensitive time. The SOE would look to others, whether already in Italy or still awaiting the cold thrill of insertion behind enemy lines.

Among those still in enemy territory were a number of Australian ex-POWs who resisted the temptation – in some cases even the advice – to leave for Switzerland before another bitter winter gripped northern Italy. On the night of 17–18 November 1944, and as a sign to the partisans that the SOE had not forgotten them, a new mission by the name of Cherokee was parachuted into Piedmont. That original team of four, led by Major Alastair MacDonald, was supplemented by two reinforcements dropped in at the end of December. The men were infiltrated to a location just south-west of Biella by parachute.[2] Disaster struck when MacDonald was captured by German forces in January, and yet the mission was a success, not least because of the help given by Australians already on the ground. MacDonald, who survived a stint in San Vittore prison, later heaped praise on 'our stalwart ex-POW Keith Jones'.[3] MacDonald's Cherokee comrade Patrick Amoore recalled that Jones carried his own Bren gun with him wherever he went and 'was very determined not to be captured again'.[4] The man who proved so helpful to Cherokee was in fact Keith Stanley Jones, formerly of 2/24 Battalion, who was captured at Tobruk back in May of 1941 but now clearly relished the opportunity to take the war up to the enemy all over again, first with one of Moscatelli's Garibaldini divisions and then lending help to Cherokee. Jones remained in Italy until the final victory was achieved.[5]

Then there was Edward Althey 'Big Bill' Smith, captured at Ruin Ridge in July 1942, and still serving with the SOE and partisans as late as April 1945. He, too, gave invaluable help to Cherokee, and with one of the mission members 'made lighting strikes at Livorno and Tronzano, destroying two locomotives; they also dropped a mains electric pylon and damaged a railway bridge at Sala Sola [Salussola] which caused major disruption'.[6] On another occasion, together with partisans and two of the Cherokee team, he helped blow a couple of bridges in the Val d'Aosta while a train was still on them. After the detonations, partisans attacked the train with bazooka shells, 'thereby making a real mess of things'.[7]

Bert Tabram, a Victorian from 2/24 Battalion captured in Africa in May 1941, was an ex-POW who had joined partisans in the middle of 1944, and then for several weeks at the end of 1944 and early 1945 risked his life for the Cherokee mission. After the capture of mission chief MacDonald, Tabram did crucial work in protecting and guiding MacDonald's deputy Amoore. That task completed, Tabram returned to the partisans and was still active in Italy's far north when the Americans finally arrived.[8]

Through the last part of 1944 and the first of the year that followed, SOE operations in Italy were guided by troubling developments in mainland Greece. The German withdrawal there had triggered unwanted political consequences, as Greek communists moved to fill the vacuum. The SOE had long had a presence in

Greece, but when regular British troops turned up in October, the communists refused to surrender arms to them. Internally, too, the Greek resistance was beginning to fray, as civil war broke out between communist partisans and their monarchist counterparts.[9]

This, then, was the nightmare scenario that confronted Italy. The last thing the British and Americans wanted in Italy was for the communists to ride to power on the back of a German withdrawal. The BLOs and other Allied representatives walked a political tightrope, not wishing to dampen enthusiasm for the war effort, but needing to impress on partisans that the campaign was led by Allied military forces, who would brook no rivalry from indigenous resistance, no matter how well intentioned. With the invaluable contribution of SOE, it was a tightrope act performed with skill, determination and, ultimately, success. Along the way there were deeply held political suspicions, military blunders, and the kind of horrific violence that only the conditions of civil war can engender.

Unlike in Greece, however, the Italian antifascist alliance held firm through a trying winter, so that the following spring became a series of triumphs for the partisans and their Allied collaborators. The SOE's estimate was that in the course of the month of April alone the partisans took over 40 000 German and fascist prisoners and liberated over 100 towns.[10] Stretched beyond their limits, the remaining German forces in Italy were being rapidly deployed north to the Reich, by now an unwilling host to a number of armies intent on its destruction. The German presence in Italy evaporating, the fall of Mussolini's RSI and the disintegration of its fighting forces was just a matter of time. Only the most ardent of fascists would willingly offer their lives for an ideology whose time had already passed.

His situation hopeless, as early as March 1945 Karl Wolff was sending out the first peace feelers. Then on 12 April Field Marshal Alexander – as he was now – launched the Allies' final offensive in Italy, while German forces streamed north through the Brenner Pass in the north-east. In reality, many of the towns and cities had fallen into partisan hands before the Allies arrived. That was especially true of Piedmont and Lombardy in the north-west, the German forces there keen not to be trapped and subjected to the wrath of the local populations. Mussolini was not so lucky. From the middle of April he based himself in Milan, where his RSI collapsed around him. With the CLNAI exerting its authority there, and with German forces in full retreat by 25 April, Mussolini and his mistress sought to conjure their own late escape into Switzerland. Two days later, the two of them, travelling with a convoy of fascists, were caught by partisans near Lake Como and later shot dead. Their bodies were among those dangled upside down on meat hooks from the girders of a Milanese petrol station.

As fascism's defeat was placed on grotesque display, German forces formally signed their surrender on 29 April. Further north, in Germany itself, the Nazi behemoth would issue its last groans for a few days yet, but for Italy, the war was now over.

In Crete the war limped toward its conclusion. With the campaigns of the Western Desert long finished, Crete did not possess the strategic significance that it held through the middle of 1941. Germany committed enough resources to hold it, even after the Italian Armistice and the end of the Italian occupation of the island's eastern end, while the Allies could never justify the sort of diversion of resources that would have been required to win Crete back.

Over many months the SOE was an elusive yet trouble-some thorn in the occupiers' side. Though relations with Crete's *andartes* did not always run smoothly, SOE officers, among them the Australian Tom Dunbabin, worked tirelessly with their Cretan counterparts to hassle and harass. Here, as in Italy, the trick was to engage in sabotage and subterfuge; to avoid open confrontation. The boldest and most controversial operation of all was the kidnapping of a German general, Heinrich Kreipe. The plan was hatched by two SOE officers, Patrick Leigh Fermor and Billy Moss, and was successfully executed on 26 April 1944, when the SOE's abduction team intercepted Kreipe's staff car, kidnapped the general and eventually smuggled him to Cairo.

It was a symbolic show of strength by the SOE; tragically, it triggered a very real demonstration of force by the Germans. Then and later, the German occupation met any semblance of opposition with an iron fist. To the great frustration of the *andartes* and the SOE officers who lived and worked with them, anything more than a symbolic response was beyond their means at that time. London was playing a waiting game, just as it would in northern Italy. Decisive battles fought elsewhere would inevitably force the German withdrawal. In the case of Crete, it was a long wait. Bit by bit the Germans withdrew into their Canea stronghold, until, in May 1945, they lay down their arms in what seemed an unfittingly timid conclusion to a vicious war.

18
AFTERMATH

JOHNNY PECK MIGHT HAVE HAD QUITE A DIFFERENT WAR, or perhaps none at all. The recruiting officer in Melbourne might have wondered whether the callow 17 year old standing before him was 21, as he claimed. Thomas Blamey might have resisted the appeals of the 18-year-old Peck to be thrown into action as an infantryman. Had the *Costa Rica* been sent to the bottom of the Mediterranean with all men aboard, then Peck's war would have met a sudden, watery end. And if the *Costa Rica* had sailed to Alexandria, or if Peck had taken his place on a boat or submarine departing the south coast of Crete, he might have been part of the reconstituted 2/7 Battalion, the 'fiery phoenix', and sent off to the jungles of New Guinea to fight a different war and a different enemy. But his escapades and misadventures in Europe had conspired to ensure that, for him at least, there would be no sequel in the Pacific War.

As things unfolded, by the end of 1944 Johnny Peck's war was, in effect, over. Withdrawn from the field of battle, his life changed in other, equally profound ways. In London before the year was out he met and fell in love with a Birmingham-born Englishwoman. She was, as he put it in a letter home from the AIF Reception Camp in Eastbourne, 'the most beautiful, most divine, delicious, enchanting, glorious girl'.[1] Brenda was serving with the Auxiliary Territorial Service, the women's branch of the British Army, and was deployed on the large guns in St John's Wood, tasked with intercepting V1 and V2 flying bombs. The romance developed with the impatience known best to people painfully aware of the fragility of life. Within about three weeks they were married,[2] after which Peck spent ten days of his honeymoon in bed with tonsillitis.[3] Nonetheless, love had blossomed, and soon Brenda was pregnant.

Before settling into family life, Peck had business to attend to in Australia – loose ends of both a family and an official nature needed to be tied. A source of constant frustration during his captivity had been the paucity of news from home, so when he arrived back in Australia in April 1945, he was eager to catch up on the latest from his family. Altogether five Pecks had served with honour in the war – Johnny, his father Chief Petty Officer Peck (Flinders Naval Depot) and brothers Mervin Peck (HMAS *Canberra*), Joffre Peck (HMAS *Hobart*) and Lock Peck (7th Division AIF) – and all had managed to survive. No doubt Johnny was hugely relieved that the war had ended well for everyone, but there was no question that he would return to the bosom of the Crib Point clan. Brenda and then a son he had not seen, Tony, were waiting for him back in Britain.

Although there was no question of sending him back into battle, Peck was still a member of the armed forces. In the service of the SOE in Italy he had been promoted in the field, but in quietly transferring back into the Australian Army, that elevation no longer applied. Over the following months he undertook officer training, so that by Christmas of 1945 he had been promoted to a commissioned rank. He was now Lieutenant Peck.[4]

In January of the following year the War Office in London recommended Peck for a Military Medal, the Other Ranks' equivalent of the Military Cross. The summary citation pointed of course to Peck's own escape efforts as well as his aid to others. Most of it was devoted to what happened *after* he escaped from San Vittore and made his way to Switzerland:

PECK escaped to Switzerland and volunteered for training as sabotage instructor. Entered Italy and was attached Italian Patriot Brigade. After period this work PECK returned Switzerland for instructions.

PECK again returned Italy and commanded Patriot Battalion which fought determinedly until ammunition exhausted. PECK returned Switzerland.

PECK's leadership and training of patriots knowledge instruction use sabotage stores decisive contribution to effective operations Patriot force under his command.

Above duties voluntarily undertaken under conditions considerable hazard and physical hardship.[5]

That citation never saw the light of day. Instead of a Military Medal, Peck was awarded the higher-ranked Distinguished Conduct Medal. This time the citation referred to his many escapes, his aid to other escapers and his imprisonment by the Gestapo, ending with his arrival in Switzerland on 22 May 1944.[6] It was strangely silent on the heroics he had performed in the service of the SOE, by now, it seems, a matter to be consigned to oblivion.

That quiet suppression of Peck's battlefield valour experienced a sequel decades later, when the Italian government via its Canberra embassy sought to confer on Peck an 'Italian Military Award for Bravery' in recognition of his efforts to save the Free Republic of Ossola as an officer in the partisan Valdossola Division. The stumbling block this time was a sharp-eyed Canberra bureaucrat who consulted the 'British Regulations concerning the Acceptance and Wearing of Foreign Awards'. Those regulations insisted that awards of this kind were not to be given officers visiting foreign countries, and they were not to be considered in relation to events more than five years in the past. That was in 1977, so on both counts Peck was ineligible, as the Australian Department of Foreign Affairs informed Peck's presumably bemused would-be benefactors.[7]

Happily there had been one other distinction. A Victory March was planned for June 1946 in London, and it was decided that Johnny Peck should represent Victoria. It was a great honour, and on top of that would enable him to return to Brenda and to see Tony for the first time. But his return to the UK of 1946 was marred by tragedy. Two days out of Freetown in West Africa, cabled news told him of the death of Tony, the result of infantile convulsion brought on by meningitis. As a soldier Peck was accustomed to death, had witnessed it at close hand countless times. On this occasion, though, word of a death far away hit him harder than anything he had known.

In England his military career formally ended. Of course he would do his duty and take his part in the Australian contingent in the Victory Parade. But with the war over, he resolved that he, too, must move on, so he formally severed his ties with the AIF.[8] It was 8 July, by which time he had served continuously for 2398 days, 1998 of them outside Australia.[9]

Peck was drawn back to Italy, whose language and people he had come to love. His vision was to settle there with Brenda and to use his contacts, his ready affability and his language skills to make a career in business.[10] He and Brenda settled in Milan, where the people were as warm as ever. But as it hauled itself from the ashes of war, Italy was no easy place in which to build a new life. In his own self-deprecating assessment, Peck 'was not worth tuppence as a businessman', and the couple decided to leave and try their luck in Australia. They left as a family of three, first daughter Barbara having been born, and then, in their provisional home of England, the family expanded further, ultimately to five daughters. Peck's planned return to his homeland, delayed by fatherhood, never happened. He tended his family and built a new life in the UK.[11]

There he found work as an electrical engineer, working on switch equipment produced by a company in Stafford. Then he switched to the export department, eventually rising through the ranks to export manager. Yet in his own assessment his greatest career success was in the field of translation. He was a member of the Council for National Academic Awards, responsible for the accreditation of tertiary education institutions in the UK. Though without a degree himself – indeed, almost entirely self-educated – he came to sit on regional advisory councils dealing with matters of higher education. For him, this was 'a greater achievement than all the wars you could mention'.[12] Yet in no small way it was also an achievement which was intimately connected with his wartime experiences. From his leisurely days under Blamey's tutelage in Jerusalem through to his embroilment in partisan warfare in Italy, his facility in languages had guided his war, perhaps even saved his own life and the lives of many others.

Though he never dwelt on the war, it never left him. In silent acknowledgment that the closest of his brushes with death framed his life, he named his house in Staffordshire 'San Vittore'. And over the years his thoughts turned to the war, and he turned to friends and acquaintances to help him dredge wartime memories from the ever-deepening waters. Eventually he returned to Crete and met up with George Psychoundakis, the 'Cretan Runner' who had helped him through his darkest time on the island. As Psychoundakis recalled his efforts, it was reported, 'John Peck, with great emotion, confirmed George's story. Once again Cretans, in gratitude, with gratitude will open their arms to receive "Yiannis".'[13]

As for the men of the 2/7th and other battalions who, due to the bravery and hospitality of George Psychoundakis and so many like him managed to get back to Egypt, new challenges awaited them. One of them was Reg Saunders, who got off Crete in May 1942. As part of the reconstituted 'mud on bloods', he found himself in New Guinea fighting the Japanese, now as a sergeant. In November 1944 he was commissioned – the first Aboriginal Australian to achieve that distinction – and served out the final months of the war as a platoon commander. Further service in the Korean War awaited, as did, eventually, an MBE.

Two of the men with whom Johnny Peck had found himself stuck on Crete were David Pettigrew and Bill Ledgerwood.

Pettigrew was in a group of men smuggled off Crete on 6 May 1943, after nearly two years on the run. By 8 May he was in Tobruk. Ledgerwood took even longer, not arriving in Egypt until June 1943. By this time the Australian army forces had departed the Middle East. Back in Australia Ledgerwood rejoined the 2/7th and was soon fighting the Japanese in the jungles of New Guinea, where he earned himself a Military Medal.[14]

Ladislao Kürti, the Czech Jew with whom Peck had swapped his uniform for onions and cigarettes as he prepared his escape from Rhodes, stayed in touch for a time. Kürti, too, had ended up in Italy, where he was eventually liberated by Allied forces from a camp at Ferramonti. Then he volunteered for the Czech army, hoping for the chance to fight Germans. The war over, he made his way back to Czechoslovakia, where, as he told Peck, 'I found nobody and nothing and came to Prague, where I met accidentally my sisters, turning back from German concentration camps.' He hoped one day to be able to visit the grave of his mother in Germany.[15] Kürti's last letter to Peck, in 1950, was from Guatemala.[16]

An acquaintance from San Vittore got in touch with Peck after the war, an Englishman by the name of Ronald Lewis-Heath. He knew as well as anyone of the horrors Peck had endured in the prison wing which the German security forces had converted to their own version of hell. Peck, he hoped, would 'recuperate from the disgraceful treatment you received from the hooligans all of whom should be baked slowly ? ? ?!!'[17]

There were others, too, who managed to survive the horrors of San Vittore. The Canadian George Paterson emerged from his second stint in the Milan prison when the Germans bargained a prisoner exchange before the end of the war. Giuseppe Bacciagaluppi, the key figure in the escape network for former POWs, managed to escape from San Vittore. After the war he steered clear of politics, and as director of the Italian national autodrome at Monza threw himself into the world of car racing.[18]

Cino Moscatelli did make a career in politics, but British fears that the communists might make a grab for power proved unfounded. On 28 April 1945 he and his *Garibaldini* marched triumphantly into Milan; thereafter Moscatelli, still a communist, accepted and participated in the creation of a new government along western democratic lines. Italy mercifully avoided the bitter civil war which plagued mainland Greece after the Germans departed.

Others of Peck's network of Italian acquaintances were not so fortunate. He learned at the end of the war that two of his associates, Mandelli and Balzarini, had been executed on 14 July 1944 at the notorious Fossoli concentration camp in Emilia-Romagna, while two others, De-Grandi and Satriani, were hauled north to Germany and executed at Dachau the following month. Johnny Peck's nemesis Lupano, who under duress betrayed the Peck network, was also despatched to Fossoli, and from there to Mauthausen in Austria, where it seems he was murdered. Oreste and Ines Ferrari, captured with Peck in Luino in February 1944, were among the lucky ones to survive their time in the Reich and rebuild their lives in Italy after the war.[19]

On the other side of World War II's divide, history's judgement of Johnny Peck's fascist tormentors was not as harsh as it might have been. Vittorio Calcaterra, the commandant of PG 57, died before he could be tried for war crimes.[20] Albert Kesselring did face court and was sentenced to death, but his sentence was commuted and he was a free man by 1952. Karl Wolff was tried in 1948 and given a sentence of four years, and then faced court again in 1964, when his role in the deportation of hundreds of thousands of Jews from Italy to the Nazi death camps was brought to light. This time he got 15 years, but he was a free man again after just five. Willi Tensfeld, the scourge of partisans in Italy's north-west and victor over the Free Republic of Ossola, was captured by British forces, tried by a military court in Padua and acquitted. As for Milan's Gestapo boss Theo Saevecke, he was captured by the Allies and spent time in Dachau – by now converted for new uses by US occupation forces. Neither the Americans nor the British showed any interest in prosecuting Saevecke, though they were well aware of the kinds of crimes in which he had participated. From 1947 at the latest, he was working for the CIA.[21]

The last time Johnny Peck saw his fellow BLO Frank Jocumsen was in Italy in late 1944, probably on the eve of the battle for the Free Republic of Ossola. A photograph shows them together on the main square of Domodossola. Some weeks later than Peck, on 7 December, Jocumsen too crossed over into Switzerland for a debriefing with Jock McCaffery. By that time 'il australiano' had served for some 13 months as Cino Moscatelli's right-hand man. Peck for a time knew nothing of Jocumsen's last weeks with Moscatelli and of what happened next to the Queenslander. Moscatelli's forces had skilfully avoided the wrath of the Germans in the wake of the Ossola disaster, retreating into the mountains and biding their time. As the end of the war approached, the SOE knew all too well that the politically astute Moscatelli was a force they had to deal with, one way or the other. Jocumsen accordingly was given training and sent via France to Rome to receive his commission and await further orders in advance of a re-infiltration.[22]

Intriguingly, as records show, an advocate of Jocumsen's redeployment with Moscatelli was the communist spy Kim Philby. At that time Philby was working for Section V of MI6, responsible for offensive counter-intelligence in Italy and other parts of the Mediterranean. On 7 February 1945 Philby broached the topic of Jocumsen with John Senter, head of SOE security. He pointed to the potential intelligence benefits of re-establishing Jocumsen's relationship with Moscatelli. Jocumsen, Philby wrote, is an 'extremely tough type who apparently enjoys Partisan life and definitely wants to go back. He has seen Moscatelli rub out his original comrades in the band one by one, but he knows that he himself is useful to Moscatelli because of his liaison with SOE. He seems confident that he can handle Moscatelli and that when he ceases to be useful to him he can manage to be one jump ahead.'[23] Philby was perhaps savouring the prospect of passing on to his Soviet handlers any intelligence Jocumsen might be able to glean.

Persuaded as to the potential advantages of sending Jocumsen back to Piedmont, and aware no doubt also of the grave risks he would face there, SOE made preparations to reinsert Jocumsen into Piedmont as a BLO, this time in the service of SOE's Maryland mission in Italy rather than McCaffery's Berne outfit. It never happened. One possible reason for the premature conclusion to Jocumsen's SOE career can be gleaned from the recollections of Jock McCaffery, who maintained a keen interest in his former protégé. An incident occurred which suggested that after many months of largely following his own initiative, a return to the rigours of daily military discipline would not sit easily with Jocumsen. In Rome at that time, as McCaffery recalls, 'it was calculated that there were some thirty thousand deserters of varied origin, and when two American military policemen saw one evening this character sporting an Aussie hat, a non-descript uniform, and a pistol in a side-holster, they grabbed him from behind. Some minutes later this outraged and affronted tourist had stretched them both on the pavement and proceeded quietly on his way.'[24]

After that there was no redeployment into the German-occupied north, though in the longer term this did nothing to stifle the Italians' gratitude for Jocumsen's contribution to their liberation. In time the Piedmontese town of Borgosesia gave him honorary citizenship, and he was awarded the *Medaglia d'Oro*, Italy's highest award for valour. Nonetheless, when Johnny Peck contacted him soon after both men had returned to Australia, Jocumsen was palpably irritated at the way he had been treated, and about to leave the armed forces for good. 'Political reasons', in his view, had dictated that his re-infiltration was to be delayed until Allied ground forces reached Moscatelli first. Unwilling to cool his heels indefinitely in Rome, Jocumsen's response, as he told Peck, was, 'I naturally did not want that and got Browned off and asked to be sent home to Australia cutting my nose off to spite my face and you can imagine how much thanks I have received from Australian Military who do not recognize my Rank in British Field Security.'[25]

Not wishing to close his correspondence on a sour note, Jocumsen assured his friend that in his Rome debriefings he had given glowing reports of Peck's work in Italy. Then he asked, 'Have you written your book yet John?' before adding, 'Yours and my experiences together should make good reading.'[26] When Johnny Peck died in 2002, his book was still unwritten.

NOTES

CHAPTER 1: WOOLLAHRA TO TOBRUK

1   Keith T Peck, *'The Kemp Connection': The Family Story of George and Louisa Kemp*, Riverwood: KT Peck, 1993, pp. 396–97.
2   John Desmond Peck, interview with Heidi Egger, Manchester, 11 February 2001, Peck family collection.
3   Peck, interview with Egger.
4   Peck, interview with Egger.
5   John Desmond Peck to his parents, 18 December 1939, Peck, John Desmond 'Des' (Lieutenant), DCM, 1919–2002, personal papers, AWM, PR03098, 1/1.
6   Peck to his parents, 7 March 1940, AWM, PR03098, 1/1.
7   Peck to his parents, 18 March 1940, AWM, PR03098, 1/1.
8   Peck to his parents, 2 September 1940, AWM, PR03098, 1/1.
9   Peck to his parents, 2 September 1940, AWM, PR03098, 1/1.
10 Peck to his parents, 2 September 1940, AWM, PR03098, 1/1.
11 John Desmond Peck, interview with Conrad Wood, London, 30 May 1996, Imperial War Museum (IWM), 16667, reel 1.
12 Pietro Badoglio, *L'Italia nella Seconda Guerra Mondiale*, Mondadori, Milan, 1946, p. 37.
13 Peck to his parents, 18 March 1940, AWM, PR03098, 1/1.
14 Peck, interview with Wood, IWM, reel 1.
15 WP Bolger and JG Littlewood, *The Fiery Phoenix: The Story of the 2/7 Australian Infantry Battalion 1939–1946*, 2/7 Battalion Association, Melbourne, 1983, p. 5.

16 Bolger and Littlewood, *The Fiery Phoenix*, pp. 5, 7.

17 Unit War Diary of 2/7 Infantry Battalion, November 1940 – January 1941, p. 65, AWM52, 8/3/7/4.

18 Unit War Diary of 2/7 Infantry Battalion, p. 66.

19 Gavin Long, *The Six Years War: A Concise History of Australia in the 1939–1945 War*, Australian War Memorial and the Australian Government Printing Service, Canberra, 1973, p. 56.

20 Unit War Diary of 2/7 Infantry Battalion, p. 69.

21 Peck to family, 6, 7 or 8 January 1941, AWM, PR03098, 1/1.

22 Peck to family, 6, 7 or 8 January 1941, AWM, PR03098, 1/1.

23 Peck, interview with Wood, IWM, reel 1.

24 Bolger and Littlewood, *The Fiery Phoenix*, p. 41.

25 Stan Savige to Theo Walker, Bardia, 8 January 1941, Unit War Diary of 2/7 Infantry Battalion, p. 108.

26 Unit War Diary of 2/7 Infantry Battalion, p. 70.

27 Bolger and Littlewood, *The Fiery Phoenix*, p. 52.

28 Peck, interview with Wood, IWM, reel 1.

CHAPTER 2: ANZACS IN GREECE

1 John Coates, 'Greece', in Peter Dennis et al. (eds), *The Oxford Companion to Australian Military History*, 2nd edn, Oxford University Press, Melbourne, 2008, p. 241. For more detailed discussions of the Australian participation in the campaign in Greece see especially Peter Ewer, *Forgotten Anzacs: The Campaign in Crete*, Scribe, Melbourne, 2008; Maria Hill, *Diggers and Greeks: The Australian Campaigns in Greece and Crete*, UNSW Press, Sydney, 2010; and Gavin Long, *Greece, Crete and Syria: Australia in the War of 1939–1945. Series 1 – Army. II*, Australian War Memorial, Canberra, 1953.

2 On 12 April Blamey renamed his corps the Anzac Corps.

3 Cited in Detlef Vogel, 'German Intervention in the Balkans', in Research Institute for Military History (ed.), *Germany and the Second World War, Vol. III, The Mediterranean, South-east Europe, and North Africa 1939–1941*, transl. Dean S McMurry, Ewald Osers and Louise Wilmot, Clarendon Press, Oxford, 1995, p. 501.

4 'Report of Activities of 2/7 Australian Infantry Battalion 1 April to 4 June 1941', AWM52, 8/2/17, 17 Infantry Brigade Reports Greece and Crete.

5 'Report of Activities of 2/7 Australian Infantry Battalion'.

6 John Desmond Peck, interview with Conrad Wood, 30 May 1996, Imperial War Museum (IWM), 16667, reel 2.

7 Cited in Harry Gordon, *The Embarrassing Australian: The Story of an Aboriginal Warrior*, Lansdowne Press, Melbourne, 1962, p. 63.

8 SG Savige, 'Report on Campaign in Greece and Crete', War Diary of 17th Brigade, AWM52, 8/2/17.

9 WP Bolger and JG Littlewood, *The Fiery Phoenix: The Story of the 2/7 Australian Infantry Battalion 1939–1946*, 2/7 Battalion Association, Melbourne, 1983, p. 79.

10 Savige, 'Report on Campaign in Greece and Crete'.

11 Bolger and Littlewood, *The Fiery Phoenix*, p. 80.

12   Bolger and Littlewood, *The Fiery Phoenix*, p. 79.

13   Peck, interview with Wood, IWM, reel 2.

CHAPTER 3: THE BATTLE FOR CRETE

1   Churchill, cited in John Laffin, *Anzacs at War: The Story of Australian and New Zealand Battles*, Abelard-Schuman, London, 1965, p. 118.

2   Maria Hill, *Diggers and Greeks: The Australian Campaigns in Greece and Crete*, UNSW Press, Sydney, 2010, p. 201.

3   Stella Tzobanakis, *Creforce: The Anzacs and the Battle of Crete*, Black Dog, Melbourne, 2010, p. 15.

4   Albert Palazzo, *Battle of Crete*, Army History Unit, Canberra, 2007, p. 32.

5   Cited in Palazzo, *Battle of Crete*, p. 34.

6   Palazzo, *Battle of Crete*, p. 34.

7   Palazzo, *Battle of Crete*, pp. 53–54.

8   Palazzo, *Battle of Crete*, p. 60.

9   Palazzo, *Battle of Crete*, p. 125.

10   Peter Ewer, *Forgotten Anzacs: The Campaign in Crete*, Scribe, Melbourne, 2008, p. 281.

11   Peter Monteath, *POW: Australian Prisoners of War in Hitler's Reich*, PanMacmillan, Sydney, 2011, p. 76.

12   Ewer, *Forgotten Anzacs*, p. 295.

13   Callum MacDonald, *The Lost Battle: Crete, 1941*, The Free Press, New York, 1993, p. 170.

14   Monteath, *POW*, p. 80.

15   Ewer, *Forgotten Anzacs*, p. 311.

16   Ewer, *Forgotten Anzacs*, p. 315.

17   For an incisive analysis of the deficiencies in the planning of the defence of Maleme in particular and Crete generally, see especially Palazzo, *Battle of Crete*.

18   Eric Davies, interview with Peter Ewer, 31 August 2006, in Ewer, *Forgotten Anzacs*, p. 299.

19   Jim Henderson, *22 Battalion*, Official History of New Zealand in the Second World War, War History Branch, Department of Internal Affairs, Wellington, 1958, p. 48.

20   John Desmond Peck, interview with Conrad Wood, London, 30 May 1996, Imperial War Museum (IWM), 16667, reel 2.

21   Ewer, *Forgotten Anzacs*, p. 316.

22   Ewer, *Forgotten Anzacs*, p. 318.

23   Ewer, *Forgotten Anzacs*, p. 319.

24   Palazzo, *Battle of Crete*, p. 160.

25   Ewer, *Forgotten Anzacs*, pp. 320–21.

26   Ewer, *Forgotten Anzacs*, p. 321.

27   Ewer, *Forgotten Anzacs*, p. 324.

28   Peck, interview with Wood, IWM, reel 2.

29   Michael Sweet and Ian Frazer, 'Introduction', in James De Mole Carstairs, *Escape from Crete: War Diary 1941*, Michael Sweet and Ian Frazer (eds), Society of Cretan Historical Studies, Heraklion, 2016, p. 18.

30 The New Zealand Division in Greece, Report of Major General B Freyberg, Commanding 2 NZEF, 28 August 1941, ANZ EA 1 18/19/3 1, cited in Ewer, *Forgotten Anzacs*, p. 326.

31 Ewer, *Forgotten Anzacs*, p. 328.

32 Peter Thompson, *Anzac Fury: The Bloody Battle of Crete 1941*, Heinemann, Sydney, 2010, p. 351.

33 Ewer, *Forgotten Anzacs*, p. 307.

34 Graham Power, 'The Anzacs at 42nd Street', www.grahampower.nz/media/battle-at-42nd-street--graham-power.pdf, last accessed 27 March 2017.

35 Unit War Diary of 2/7 Infantry Battalion, April–July 1941, p, 157, AWM52, 8/3/7.

36 Thompson, *Anzac Fury*, p. 355.

37 Ewer, *Forgotten Anzacs*, p. 330.

38 JF Cody, *28 (Maori) Battalion*, War History Branch, Wellington, 1953, p. 120, cited in Ewer, *Forgotten Anzacs*, p. 330.

39 Ewer, *Forgotten Anzacs*, p. 331.

40 JF Cody, *21 Battalion*, Historical Publications Branch, Wellington, 1953, cited in Power, 'The Anzacs at 42nd Street', p. 51.

41 Saunders, cited in Bolger and Littlewood, *The Fiery Phoenix*, pp. 331–32.

42 Peck, interview with Wood, IWM, reel 3.

43 Peck, interview with Wood, IWM, reel 3.

44 Peck, interview with Wood, IWM, reel 3.

45 Power, 'The Anzacs at 42nd Street', p. 55; see also Antony Beevor, *Crete: The Battle and the Resistance*, John Murray, London, 1991, p. 200

46 Gavin Long, *The Six Years War: A Concise History of Australia in the 1939–45 War*, Australian War Memorial, Canberra, 1973, p. 252.

47 Cited in Harry Gordon, *The Embarrassing Australian: The Story of an Aboriginal Warrior*, Lansdowne Press, Melbourne, 1962, p. 80.

CHAPTER 4: STRANDED AT SFAKIA

1 James De Mole Carstairs, *Escape from Crete: War Diary*, Michael Sweet and Ian Frazer (eds), Society of Cretan Historical Studies, Heraklion, 2016, p. 57.

2 John Desmond Peck, interview with Conrad Wood, 30 May 1996, Imperial War Museum (IWM), 16667, reel 3.

3 Harry Gordon, *The Embarrassing Australian: The Story of an Aboriginal Warrior*, Lansdowne Press, Melbourne, 1962, p. 85.

4 Gordon, *The Embarrassing Australian*, p. 84

5 John Peck, 'Captive in Crete', unpublished manuscript, p. 3, Peck, John Desmond 'Des' (Lieutenant), DCM, 1919–2002, personal papers, AWM, PR03098, 2/2.

6 Peck, 'Captive in Crete', p. 3.

7 Peck, 'Captive in Crete', p. 7.

8 Michael O'Brien, 'Walker, Theodore Gordon (1900–1971)', Australian Dictionary of Biography, National Centre of Biography, Australian National University, <http://adb.anu.edu.au/biography/walker-theodore-gordon-11938/text21393>, published in hardcopy 2002, last accessed 18 May 2014.

9 Graham Power, 'The Anzacs at 42nd Street', www.grahampower.nz/media/

battle-at-42nd-street--graham-power.pdf, p. 60, last accessed 27 March 2017.

10   As recounted in Gordon, *The Embarrassing Australian*, p. 87.

11   Gordon, *The Embarrassing Australian*, p. 88.

12   Leslie Le Souef, *To War without a Gun*, Artlook, Perth, 1980, p. 146.

13   Figures according to Sean Damer and Ian Frazer, *On the Run: Anzac Escape and Evasion in Enemy-Occupied Crete*, Penguin (NZ), Northshore, 2007, p. 33. Also Dan Davin, 'Crete', in New Zealand Dept of Internal Affairs, War History Branch, *Official History of New Zealand in the Second World War, 1939–1945*, Government Printer, Wellington, 1953, p. 455. The official German history gives the number of captives at 9000 Creforce soldiers and 1000 Greeks. Detlef Vogel, 'German Intervention in the Balkans', in Research Institute for Military History (ed.), *Germany and the Second World War, Vol. III, The Mediterranean, South-east Europe, and North Africa 1939–1941*, transl. Dean S McMurry, Ewald Osers and Louise Wilmot, Clarendon Press, Oxford, 1995, p. 551.

14   Damer and Frazer, *On the Run*, pp. 35–37.

15   Damer and Frazer, *On the Run*, pp. 39–40.

16   Frank Arnold Reiter went on to distinguished service in New Guinea, where he earned both an MC and a Military Medal: NAA, B883, VX4024, Reiter Frank Arnold.

17   George Burgess (NX9600) from Glen Innes in NSW was in the 2/3 Australian Infantry Battalion. Burgess seems to have struck off on his own from Lambini, 9 kilometres north-east of Preveli. Records show that he was officially registered as a prisoner of war in Crete from February 1942 but then escaped and managed to get to Egypt by June of that year: NAA, B883, NX9600, Burgess George. Les Vincent (NX13043), a member of 2/1 Battalion, hailed from Ingleburn and would have been involved in the defence of Retimo. He was reported as returned to the Middle East on 28 May 1942: NAA, B883, NX13043, Vincent Leslie Charles.

18   Gordon, *The Embarrassing Australian*, pp. 92–93.

19   Gavin Long writes that there were thousands of British troops on Crete, of whom perhaps 600 made their way to Egypt by various vessels: Gavin Long, *The Six Years War: A Concise History of Australia in the 1939–45 War*, Australian War Memorial, Canberra, 1973, p. 307. Foot and Langley suggest a figure of 'nearly a thousand' evaders: MRD Foot and JM Langley, *MI9: The British Secret Service that Fostered Escape and Evasion 1939–1945 and Its American Counterpart*, Bodley Head, London, 1979, p. 91.

20   Damer and Frazer, *On the Run*, pp. 41–42; Anthony Beevor, *Crete: The Battle and the Resistance*, John Murray, London, 1991, pp. 211–12; BH Avery, 'A War History', <https://anzac.dpc.wa.gov.au/Resources/Stories/avery_bh_20050422. pdf>.

21   Peter Thompson, *Anzac Fury: The Bloody Battle of Crete 1941*, Heinemann, Sydney, 2010, p. 385.

22   Peck, 'Captive in Crete', p. 9.

23   Peck, 'Captive in Crete', p. 9.

24   Henry Thomas Blake (VX15836) was born in Mywee in Victoria (NAA, B883, VX15836, Blake Henry Thomas); David Pettigrew (VX4663) was born in Wales

and enlisted in Mildura. For a year there was no word on Pettigrew until it was reported that he was 'free and well in enemy occupied territory in April and May' (of 1942). In May of 1943 he was reported as having arrived in Egypt: NAA, B883, VX4663, Pettigrew David.

25   Apart from the aforementioned Blake and Pettigrew, Peck names Bill Ledgerwood, Jack O'Brien and someone by the name of Alan. William Ledgerwood (VX4648) was born in Agra in India in 1906.: NAA, B883, VX4648 Ledgerwood William. John O'Brien (VX17803) was destined to become a prisoner of war: NAA, B883, VX17803 O'Brien John.

26   NAA, B883, VX4648 Ledgerwood William.

27   Bill Bunbury, *Rabbits and Spaghetti: Captives and Comrades, Australians, Italians and the War*, Fremantle Arts Centre Press, Fremantle, 1995, p. 101.

28   WP Bolger and JG Littlewood, *The Fiery Phoenix: The Story of the 2/7 Australian Infantry Battalion 1939–1946*, 2/7 Battalion Association, Parkdale, n.d., pp. 114–17. Thomson's account of their voyage across the Libyan Sea is included in 17 Brigade's Unit Diary, AWM52, 8/2/17, 17 Infantry Brigade Reports Greece and Crete.

29   Peck, 'Captive in Crete', p. 12.

30   Peck, 'Captive in Crete', p. 14.

31   Peck, 'Captive in Crete', p. 16.

32   Peck, 'Captive in Crete', pp. 15–16.

33   Peck, 'Captive in Crete', p. 16.

34   Peck, 'Captive in Crete', p. 17.

35   Peck, 'Captive in Crete', p. 18.

CHAPTER 5: CAPTIVE IN CRETE

1   'Australian prisoners of war: Second World War – prisoners in Europe', Encyclopedia of the Australian War Memorial, < https://www.awm.gov.au/ encyclopedia/pow/ww2/>, last accessed 27 March 2017.

2   John Peck, 'Captive in Crete', unpublished manuscript, p. 20, Peck, John Desmond 'Des' (Lieutenant), DCM, 1919–2002, personal papers, AWM PR03098, 2/2.

3   Peck, 'Captive in Crete', pp. 22, 25.

4   John Desmond Peck to his parents, 12 August 1941, Peck, John Desmond 'Des' (Lieutenant), DCM, 1919–2002, personal papers, AWM, PR03098, 1/1.

5   Peck, 'Captive in Crete', p. 22.

6   Peck, 'Captive in Crete', p. 23.

7   Peck, 'Captive in Crete', p. 24.

8   Peck, 'Captive in Crete', pp. 24–25.

9   Peck, 'Captive in Crete', p. 25.

10   Peck, 'Captive in Crete', p. 26.

11   Peck, 'Captive in Crete', p. 27.

12   World War II Nominal Roll, < http://www.ww2roll.gov.au/Veteran. aspx?ServiceId=A&VeteranId=420871>.

13   Charles Jager, *Escape from Crete*, Floradale, Sydney, 2004, p. 206.

14   Jager, *Escape from Crete*, p. 203.

15 Peck, 'Captive in Crete', p. 27.
16 Peck 'Captive in Crete', p. 28.
17 Peck 'Captive in Crete', p. 29.
18 Peck 'Captive in Crete', p. 29.
19 Stephen Warner was born in Tasmania and served in the 2/7 Battalion until his death at the age of 33: NAA, B883, VX16773, Warner Stephen George. Harvey Arnold Newnham was born in Camberwell in Melbourne in 1919; he was killed in action on 24 May 1941: NAA, B883, VX5474 Newnham Harvey Arnold.
20 Peck, 'Captive in Crete', p. 30.
21 Peck, 'Captive in Crete', p. 31.
22 Peck, 'Captive in Crete', p. 32.
23 Peck, 'Captive in Crete', p. 33.
24 Peck, 'Captive in Crete', p. 33.

CHAPTER 6: ON THE RUN

1   AC Simonds, 'MI9 "Tailpieces"', TNA, WO 208/3253, Summary of MI9 Activities in the Eastern Mediterranean 1941–1945.
2   The figure of about 1000 is used by GG Kiriakopoulos, *The Nazi Occupation of Crete 1941–1945*, Praeger, Westport CT, 1985, p. 359, and Nikos Kokonas suggests more than a thousand: see NA Kokonas (ed.), *The Cretan Resistance 1941–1945: The Official British Report of 1945 Together with Comments by British Officers Who Took Part in the Resistance*, NA Kokonas, Retimo, 1991, p. 27. Australia's official war historian Gavin Long suggests that the Anzacs alone numbered about 1000, which he breaks down into 600 Australians and 400 New Zealanders: see Gavin Long, *Greece, Crete and Syria*, Australian War Memorial, Canberra, 1953, p. 312. See also Sean Damer and Ian Frazer, *On the Run: Anzac Escape and Evasion in Enemy-Occupied Crete*, Penguin (NZ), Northshore, 2007, p. 73.
3   MRD Foot and JM Langley, *MI9: The British Secret Service that Fostered Escape and Evasion 1939–1945 and Its American Counterpart*, Bodley Head, London, 1979, pp. 34–35.
4   Kokonas, *The Cretan Resistance*, p. 32.
5   TNA, WO 208/3253, cited in Damer and Frazer, *On the Run*, p. 70.
6   Thaddeus Holt, *The Deceivers: Allied Military Deception in the Second World War*, Scribner, London, 2004, pp. 26–30.
7   Nicholas Rankin, *Churchill's Wizards: The British Genius for Deception, 1914–1945*, Faber & Faber, London, 2008, p. 178.
8   Foot and Langley, *MI9*, p. 88.
9   Damer and Frazier, *On the Run*, p. 71.
10 Anthony Beevor, *Crete: The Battle and the Resistance*, John Murray, London, 1991, p. 241. After the war Pool became British consul in Canea; he died in Athens in 1946: see Xan Fielding, *Hide and Seek: The Story of a War-time Agent*, Secker & Warburg, London, 1954, p. 25.
11 TNA, ADM 236/30 Thrasher.
12 Kokonas, *The Cretan Resistance*, p. 32.
13 Recommendation for Decoration or Mention in Despatches for Frances Grant

Pool, TNA, ADM 1/11477, Withdrawal from Crete – Temporary Lieutenant Commander FG Pool.

14 Beevor, *Crete*, p. 242.

15 John Peck, 'Captive in Crete', unpublished manuscript, p. 36, Peck, John Desmond 'Des' (Lieutenant), DCM, 1919–2002, personal papers, PR03098, 2/2.

16 Peck, 'Captive in Crete', p. 37.

17 Peck, 'Captive in Crete', p. 38.

18 Peck, 'Captive in Crete', pp. 39-40.

19 Peck, 'Captive in Crete', p. 42.

20 Peck, 'Captive in Crete', p. 43.

21 Peck, 'Captive in Crete', p. 44.

22 Peck, 'Captive in Crete', p. 44.

23 Peck, 'Captive in Crete', p. 45.

24 Peck, 'Captive in Crete', p. 45.

25 Peck, 'Captive in Crete', p. 46.

26 Peck, 'Captive in Crete', p. 47.

27 Peck, 'Captive in Crete', p. 47.

28 Peck. 'Captive in Crete', p. 48.

29 Peck, 'Captive in Crete', p. 48.

30 Beevor, *Crete*, p. 241.

31 Geoffrey Edwards, *The Road to Prevelly*, Geoffrey Edwards, Perth, 1989, pp. 48–49.

32 Beevor, *Crete*, p. 242

33 Damer and Fraser, *On the Run*, pp. 254–55.

34 Beevor, *Crete*, p 242.

35 Damer and Fraser, *On the Run*, p. 104.

36 Fielding, *Hide and Seek*, p. 43.

37 Damer and Fraser, *On the Run*, p. 75.

38 Peck, 'Captive in Crete', p. 49.

39 Peck, 'Captive in Crete', p. 49.

CHAPTER 7: SPECIAL OPERATIONS

1 Sean Damer and Ian Frazer, *On the Run: Anzac Escape and Evasion in Enemy-Occupied Crete*, Penguin (NZ), Northshore, 2007, pp. 107–108, 257.

2 NA Kokonas, *The Cretan Resistance 1941–1945: The Official British Report of 1945 Together with Comments by British Officers Who Took Part in the Resistance*, NA Kokonas, Rethymnon, 1991, p. 157; Michael Sweet, 'Jim Carstairs' Cretan Odyssey', *Neos Kosmos*, 8 April 2016, <http://neoskosmos.com/news/en/Jim-Carstairs-Cretan-odyssey>, last accessed 28 March 2017.

3 Damer and Frazer, *On the Run*, pp. 125–26, 257–59.

4 Damer and Frazer, *On the Run*, pp. 125–26.

5 Damer and Frazer, *On the Run*, p. 133.

6 Xan Fielding, cited in Damer and Frazer, *On the Run*, p. 172.

7 Damer and Frazer, *On the Run*, pp. 196–98.

8 Cited in Nigel Morris, 'The Special Operations Executive 1940–1946', <www.bbc.co.uk/history/worldwars/wwtwo/soe_01.shtml>, last accessed 1 June 2014.

9   Anthony Beevor, *Crete: The Battle and the Resistance*, John Murray, London, 1991, pp. 141–42; Kokonas, *The Cretan Resistance*, p. 31

10   Patrick Leigh Fermor, 'The Magnetic John Pendlebury', <https://patrickleighfermor.org/2011/08/13/the-magnetic-john-pendlebury/>, last accessed 28 March 2017.

11   Kokonas, *The Cretan Resistance*, p. 153.

12   Nigel West, *Secret War: The Story of SOE, Britain's Wartime Sabotage Organisation*, Hodder & Stoughton, London, 1992, p. 159.

13   Fraser and Damer, *On the Run*, p. 124; Kokonas, *The Cretan Resistance*, pp. 14, 33.

14   West, *Secret War*, p. 159

15   Beevor, *Crete*, p. 244.

16   'Summary of MI9 Activities in the Eastern Mediterranean 1941–1945', TNA, WO 208/3253.

17   NAA, AWM63, 175/500/45, Escaped Prisoner of War VX12521 Private WM Bazely [sic], 2/5 Australian Infantry Battalion and NX3461 Gunner J Brewer, 2/1 Australian Field Regiment – employed on intelligence duties, Advanced HQ 'A' Force, Cairo. See also AWM76, B37, Official Historian 1939–1945 War, biographical files – Baylos FW, Bayliss HE, Bayne AM, Bazely AW, Beadman WS, Beale LE, Beale R, and AWM63, 122/500/15 VX12521 Pte (Private) WM Bazeley – 2/5 Aust Inf Bn (Australian Infantry Battalion) – Attachment for special duty.

18   'Summary of MI9 Activities in the Eastern Mediterranean 1941–1945', TNA, WO 208/3253.

19   World War II Nominal Roll, <www.ww2roll.gov.au/Veteran.aspx?ServiceId=A&VeteranId=737648>, last accessed 28 March 2017.

20   NAA, B883, WX976 Greenaway George James.

21   George Psychoundakis, *The Cretan Runner: His Story of the German Occupation*, transl. Patrick Leigh Fermor, John Murray, London, 1978.

22   Kokonas, *The Cretan Resistance*, p. 36.

23   John Peck, 'Captive in Crete', unpublished manuscript, p. 50, Peck, John Desmond, 'Des' (Lieutenant), DCM, 1919–2001, personal papers, AWM, PR03098, 2/2.

24   Peck, 'Captive in Crete', p. 50.

25   Peck, 'Captive in Crete', p. 51.

26   Peck, 'Captive in Crete', p. 52.

27   Peck, 'Captive in Crete', p. 53.

28   Peck, 'Captive in Crete', p. 53.

29   Xan Fielding, *Hide and Seek: The Story of a War-time Agent*, Secker & Warburg, London, 1954, p. 194.

30   Peck, 'Captive in Crete', p. 54.

31   Peck, 'Captive in Crete', p. 55.

32   Peck, 'Captive in Crete', p. 57.

33   Peck, 'Captive in Crete', p. 58

34   Peck, 'Captive in Crete', p. 60.

35   Peck, 'Captive in Crete', p. 60.

36   Peck, 'Captive in Crete', pp. 60–61.

37 Psychoundakis, *The Cretan Runner*, p. 61.

38 Peck, 'Captive in Crete', p. 61.

39 Peck, 'Captive in Crete', p. 62.

40 Peck. 'Captive in Crete', pp. 62–63.

41 Peck in an interview suggested that the SOE officer who arranged for him to be taken to the vicinity of Timbaki for extraction by submarine was Patrick Leigh Fermor: John Desmond Peck, interview with Conrad Wood, London, 30 May 1996, Imperial War Museum, 16667, reel 5.

42 Peck, 'Captive in Crete', p. 63.

43 Psychoundakis, *The Cretan Runner*, p. 66.

44 Psychoundakis, *The Cretan Runner*, p. 67.

45 Peck, 'Captive in Crete', pp. 64–65.

46 Fermor's footnote in Psychoundakis, *The Cretan Runner*, p. 67.

47 Peck, 'Captive in Crete', p. 65.

48 Report by JD Peck (Australian Army) who arrived UK 4 November 1944, 14 November 1944, TNA,WO 208/4265, War Office: Directorate of Military Operations and Intelligence; Ministry of Defence, Defence Intelligence Staff: Files. Prisoner of War Reports.

CHAPTER 8: FAREWELL TO CRETE

1 John Desmond Peck, 'Captive in Crete', unpublished manuscript, p. 66, Peck, John Desmond 'Des' (Lieutenant), DCM, 1919–2002, personal papers, AWM, PR03098, 2/2.

2 Obituary for Arnold Gourevitch, <www.telegraph.co.uk/news/ obituaries/1458522/Arnold-Gourevitch.html>, last accessed 7 July 2014.

3 EJ Maguire, obituary for Kiernan Dorney, <www.surgeons.org/member-services/ in-memoriam/kiernan-dorney/>, last accessed 7 July 2014.

4 Both did eventually get off the island. Dorney went on to fight at El Alamein and then in the Pacific War, where he earned a DSO. Gourevitch also took part in the Battle of El Alamein. After that he participated in the invasion of Italy and earned an MC: see obituaries above.

5 Peck, 'Captive in Crete', pp. 66–67.

6 Peck, 'Captive in Crete', p. 67.

7 Peck, 'Captive in Crete', p. 67.

8 Peck, 'Captive in Crete', p. 68.

9 Peck, 'Captive in Crete', p. 68

10 Peck, 'Captive in Crete', p. 68.

11 Peck, 'Captive in Crete', p. 68.

12 Peck, 'Captive in Crete', p 68. Monty Woodhouse was responsible for the central area from November 1941 to the middle of April 1942. NA Kokonas (ed.), *The Cretan Resistance 1941–1945: The Official British Report of 1945 Together with Comments by British Officers Who Took Part in the Resistance*, NA Kokonas, Retimo, n.d., p. 147.

13 Sean Damer and Ian Frazer, *On the Run: Anzac Escape and Evasion in Enemy-Occupied Crete*, Penguin (NZ), Northshore, 2007, p. 259.

14 Harry Gordon, *The Embarrassing Australian: The Story of an Aboriginal Warrior,*

Lansdowne Press, Melbourne, 1962, pp. 98–99.

15 Peck, 'Captive in Crete', p. 68.
16 Peck, 'Captive in Crete', p. 69.
17 Peck, 'Captive in Crete', p. 69.
18 Peck, 'Captive in Crete', p. 69.
19 Peck, 'Captive in Crete', p. 69; Peter Thompson, *Anzac Fury: The Bloody Battle of Crete 1941*, Heinemann, Sydney, 2010, p. 422.
20 Thompson, *Anzac Fury*, p. 42; Peck, 'Captive in Crete', p. 70.
21 Peck, 'Captive in Crete', p. 70.
22 Peck, 'Captive in Crete', p. 71. For details of the colourful war of Roy Natusch, a POW who, like Johnny Peck, became an agent in German-occupied Europe, see his obituary by Paul London and Gerry Carman, 'Double Dutchman's nine lives: Roy Natusch, 1918–2009', <http://www.smh.com.au/comment/obituaries/double-dutchmans-nine-lives-20090503-arfg.html>, last accessed 28 March 2017.
23 Peck, 'Captive in Crete', p. 71. Peck suggested that the Czechs were Jewish in an interview: see John Desmond Peck, interview with Heidi Egger, 8 July 2000, Manchester, Peck family collection.
24 Peck, 'Captive in Crete', p. 71.

CHAPTER 9: TO ITALY

1 POW Report by Private John Desmond Peck, VX9534, Wil (Switzerland), 12 July 1944, TNA, WO 208/4273, War Office: Directorate of Military Operations and Intelligence, and Directorate of Military Intelligence; Ministry of Defence, Defence Intelligence Staff: Files. Prisoners of War Reports: Escapes via Switzerland.
2 John Desmond Peck, interview with Heidi Egger, Manchester, 10–11 February 2001, Peck family collection.
3 Bill Bunbury, *Rabbits and Spaghetti: Captives and Comrades, Australians, Italians and the War*, Fremantle Arts Centre Press, Fremantle, 1995, p. 103.
4 POW Report by Private John Desmond Peck, VX9534, Wil (Switzerland), 12 July 1944.
5 Bunbury, *Rabbits and Spaghetti*, p. 103.
6 Peter Stanley, 'Remembering 1942: Ruin Ridge 26–27 July 1942', transcript of a talk given 28 July 2002, <www.awm.gov.au/education/talks/1942-ruin-ridge/>, last accessed 28 March 2017.
7 'Attack on the Nino Bixio, 17 August 1942', <http://www.nzhistory.net.nz/page/attack-nino-bixio>, last accessed 28 March 2017.
8 'Australians on board "Nino Bixio"', <www.aifpow.com/__data/assets/pdf_file/0011/2405/Nino_Bixio_163_Aus_-_41_killed_122_survived2.pdf>, last accessed 30 March 2017.
9 POW Report by Private John Desmond Peck, VX9534, Wil (Switzerland), 12 July 1944.
10 John Peck, manuscript notes, Peck, John Desmond 'Des' (Lieutenant), DCM, 1919–2002, personal papers, AWM, PR03098, 3/1.
11 Report No. 5 On Inspection of Prisoners of War Camp No. 57, 20 July 1942,

TNA, WO 361/1893, 'Prisoners of war, Italy: Camp 57, Gruppignano; International Red Cross reports on conditions'. The exact figures were: 1609 prisoners, of them 976 Australians, including 904 ORs, 70 NCOs and 2 officers. The next biggest group were New Zealanders (444) followed by Cypriots (105) and Indians (36).

12   AE Field, 'Prisoners of the Germans and the Italians', in Barton Maughan, *Tobruk and El Alamein*, Australian War Memorial, Canberra, 1966, p. 760.

13   ICRC report on Gruppignano Camp, 9 December 1941, NAA (Melbourne), MP1049/5, 1951/2/36, Prisoners of war camp – British prisoners in Italy.

14   Roger Absalom, '"Another Crack at Jerry"? Australian prisoners of war in Italy 1941–1945', *Journal of the Australian War Memorial*, 14 (1989), p. 24.

15   See for example, Roger Absalom, '"Another crack at Jerry"?', p. 24; also Department of the Army, Minute Paper, July 43. Subject: Interrogation of PWs and Escapees from Enemy Occupied Territory, NAA, MP385/7, 53/101/72, Treatment of Prisoners of War.

16   WX1982. Symons served in the 2/32 Infantry Battalion.

17   After the war Soddini was put on trial and sentenced to death, but after interventions by the Italian Prime Minister De Gasperi and the Vatican, the sentence was commuted to life imprisonment: see Richard Lamb, *War in Italy 1943–1945: A Brutal Story*, Penguin, London, 1995, p. 173

18   Peck, interview with Egger.

19   Peck to his parents, letter from PG 57, undated, Peck, John Desmond 'Des' (Lieutenant), DCM, 1919–2001, personal papers, AWM, PR03098, 1/1.

20   Massimiliano Tenconi, 'Prigionia, sopravvivenza e Resistenza. Storie di australiani e neozelandesi in provincia di Vercelli (1943–1945)', *L'impegno*, 28, 1 (June 2008), p. 27.

21   Luigi Moranino, foreword to testimony of Sergio Rigalo in *L'impegno*, 9, 1 (April 1989), cited in Malcolm Webster, *An Italian Experience*, Malcolm Webster, Melbourne, 1995, p. 153.

22   Peck to his parents, May 1942, Peck, John Desmond 'Des' (Lieutenant), DCM, 1919–2001, personal papers, AWM, PR03098, 1/1.

23   Luigi Moranino, 'Il campo di prigionia PG106', *L'impegno*, 9, 1 (April 1989).

24   Giorgio Nascimbene, *Prigionieri di guerra: L'anabasi dei prigionieri alleati che nel 1943 fecero parte dei campi di lavoro nelle risaie vercellesi e dintorni*, Società Operaia di Mutuo Soccorso Villata 1884, Vercelli, 2004, p. 53.

25   Nascimbene, *Prigionieri di guerra*, p. 31.

26   John Desmond Peck, 'POW Report', PW/EX/SWITZ/1013, AWM, PR03098, 1/2.

27   Tenconi, 'Prigionia, sopravvivenza e Resistenza', pp. 27–49, 32.

28   Peck, interview with Egger.

29   Report by JD Peck (Australian Army) who arrived UK 4 November 1944, 14 November 1944, TNA, WO 208/4265, War Office: Directorate of Military Operations and Intelligence; Ministry of Defence, Defence Intelligence Staff: Files. Prisoner of War Reports.

30   John Desmond Peck, interview with Conrad Wood, London, 30 May 1996, Imperial War Museum, 16667, reel 5.

31 Peck to his parents, Vercelli, 7 May 1943, Peck, John Desmond 'Des' (Lieutenant), DCM, 1919–2001, personal papers, AWM, PRO3098, 1/1.

32 Roger Absalom and John Peck, Questions and answers re Peck's experiences in Italy, AWM, PR03098, 9/1.

33 Peck to his mother, 18 July 1943, Peck, John Desmond 'Des' (Lieutenant), DCM, 1919–2001, personal papers, AWM, PRO3098, 1/1.

34 Nascimbene, *Prigionieri di guerra,* p. 53.

35 POW Report, Private John Desmond Peck, VX9534, Wil (Switzerland), 12 July 1944. In his POW report Peck records being in two prisons in late August and early September. From 20 August he was confined to a place he calls 'Sali'; from 3 September he was in the Vercelli civilian prison. The name of the civilian prison is given in Nascimbene, *Prigionieri di guerra*, p. 31.

CHAPTER 10: ARMISTICE

1 Gerhard Schreiber, 'Das Ende des nordafrikanischen Feldzugs', in Karl-Heinz Frieser (ed.), *Das Deutsche Reich und der Zweite Weltkrieg. Bd. 8. Die Ostfront 1943/44. Der Krieg im Osten und an den Nebenfronten*, Deutsche Verlagsanstalt, Munich, 2007, p. 1115.

2 Richard Lamb, *War in Italy 1943–1945: A Brutal Story*, Penguin, London, 1995, p. 14.

3 Nadja Bennewitz and Heike Herzog, 'La Resistenza – der Widerstand in Italien 1943–45', in Wolfgang Most (ed.), *La Resistenza: Beiträge zu Faschismus, Deutscher Besatzung und zum Widerstand in Italien*, Schriftenreihe des Vereins zur Förderung alternativer Medien e.V., Erlangen, 2006, p. 5.

4 Lamb, *War in Italy*, p. 19; David Stafford, *Mission Accomplished: SOE and Italy 1943–1945*, Vintage, London, 2012, p. 8.

5 Lamb, *War in Italy*, p. 22.

6 Lamb, *War in Italy*, p. 176.

7 Lamb, *War in Italy*, p. 177.

8 Gustavo Corni, 'Italy', in Bob Moore (ed.), *Resistance in Western Europe*, Berg, Oxford, 2000, pp. 157–87, p. 158.

9 Federico Chabod, *A History of Italian Fascism*, Cedric Chivers, Bath, 1974, p. 102.

10 Chabod, *A History of Italian Fascism*, p. 109.

11 Lamb, *War in Italy*, p. 23.

12 Lamb, *War in Italy*, pp. 23–24.

13 Cited in Malcolm Webster, *An Italian Experience*, Malcolm Webster, Wheelers Hill, Vic., 1995, p. 147.

14 Adrian Gilbert, *POW: Allied Prisoners in Europe, 1939–1945*, John Murray, London, 2006, p. 283.

15 Cited in Tom Carver, 'Second World War blunder that doomed 50,000 British PoWs', *Guardian*, 1 November 2009, <http://www.theguardian.com/world/2009/nov/01/second-world-war-british-pows>, last accessed 11 January 2016. There is a temptation to blame the mistake on Montgomery: see especially MRD Foot and JM Langley, *MI9: The British Secret Service that Fostered Escape and Evasion 1939–1945 and its American Counterpart*, Book Club Associates, London, 1979, p. 156

16   Tom Carver, *Where the Hell Have You Been?: Monty, Italy and One Man's Great Escape*, Short Books, London, 2010, p. 108.

17   Cited in Carver, 'Second World War blunder that doomed 50,000 British PoWs'.

18   Cited in Lamb, *War in Italy*, p. 163.

19   Cited in Lamb, *War in Italy*, p. 163.

20   Lamb, *War in Italy*, p. 161.

21   Recollections of Thom Williams and Jim Goddard, in Webster, *An Italian Experience*, pp. 114–15.

22   Brian Lett, *An Extraordinary Italian Imprisonment: The Brutal Truth of Campo 21*, Pen and Sword, Barnsley, 2014, p. 192.

23   One of them was the Australian airman Robert Sydney Jones. Shot down in North Africa in January 1942, he was languishing in Bologna at the time of the Armistice. With 11 others – all Australians except for two Englishmen – he managed to cut out a section in the side of the car and jump to freedom. With the help of well-disposed Italians, he climbed into Switzerland: see Account of Escape of F/Lt Robert Sydney Jones, RAAF, 3 Sqn DAF, RAF, TNA, WO 208/3323. Jones went on to leave Switzerland in September of the following year to work with American forces in occupied Italy.

24   Gilbert, *POW*, p. 288.

25   Gilbert, *POW*, p. 287.

26   Massimiliano Tenconi, 'Prigionia, sopravvivenza e Resistenza. Storie di australiani e neozelandesi in provincia di Vercelli (1943–1945)', *L'impegna*, 28, 1 (June 2008), pp. 27–49, 33.

27   Giorgio Nascimbene, *Prigionieri di guerra: L'anabasi dei prigionieri alleati che nel 1943 fecero parte dei campi di lavoro nelle risaie vercellesi e dintorni*, Società Operaia di Mutuo Soccorso Villata 1884, Vercelli, 2004, p. 31.

28   Nascimbene, *Prigionieri di guerra*, p. 32.

29   Nascimbine, *Prigionieri di guerra*, p. 32.

30   Nuto Ravelli, *Il mondo dei vinti Testimonianze di vita Contadina*, Einaudi, Turin, 1977, p. 117.

31   Roger Absalom, *A Strange Alliance: Aspects of Escape and Survival in Italy 1943–1945*, Leo Olschki, Florence, 1991, p. 20.

32   John Desmond Peck, interview with Heidi Egger, Manchester, 8 July 2000, Peck family collection.

33   The story is recounted in Webster, *An Italian Experience*, p. 185.

34   Lamb, *War in Italy*, p. 167.

35   AWM54, 781/6/6, 'Parker file', Appendix C. This report suggests that, in contrast, just 58 Australians who exited Italian POW camps successfully reached Allied lines.

36   'Historical record of I.S.9', <http://arcre.com/archive/mi9/is9 - III>, last accessed 29 March 2017.

37   Stafford, *Mission Accomplished*, p. 53.

38   Christopher M Woods, 'No. 1 Special Force', in Donatella Ghini and Patrick Leech (eds.), *No. 1 Special Force and Italian Resistance: Proceedings of the Conference Held at Bologna, 28–30 1987, Vol. II*, CLUEB, Bologna, 1990, p. 36.

39   Stafford, *Mission Accomplished*, p. 53.

40 Lamb, *War in Italy*, p. 167.

41 TNA, WO208/3416, MI9.

CHAPTER 11: THE ESCAPE ARTIST

1   John Desmond Peck and Roger Absalom, Questions and answers re Peck's experiences in Italy, John Desmond 'Des' (Lieutenant), DCM, 1919–2002, personal papers, AWM, PR03098, Peck 9/1.

2   NAA, B2458, 211001, Webb, Claude Earnest.

3   NAA, B2458, 211001, Webb, Claude Earnest.

4   This according to Edgar Triffet, in 'Interrogation of Sgt TRIFFET. Edgar, AIF, 26th November, 1944', TNA, WO 208/4273, War Office: Directorate of Military Operations and Intelligence, and Directorate of Military Intelligence; Ministry of Defence, Defence Intelligence Staff: Files. Prisoners of War Reports: Escapes via Switzerland.

5   Peck and Absalom, Questions and answers re Peck's experiences in Italy.

6   POW Report by Private John Desmond Peck, VX9534, Wil (Switzerland), 12 July 1944, TNA, WO 208/4273.

7   Massimiliano Tenconi, 'Prigionia, sopravvivenza e Resistenza. Storie di australiani e neozelandesi in provincia di Vercelli (1943–1945)', *L'impegno*, 28, 1, (June 2008), pp. 35–37.

8   List of documents provided by John Peck, 19 January 1987, compiled by Roger Absalom, AWM, PR03098, 9/1.

9   Giorgio Nascimbene, *Prigionieri di guerra: L'anabasi dei prigionieri alleati che nel 1943 fecero parte dei campi di lavoro nelle risaie vercellesi e dintorni*. Società Operaia di Mutuo Soccorso Villata 1884, Vercelli, 2004, pp 159–60.

10 Tenconi, 'Prigionia, sopravvivenza e Resistenza', pp. 35–37.

11 Note on the judicial enquiry and subsequent trial of Oreste Barbero et al., accused of aiding and abetting John Peck's activities, AWM PR03098, 9/1.

12 Tenconi, 'Prigionia, sopravvivenza e Resistenza', pp. 35–37.

13 Personal correspondence, Bill Rudd to Ken Fenton, in Ken Fenton, *Anzacs at the Frontiers 1941–45: Northern Italy*, vol. 1, Ken Fenton, Nelson, 2008, p. 182.

14 Roger Absalom, *A Strange Alliance: Aspects of Escape and Survival in Italy 1943–1945*, Leo Olschki, Florence, 1991, p. 51.

15 Parker's service record shows that he was captured and sent to Germany in January 1944: NAA, B883, VX33048, Parker James Henry.

16 AWM, PR03098, 4/1.

17 Ken O'Leary to Peck, undated, AWM, PR03098, 4/1.

18 POW Report by LM Jarvis, Wil (Switzerland), 13 July 1944, TNA, WO 208/4255, War Office: Directorate of Military Operations and Intelligence, and Directorate of Military Intelligence; Ministry of Defence, Defence Intelligence Staff: Files. Prisoners of War Reports: Escapes via Switzerland.

19 Absalom, *A Strange Alliance*, p. 51.

20 Personal correspondence, Rudd to Fenton, in Fenton, *Anzacs at the Frontiers*, p. 182.

21 Personal correspondence, Rudd to Fenton, in Fenton, *Anzacs at the Frontiers*, p. 182.

22   POW Report by Private John Desmond Peck, VX9534, Wil (Switzerland), 12 July 1944.

23   POW Report Private John Desmond Peck, VX9534, Wil (Switzerland) 12 July 1944.

24   Rudd to Fenton, in Fenton, *Anzacs at the Frontiers*, p. 182

25   POW Report Private John Desmond Peck, VX9534, Wil (Switzerland) 12 July 1944.

26   Absalom, *A Strange Alliance*, p. 39.

27   POW Report Private John Desmond Peck, VX9534, Wil (Switzerland), 12 July 1944. On the operations of the central committee in Milan, see especially 'Final Report on the Activity of the Committee of National Liberation of Northern Italy CLNAI, on behalf of Allied Prisoners of War', TNA WO 208/3479, Activity of Committee of National Liberation of Northern Italy (CLNAI) on Behalf of Allied POWs: Final Report.

28   Laurence Lewis, *Echoes of Resistance: British Involvement with the Italian Partisans*, Costello, Tunbridge Wells, 1985, p. 32.

29   John Desmond Peck, interview with Heidi Egger, Manchester, 11 February 2001, Peck family collection.

30   Peck, interview with Egger.

31   Richard Lamb, *War in Italy 1943–1945: A Brutal Story*, Penguin, London, 1995, p. 165.

32   Peck, interview with Egger.

33   Peck, interview with Egger.

34   Peck, interview with Egger.

35   Peck, interview with Egger.

36   Peck, interview with Egger.

37   Peck, interview with Egger.

38   Peck, interview with Egger.

39   Peck, interview with Egger.

40   Peck, interview with Egger.

41   Peck, interview with Egger.

42   Peck, interview with Egger.

43   Peck, interview with Egger.

44   Lewis, *Echoes of Resistance*, p. 32.

45   Absalom, *A Strange Alliance*, p. 43

46   Nascimbene, *Prigionieri di guerra*, p. 76.

47   Peck and Absalom, Questions and answers re Peck's experiences in Italy, AWM PR03098, 9/1.

48   Giorgio Nascimbene, *Prigionieri di guerra*, p. 76.

CHAPTER 12: PARTISANS

1   Roger Absalom, *A Strange Alliance: Aspects of Escape and Survival in Italy 1943–1945*, Leo Olschki, Florence, 1991, p. 309.

2   TNA, WO 208/3396, cited in Richard Lamb, *War in Italy 1943–1945: A Brutal Story*, Penguin, London, 1995, p. 170.

3   TNA, WO 204/7283, cited in Lamb, *War in Italy*, p. 207.

4   David Travis, 'Communism and resistance in Italy, 1943–8', in Tony Judt (ed.), *Resistance and Revolution in Mediterranean Europe 1939–1948*, Routledge, London, 1989, p. 90.

5   Travis, 'Communism and resistance in Italy, 1943–8', p. 90.

6   Laurence Lewis, *Echoes of Resistance: British Involvement with the Italian Partisans*, Costello, Tunbridge Wells, 1985, p. 24.

7   Carlo Gentile, *Wehrmacht und Waffen-SS im Partisanenkrieg: Italien 1943–1945*, Ferdinand Schöningh, Paderborn, 2012, pp. 52–53.

8   Gentile, *Wehrmacht und Waffen-SS im Partisanenkrieg*, p. 52.

9   Gustavo Corni, 'Italy', in Bob Moore (ed.), *Resistance in Western Europe*, Berg, Oxford, 2000, p. 164.

10 Gentile, *Wehrmacht und Waffen-SS im Partisanenkrieg*, p. 52.

11 Travis, 'Communism and resistance in Italy, 1943–8', p. 91.

12 Malcolm Webster, *An Italian Experience*, Malcolm Webster, Melbourne, 1995, p. 201.

13 Ken Fenton, *Alamein to the Alps: War in the Piedmont with Mission Cherokee and the Lost Anzacs 1943–1945*, Frontier Press, Nelson, 2011, p. 287.

14 For a full list of the names see the website established by Bill Rudd et al., Anzac POW Freemen in Europe, <www.aifpow.com/__data/assets/pdf_file/0015/22740/3853_Anzac_European_Freemen_10-4-14.pdf>, last accessed 3 April 2017.

15 Lynette Oates and Ian Sproule, *Australian Partisan: A True Story of Love and War*, Australian Military History Publications, Loftus, NSW, 1997, p. 32.

16 Interrogation of Sgt Triffet, Edgar, AIF, 26 November 1944, TNA, WO 208/4273, War Office: Directorate of Military Operations and Intelligence, and Directorate of Military Intelligence; Ministry of Defence, Defence Intelligence Staff: Files. Prisoners of War Reports: Escapes via Switzerland.

17 Roger Absalom, '"Another crack at Jerry?" Australian prisoners of war in Italy 1941–45', *Journal of the Australian War Memorial*, 17 (1989), p. 26.

18 Absalom, *A Strange Alliance*, p. 57.

19 Interrogation of Sgt Triffet, Edgar, AIF, 26 November 1944, TNA, WO 208/4273.

20 Webster, *An Italian Experience*, pp. 52–75.

21 Webster, *An Italian Experience*, pp. 52–75, 226–27, 239.

22 John Rowe and Keith Hooper, 'Partisan – the Story of WX5292 Cpl John Wilfred Rowe as Told to Keith Hooper', 1982, AWM, PR84/24.

23 Rowe recalls an Australian called 'Frank Bowan', but no such name exists among the lists of Australian POWs in Europe. It is possible the man in question was the New Zealander Frank Bowes.

24 Rowe and Hooper, 'Partisan'.

25 Rowe and Hooper, 'Partisan'. Among them were Bert Keats, Doug Henderson and Bill Smith.

26 Stan Peebles, letter to Bill Rudd, undated (1999), courtesy Bill Rudd.

27 Stanley Eric Peebles, Statutory Declaration, 14 December 1967, NAA, B883, VX31755, Peebles Stanley Eric.

28 Department of Veterans' Affairs, 'WX14427 Harold Davis 2/32 Battalion', <http://www.dva.gov.au/i-am/aboriginal-andor-torres-strait-islander/our-mob-

serving-country-100-years-and-beyond/wx14427>, last accessed 29 March 2017. On Davis in Italy see also Marco Soggetto, *Braccati Prigionieri di Guerra alleati in Piemonte e Valle D'Aosta*, Aviani & Aviani, Udine, 2013, pp. 172–73, 195–96, 198–202, 204–209, 244–45.

29   Service Record of Harold R Davis, NAA, B883, WX14427.

30   Jocumsen is mentioned by this name in Pietro Secchia and Cino Moscatelli, *Il Monte Rosa è Sceso a Milano: la Resistenza nel Biellese nella Valsesia e nella Valdossola*, Einaudi, Turin, 1958, p. 91.

31   Secchia and Moscatelli, *Il Monte Rosa è Sceso a Milano*, pp. 129, 135.

32   Edgardo Sogno, *Guerra senza Bandiera: Cronaca della Franchi nella Resistenza*, Mursia, Milan, 1970, p. 204.

33   DJ Nicholls, 'A British PoW Becomes a Partisan, 1943–1945', WW2 People's War, p. 7, <www.bbc.co.uk/history/ww2peopleswar/stories/41/a2001141.shtml>, last accessed 29 March 2017. For further information on Frank Jocumsen I am indebted to his sons Ross and Ian and to Katrina Kittel. For further information, see also Bill Rudd et al., *AIF in Switzerland: A Compendium*, n.p., n.d.; copy held in AWM library. See also Ken Fenton, *Anzacs at the Frontiers 1941–45: Northern Italy*, vol. 1, Ken Fenton, Nelson, 2008, pp. 305–314; Absalom, *A Strange Alliance*, pp. 61–62.

34   Susan Jacobs, *Fighting with the Enemy: New Zealand POWs and the Italian Resistance*, Penguin, Auckland, 2003, p. 117.

CHAPTER 13: GUEST OF THE GESTAPO

1   Report by JD Peck (Australian Army) who arrived UK 4 November 44, 14 November 1944, p. 3, TNA, WO 208/4265, War Office: Directorate of Military Operations and Intelligence; Ministry of Defence, Defence Intelligence Staff: Files. Prisoner of War Reports.

2   Report by JD Peck (Australian Army) who arrived UK 4 November 44, 14 November 1944, p. 3.

3   The division of labour in Italy between Wehrmacht and security forces was largely settled in April 1944, when Kesselring and Wolff between themselves devised a scheme which recognised Kesselring's overall authority in Italy and guaranteed the Wehrmacht's primacy in operational zones, but gave a key role to security forces elsewhere: Carlo Gentile, *Wehrmacht und Waffen-SS im Partisanenkrieg: Italien 1943–1945*, Ferdinand Schöningh, Paderborn, 2012, p. 78; see also Gerhard Schreiber, 'Das Ende des nordafrikanischen Feldzugs', in Karl-Heinz Frieser (ed.), *Das Deutsche Reich und der Zweite Weltkrieg. Bd. 8. Die Ostfront 1943/44. Der Krieg im Osten und an den Nebenfronten*, Deutsche Verlagsanstalt, Munich, 2007, p. 1135.

4   Federico Ciavattone, 'Counterinsurgency in the Italian Social Republic, 1943–1945', in Daniel Macías Fernández and Fernando Puell de la Villa (eds), *David contra Goliat: Guerra y Asimetría en la Edad contemporánea*, Instituto Universitario General Gutiérrez Mellado, Madrid, 2014, p. 254.

5   Ciavattone, 'Counterinsurgency in the Italian Social Republic', p. 253.

6   Gentile, *Wehrmacht und Waffen-SS im Partisanenkrieg*, p. 59.

7   Richard Bosworth, *Mussolini*, Edward Arnold, London, 2002, p. 524.

8   Cited in Charles F Delzell, *Mussolini's Enemies: The Italian Anti-Fascist Resistance*, Princeton University Press, Princeton, 1961, p. 403.

9   Federico Ciavattone, 'Counterinsurgency in the Italian Social Republic', p. 273.

10   David Stafford, *Mission Accomplished: SOE and Italy 1943–1945*, Vintage, London, 2012, p. 121; Delzell, *Mussolini's Enemies*, p. 376.

11   Herbert George Lewis (Bert) Wainewright, transcript of oral history recording, interviewed by Brian Wall, 28 March 1989, AWM, Keith Murdoch Sound Archive, S00570, p. 16.

12   Oberleutnant der Schutzpolizei, Sicherungsabschnitt 23 an den SS- und Polizeiführer Oberitalien-West, Monza, 24 December 1943, AWM, PR03098, Peck, John Desmond 'Des' (Lieutenant), DCM, 1919–2002, personal papers, 4/9.

13   John Desmond Peck, interview with Heidi Egger, Manchester, 10 February 2001, Peck family collection.

14   Roger Absalom, 'Note on the judiciary enquiry and subsequent trial of Oreste Barbero et al. accused of aiding and abetting John Peck's activities', AWM, PR03098, 9/1.

15   Giorgio Nascimbene, *Prigionieri di guerra: L'anabasi dei prigionieri alleati che nel 1943 fecero parte dei campi di lavoro nelle risaie vercellesi e dintorni*. Società Operaia di Mutuo Soccorso Villata 1884, Vercelli, 2004, pp. 160–161.

16   Report by JD Peck (Australian Army) who arrived UK 4 November 44, 14 November 1944, p. 3.

17   Traduzione di arrestati nelle carceri di Torino, 19 January 1944, AWM, PR03098, 4/5.

18   Peck, interview with Egger.

19   Roger Absalom, 'Note on the judiciary enquiry'.

20   Roger Absalom, 'Note on the judiciary enquiry'.

21   John Desmond Peck, interview with Conrad Wood, London, 30 May 1996, Imperial War Museum, 16667, reel 6.

22   John Desmond Peck, untitled manuscript, Peck, John Desmond 'Des' (Lieutenant), DCM, 1919–2002, personal papers, AWM, PR03098, 3/1.

23   Peck, untitled manuscript.

24   Peck, untitled manuscript.

25   Peck, untitled manuscript.

26   Peck, untitled manuscript.

27   Peck, untitled manuscript.

28   Peck, untitled manuscript.

29   Peck, untitled manuscript.

30   Peck, untitled manuscript.

31   Peck, untitled manuscript.

CHAPTER 14: ESCAPE FROM SAN VITTORE

1   Report by JD Peck (Australian Army) who arrived UK 4 November 1944, p. 3, TNA, WO 208/4265, War Office: Directorate of Military Operations and Intelligence; Ministry of Defence, Defence Intelligence Staff: Files. Prisoner of War Reports.

2   Report by JD Peck (Australian Army) who arrived UK 4 November 1944, p. 3.

3   Report by JD Peck (Australian Army), who arrived UK 4 November 1944, p. 3.

4   'Vittore el Moro', <https://it.wikipedia.org/wiki/Vittore_il_Moro>, last accessed
       30 March 2017.

5   'Theo Saevecke', <https://de.wikipedia.org/wiki/Theo_ Saevecke>; Ernst
       Klee, *Personenlexikon zum Dritten Reich: Wer war was vor und nach 1945*, Fischer
       Taschenbuch, Frankfurt am Main, 2005, p. 518; Timothy Naftali, 'The CIA
       and Eichmann's Associates', in Richard Breitman, Norman JW Goda, Timothy
       Naftali, Robert Wolfe (eds), *US Intelligence and the Nazis*, Cambridge University
       Press, Cambridge, 2005, pp. 337–74.

6   Cited in Dieter Schenk, *Auf dem rechten Auge blind: Die braunen Wurzeln des BK*,
       Kiepenheuer & Witsch, Cologne, 2001, p. 237 .

7   AS MI – Cabinet prefecture second section, envelope 396, file category 37,
       document dated 11 February 1944, 'Notes to the Duce. Judicial Prisons', by
       Mario Bassi, cited in 'Carcere di San Vittore', <https://it.wikipedia.org/wiki/
       Carcere_di_San_Vittore>, last accessed 30 March 2017.

8   Interrogation Report on Three German Deserters from 2 COY, 3 Para Rifle Regt,
       taken at S. Sepolcro on 15 Aug 44, National Archives and Records Administration
       (NARA), RG407 Fifth Army WWII Int Reports Entry 427 Box 2223 (courtesy
       Katrina Kittel).

9   Interrogation Report on Three German Deserters.

10   Report by JD Peck (Australian Army) who arrived UK 4 November 44, p. 3.

11   Cecil Roseberry, 'Allied Forces and the Italian Resistance 1943–1945', p. 5, TNA,
       PRO HS7/59, History of the Italian Section.

12   In the sources the spelling of the Canadian's name is inconsistent; it sometimes
       appears as 'Patterson'.

13   David Stafford, *Mission Accomplished: SOE and Italy 1943–1945*, Vintage,
       London, 2012, p. 211. A fictionalised account of Paterson's wartime experience
       appears in John Windsor, *The Mouth of the Wolf*, Hodder & Stoughton, London,
       1967.

14   Report by JD Peck (Australian Army) who arrived UK 4 November 1944, p. 8.

15   POW Report of Private John Desmond Peck, VX9534, Wil (Switzerland),
       12 July 1944, TNA, WO 208/4273, War Office: Directorate of Military
       Operations and Intelligence, and Directorate of Military Intelligence;
       Ministry of Defence, Defence Intelligence Staff: Files. Prisoner of War
       Reports: Escapes via Switzerland.

16   Roger Absalom, 'List of documents provided by John Peck, 19 January 1987',
       AWM, PRO 3098, Peck, John Desmond 'Des' (Lieutenant), DCM, 1919–2002.
       personal papers, 9/1; also POW Report of Private John Desmond Peck, VX9534,
       Wil (Switzerland), 12 July 1944.

17   Roger Absalom, 'List of documents provided by John Peck, 19 January 1987'.

18   British Legation Berne to Eden, 20 October 1944, TNA, FO 916/984, Escape of
       Prisoners of War in Italy.

19   Cablegram, Secretary of State for Dominion Affairs to Prime Minister of
       Australia, 15 September 1943, NAA, A5954, 670/7, Prisoners of War in Italy
       – Transfer to Germany and Escape to Switzerland consequent upon Italian
       Capitulation.

20   Johnny Peck and Roger Absalom, 'Questions and answers re Peck's experiences in Italy', AWM PR03098, 9/1.
21   John Desmond Peck to his parents, Wil (Switzerland), 27 June 1944, Peck, John Desmond 'Des' (Lieutenant), DCM, 1919–2002, personal papers, AWM PR03098, 1/1.
22   Peck to his parents, Wil, 26 July 1944.
23   Ken Fenton, *Anzacs at the Frontiers 1941–1945: Northern Italy*, vol. I, Ken Fenton, Nelson, 2008, pp. 198–99.
24   Lynette Oates and Ian Sproule, *Australian Partisan: A True Story of Love and War*, Australian Military History Publications, Loftus, NSW, 1997, p. 65; Ken Fenton, *Alamein to the Alps: War in the Piedmont with Mission Cherokee and the Lost Anzacs 1943–1945*, Frontier Press, Nelson, 2011, p. 313; Herbert George Lewis Wainewright, interview with Brian Wall, 28 March 1989 (transcript), AWM Sound Archive, S00570, p. 17.
25   AWM54, 781/6/6, Prisoner of War Statements – Europe.
26   TNA, WO 235/324, Defendant: Pietro Musetti. Defendant: Luigi Musetti. Place of Trial: Bologna.
27   Fenton, *Anzacs at the Frontiers*, 193 –94.
28   Statement by Giovanni Nascimbene, Varallo, 21 December 1946, TNA, WO 310/68, Verallo, Italy: shooting of Australian POWs.
29   TNA, WO 310/68.

CHAPTER 15: THE SOE IN ITALY

1   John Desmond Peck to his parents, Wil (Switzerland), 26 July 1944, Peck, John Desmond 'Des' (Lieutenant), DCM, 1919–2002, personal papers, AWM, PR03098, 1/1.
2   TNA, HS 9/155/6, John William Gallaudet Birkbeck.
3   David Stafford, *Mission Accomplished: SOE and Italy 1943–1945*, Vintage, London, 2012, p. 91; Roderick Bailey, *Target: Italy. The Secret War against Mussolini, 1940–1943 (The Official History of SOE Operations in Fascist Italy)*, Faber & Faber, London, 2014, p. 186.
4   Bailey, *Target: Italy*, pp. 186–87.
5   Bailey, *Target: Italy*, pp. 187–88.
6   Bailey, *Target: Italy*, p. 189.
7   Jock McCaffery, 'No Pipes or Drums', unpublished manuscript, p. 48, Private papers of J McCaffery OBE, IWM, Documents, 1409305/77/1.
8   Christopher M Woods, 'No. 1 Special Force', in Donatelli Ghini and Patrick Leech (eds), *No. 1 Special Force and Italian Resistance*, vol. 2, CLUEB, Bologna, 1988, p. 36.
9   McCaffery, 'No Pipes or Drums', p. 133.
10   McCaffery, 'No Pipes or Drums', p. 133.
11   Bailey, *Target: Italy*, pp. 303–306. Fortuitously Mallaby and his radio were able to play a role in Armistice negotiations.
12   Private papers of Major General Sir Colin M Gubbins KCMG DSO MC, IWM, Documents, 12618; see also Peter Wilkinson and Joan Bright-Astley, *Gubbins and SOE*, Leo Cooper, London, 1993.

13 Stafford, *Mission Accomplished*, pp. 67–68.

14 Woods, 'No. 1 Special Force', p. 37

15 TNA, HS 9/155/6, John William Gallaudet Birkbeck.

16 Patrick Howarth, *Undercover: The Men and Women of the Special Operations Executive*, Routledge & Kegan Paul, London, 1980, p. 182.

17 Howarth, *Undercover*, pp. 189–90.

18 McCaffery, 'No Pipes or Drums', p. 83.

19 Bailey, *Target: Italy*, p. 190.

20 SOE Cabinet Papers, Italy, Draft, p. 12, TNA, HS 6/776, SOE organisation in Italy.

21 Charles F Delzell, *Mussolini's Enemies: The Italian Anti-Fascist Resistance*, Princeton University Press, Princeton, 1961, p. 312

22 Richard Lamb, *War in Italy 1943–1945: A Brutal Story*, Penguin, London, 1995, pp. 204–205.

23 Lamb, *War in Italy 1943–1945*, p. 204.

24 Jock McCaffery, 'No Pipes or Drums', p. 73.

25 Cecil Roseberry, 'History of the Italian Section', p. 4, TNA, HS 7/59, Italy: Allied Forces and Italian Resistance 1943–1945.

26 McCaffery, 'No Pipes or Drums', p. 133.

27 Christopher Woods, 'SOE in Italy', in Mark Seaman (ed.), *Special Operations Executive: A New Instrument of War*, Routledge, London, 2006, p. 99.

28 SOE Cabinet Papers, Italy, Draft, p. 12.

29 Max Corvo, *The OSS in Italy 1942–1945: A Personal Memoir*, Praeger, New York, 1990, p. 303.

30 SOE Cabinet Papers, Italy, Draft, p. 12.

31 Gustavo Corni, 'Italy', in Bob Moore (ed.), *Resistance in Western Europe*, Berg, Oxford, 2000, p. 174.

32 SOE Cabinet Papers, Italy, Draft, p. 11.

33 AAS London to LHQ Melbourne, 22 January 1945, Secret, VX9534, Pte Peck J D, Escaped PW, Recommendation for award Military Medal, NAA B833, Peck Desmond John: Service Number – VX9534.

34 Delzell, *Mussolini's Enemies*, p. 364.

35 McCaffery, 'No Pipes or Drums', p. 179.

36 McCaffery, 'No Pipes or Drums', p. 179.

37 Stafford, *Mission Accomplished*, p. 211.

38 Report by JD Peck (Australian Army), who arrived UK 4 November 1944, p. 8, TNA WO 208/4265, War Office: Directorate of Military Operations and Intelligence; Ministry of Defence, Defence Intelligence Staff: Files. Prisoner of War Reports.

CHAPTER 16: THE DOOMED REPUBLIC

1 David Stafford, *Mission Accomplished: SOE and Italy 1943–1945*, Vintage, London, 2012, p. 215.

2 Stafford, *Mission Accomplished*, p. 215.

3 Kesselring's Order, 24 September 1944, as translated for the Kesselring trial, WO 235/375, in Richard Lamb, *War in Italy 1943–1845: A Brutal Story*, Penguin, London, 1995, p. 322.

4   Report by JD Peck (Australian Army), who arrived UK 4 November 1944, 14 November 1944, p. 2, TNA, WO 208/4265, War Office: Directorate of Military Operations and Intelligence; Ministry of Defence, Defence Intelligence Staff: Files. Prisoner of War Reports.

5   'The Moscatelli Formations' (document for which Jocumsen is a source), p. 9, TNA, HS 6/815, Italy. Personal Cases and Interrogations.

6   'Annotazioni', Archivio Istituto Storico Resistenza Novara Piero Fornara, Fonde Divisione Valdossola, Fascicolo John Peck.

7   Report by JD Peck (Australian Army) who arrived UK 4 November 1944, p. 2.

8   Report by JD Peck (Australian Army) who arrived UK 4 November 1944, p. 8.

9   Translation of Telegram from German C-in-C, South-West to Supreme SS and Police Chief Italy, 21 August 1944, in IWM, Private Papers of Major General Sir Colin M Gubbins KCMG DSO MC, Documents.12618, Box 1.

10   Report by JD Peck (Australian Army), who arrived UK 4 Nov 44, 14 Nov. 1944, p. 4

11   Report by JD Peck (Australian Army), who arrived UK 4 November 1944, p. 4. For an account of the episode, see also Ken Fenton, 'The Gold Mine in the Valley of the Widows', unpublished manuscript kindly provided by the author.

12   Report by JD Peck (Australian Army) who arrived UK 4 November 1944, p. 4.

13   Report by JD Peck (Australian Army) who arrived UK 4 November 1944, p. 5.

14   Report by JD Peck (Australian Army) who arrived UK 4 November 1944, p. 5.

15   Report by JD Peck (Australian Army) who arrived UK 4 November 1944, p. 5.

16   Report by JD Peck (Australian Army) who arrived UK 4 November 1944, p. 5.

17   Report by JD Peck (Australian Army) who arrived UK 4 November 1944, p. 5.

18   Report by JD Peck (Australian Army) who arrived UK 4 November 1944, p. 8.

19   'The Moscatelli Formations', p. 9.

20   Report by JD Peck (Australian Army) who arrived UK 4 November 1944, p. 8.

21   AAS London to LHQ Melbourne, 22 January 1945, Secret, VX9534 Pte Peck JD, Escaped PW, Recommendation for award Military Medal, NAA B833, VX9534, Peck Desmond John: Service Number – VX9534.

22   AAS London to LHQ Melbourne, 22 January 1945.

23   Report by JD Peck (Australian Army) who arrived UK 4 November 1944, p. 3 Apart from Peck's report, Michael Foot and JM Langley suggest in their history of MI9 that 'two Australians in Piedmont each commanded a brigade two thousand strong'. Though they do not name him, Peck would have been one of those referred to, Frank Jocumsen presumably the other: MRD Foot and JM Langley, *MI9: The British Secret Service that Fostered Escape and Evasion 1939–1945 and Its American Counterpart*, Bodley Head, London, 1979, p. 163.

24   Jock McCaffery, 'No Pipes or Drums', p. 208.

25   Malcolm Tudor, *Special Force: SOE and the Italian Resistance 1943–1945*, Emilia Publishing, Powys, 2004, p. 52.

26   Hubertus Bergwitz, *Die Partisanenrepublik Ossola. Vom 10. September bis zum 23. Oktober 1944*, Verlag für Literatur und Zeitgeschehen, Hannover, 1972, p. 16.

27   On the creation of the Free Republic of Domodossola, see Stafford, *Mission Accomplished*, pp. 208–209.

28   Jock McCaffery, 'No Pipes or Drums', p. 209.

29   Stafford, *Mission Accomplished*, p. 211.

30   Stafford, *Mission Accomplished*, pp. 211–12.

31   Stafford, *Mission Accomplished*, pp. 212–13.

32   John Windsor, *The Mouth of the Wolf*, Gray's Publishing, Sidney, British Columbia, 1967, cited in Stafford, *Mission Accomplished*, p. 212.

33   Report by JD Peck (Australian Army) who arrived UK 4 November 44, p. 8. At this time there was a socialist Matteotti Brigade in the Valdossola Division: see Bergwitz, *Die Partisanenrepublik Ossola*, p. 79.

34   Michele Beltrami, *Il governo dell'Ossola partigiana*, Sapere 2000, Rome, 1994, p. 96.

35   Enrico Massara, *Antologia dell'antifascismo e della resistenza novarese: Uomini ed episodi della lotta de liberazione,* Provincia di Novara Istituto Storico della Resistenza e della Società Contemporanea, Novara, 1984, p. 789.

36   Malcolm Tudor, *Special Force: SOE and the Italian Resistance 1943–1945*, Emilia Publishing, Woodlands, 2004, p. 51.

37   Dionigi Superti to Dino Roberto, Milan, 9 November 1946, Archivio Istituto Storico Resistenza Novara Piero Fornara, Fonde Divisione Valdossola, Fascicolo John Peck.

38   John Desmond Peck, interview with Conrad Wood, London, 30 May 1996, Imperial War Museum, 16667, reel 6.

39   Report by JD Peck (Australian Army) who arrived UK 4 November 1944, p. 8.

40   Report by JD Peck (Australian Army) who arrived UK 4 November 1944, p. 9.

41   Translation of Telegram from German C-in-C., South West, to multiple recipients, 1 October 44, IWM, Major General Sir Colin Gubbins 04/29/2, Box 1.

42   Report by JD Peck (Australian Army) who arrived UK 4 November 1944, p. 9.

43   Report by JD Peck (Australian Army) who arrived UK 4 November 1944, p. 9.

44   Report by JD Peck (Australian Army) who arrived UK 4 November 1944, p. 9.

45   Report by JD Peck (Australian Army) who arrived UK 4 November 1944, p. 9.

46   Report by JD Peck (Australian Army) who arrived UK 4 November 1944, p. 9.

47   Report by JD Peck (Australian Army) who arrived UK 4 November 1944, p. 9.

48   Report by JD Peck (Australian Army) who arrived UK 4 November 1944, p. 9.

49   Report by JD Peck (Australian Army) who arrived UK 4 November 1944, p. 9

50   Report by JD Peck (Australian Army) who arrived UK 4 November 1944, p. 9.

51   Claudio Perazzi, interview with Anna Banfi, Verbania, 16 February 2017.

52   Cited in Barbara Barclay Carter, *Italy Speaks*, Victor Gollancz, London, 1947, p. 121.

53   Paterson's report of 23 May 1945, Christopher Woods Archive, Cabinet Office London, cited in Stafford, *Mission Accomplished*, p. 213.

54   'An Outline of the History of SOE Activity in Italy 1941–1945', p. 5, TNA HS 7/59, Italy: Allied Forces and Italian resistance 1943–1945.

CHAPTER 17: VICTORY

1   John Desmond Peck and Roger Absalom, Questions and answers re Peck's experiences in Italy, AWM, PR03098, Peck, John Desmond 'Des' (Lieutenant), DCM, 1919–2002, personal papers, 9/1.

2   Alastair Macdonald and Patrick Amoore, 'The Cherokee Mission in the Biella Area', in Donatella Ghini and Patrick Leech (eds), *No. 1 Special Force and Italian Resistance: Proceedings of the Conference held at Bologna, 28–30 April 1987,* vol. II, CLUEB, Bologna, 1990. p. 69.

3   Alastair Macdonald, report on Cherokee Mission, IWM 16234, Amoore, John Patrick Strode, private papers.

4   Macdonald and Amoore, 'The Cherokee Mission in the Biella Area', p. 73.

5   NAA, B883, VX29657, Jones Keith Stanley.

6   DJ Nicholls, 'A British PoW Becomes a Partisan, 1943–1945', p. 7, WW2 People's War, <www.bbc.co.uk/history/ww2peopleswar/stories/41/a2001141.shtml>, last accessed 5 April 2017.

7   DJ Nicholls, 'A British PoW Becomes a Partisan, 1943–1945', p. 8.

8   TNA, WO344/311/1, War Office: Directorate of Military Intelligence: Liberated Prisoner of War Interrogation Questionnaires. Private Frederick John Tabram.

9   Gustavo Corni, 'Italy', in Bob Moore (ed.), *Resistance in Western Europe*, Berg, Oxford, 2000, p. 161.

10 JG Beevor, *SOE: Recollections and Reflections 1940–1945*, Bodley Head, London, 1981, p. 143.

CHAPTER 18: AFTERMATH

1   John Desmond Peck to his parents, 27 December 1944, Peck family collection.

2   John Desmond Peck, interview with Heidi Egger, Manchester, 10–11 February 2001, Peck family collection.

3   Peck to his parents, February 1945, Peck family collection.

4   NAA, B833, VX9534, Peck John Desmond.

5   AAS London to LHQ Melbourne, 22 January, Secret, VX9534 Pte Peck J D. Escaped PW. Recommendation for award Military Medal. NAA, B833, VX9534.

6   The Distinguished Conduct Medal, Private John Desmond Peck – 2/7 Aust Inf Bn, NAA, B833, VX9534.

7   NAA, A1838, 1535/18/274 Part 1, Decorations – Italy – Peck, John Desmond.

8   NAA, B833, VX9534.

9   NAA, B833, VX9534.

10 Peck, interview with Egger.

11 Peck, interview with Egger.

12 Peck, interview with Egger.

13 Translation of a story in *Chania News*, 18 May 1990, AWM, PR03098, Peck, John Desmond 'Des' (Lieutenant), DCM, 1919–2002, personal papers, 2/2.

14 NAA, B883, VX4648, Ledgerwood William.

15 Ladislao Kürti to Peck, Prague, 8 Feb 1946, AWM, PR03098, 1/5.

16 Ladislao Kürti to Peck, 21 August 1950, AWM, PR03098, 1/5.

17 Lewis-Heath to Peck, 19 September 1945, AWM, PR03098, 1/5.

18 Solaro Gabriella, 'Fondo: Bacciagaluppi Giuseppe', <http://beniculturali.ilc.cnr.it:8080/Isis/servlet/Isis?Conf=/usr/local/IsisGas/InsmliConf/Insmli.sys6.file&Obj=@Insmlid.pft&Opt=get&Type=Doc&Id=003646>, last accessed 5 April 2017.

19 Undated letter to Peck by unknown Italian correspondent, AWM, PR03098, 4/1.

20 'Campo 57', <www.awm.gov.au/exhibitions/stolenyears/ww2/italy/story2.asp>, last accessed 5 April 2017.

21 Timothy Naftali, 'The CIA and Eichmann's Associates', in Richard Breitman, Norman JW Goda, Timothy Naftali, Robert Wolfe (eds), *U.S. Intelligence and the Nazis,* Cambridge University Press, Cambridge, 2005, pp. 337–74.

22 TNA, HS 6/815, Italy. Personal Cases and Interrogations.

23 HAR Philby to John Senter, SOE, 7 February 2016, TNA, HS 6/815.

24 Jock McCaffery, 'No Pipes or Drums', unpublished manuscript, p. 182, Private papers of J McCaffery OBE, IWM, Documents,1409305/77/1.

25 Frank Jocumsen to John Peck, 28 August 1945, AWM, PR03098, 1/5.

26 Jocumsen to Peck, 28 August 1945.

BIBLIOGRAPHY

Archivio Istituto Storico Resistenza Novara Piero Fornara
Fonde Divisione Valdossola, Fascicolo John Peck

Australian War Memorial, Canberra (AWM)
AWM54, 781/6/6, Prisoner of War Statements – Europe [also known as the Parker file]
AWM54, 781/6/7, Prisoner of War Statements – Europe: Interrogation reports of
    Escaped Prisoners of War by Allied Interrogation Service, CMF 1944
AWM52, 8/2/17, HQ 17 Infantry Brigade diary
AWM52, 8/3/7, 2/7 Infantry Battalion diary
AWM63, 2nd AIF Headquarters (Middle East), registry records
AWM76, Official History, 1939–45 war, biographical files
PR84/24, John Rowe and Keith Hooper, 'Partisan – the story of WX5292 Cpl John
    Wilfred Rowe as told to Keith Hooper', 1982
PR03098, Peck, John Desmond 'Des' (Lieutenant), DCM, 1919–2002, personal papers
Rudd, Bill, et al., 'AIF in Switzerland: A Compendium', n.p., n.d.; (research centre
    library)
Wainewright, Herbert George Lewis, interview with Brian Wall, 28 March 1989
    (transcript), AWM Sound Archive, S00570

Banfi private collection, Milan
Claudio Perazzi, oral history interview with Anna Banfi, Verbania, 16 February 2017

Imperial War Museum, London (IWM)
Amoore, John, Private papers of John Patrick Strode Amoore, 16234
Gubbins, Colin, Private papers of Major General Sir Colin M Gubbins KCMG DSO
    MC, Documents, 12618
McCaffery, J, Private papers of J McCaffery OBE, Documents, 1409305/77/1
Peck, John Desmond, Oral history interview with Conrad Wood, London, 30 May
    1996, 16667

The National Archive, London (TNA)
Files from the following series:
ADM 1, Admiralty, and Ministry of Defence, Navy Department: Correspondence and
    Papers

274

FO 916, Foreign Office: Consular (War) Department, later Prisoners of War
Department: Registered Files (KW and RD Series)

HS 6, Special Operations Executive: Western Europe: Registered Files

HS 7, Special Operations Executive: Histories and War Diaries: Registered Files

WO 208, War Office: Directorate of Military Operations and Intelligence, and
Directorate of Military Intelligence; Ministry of Defence, Defence Intelligence
Staff: Files

WO 235, Judge Advocate General's Office: War Crimes Case Files, Second World War

WO 310, War Office: Judge Advocate General's Office, War Crimes Group (South East
Europe) and predecessors: Case Files (SEE and other series)

WO 344, War Office: Directorate of Military Intelligence: Liberated Prisoner of War
Interrogation Questionnaires

WO 361, War Office: Department of the Permanent Under Secretary of State:
Casualties (L) Branch: Enquiries into Missing Personnel, 1939–45 War

WO 373, War Office and Ministry of Defence: Military Secretary's Department:
Recommendations for Honours and Awards for Gallant and Distinguished Service
(Army)

National Archives of Australia (NAA)
Files from the following series:

A1838, External Affairs: Correspondence files, multiple number series

A5954, 'Shedden Collection'

B883, Second Australian Imperial Force Personnel Dossiers, 1939–1947

MP385/7, Department of Defence, Correspondence files, multiple number, security
classified series

MP1049/5 Department of Defence, correspondence files (general)

Peck family collection UK
Clippings, correspondence, photos, interviews

Primary sources (published)

Carstairs, James De Mole, *Escape from Crete: War Diary*, edited by Michael Sweet and
Ian Frazer, Society of Cretan Historical Studies, Heraklion, 2016

Edwards, Geoffrey, *The Road to Prevelly*, Geoffrey Edwards, Perth, 1989

Fielding, Xan, *Hide and Seek: The Story of a War-time Agent*, Secker & Warburg,
London, 1954

Jager, Charles, *Escape from Crete*, Floradale, Sydney, 2004

Le Souef, Leslie, *To War without a Gun*, Artlook, Perth, 1980

Oates, Lynette and Ian Sproule, *Australian Partisan: A True Story of Love and War*,
Australian Military History Publications, Loftus, NSW, 1997

Psychoundakis, George, *The Cretan Runner: His Story of the German Occupation*, transl.
Patrick Leigh Fermor, John Murray, London, 1978

Webster, Malcolm, *An Italian Experience*, the author, Melbourne, 1995

Secondary sources

Absalom, Roger, *A Strange Alliance: Aspects of Escape and Survival in Italy 1943–1945*, Leo Olschki, Florence, 1991

Absalom, Roger, '"Another crack at Jerry?" Australian prisoners of war in Italy 1941–45', *Journal of the Australian War Memorial*, vol. 17, 1989, pp. 24–32

Badoglio, Pietro, *L'Italia nella seconda guerra mondiale*, Mondadori, Milan, 1946

Bailey, Roderick, *Target: Italy. The Secret War against Mussolini, 1940–1943: The Official History of SOE Operations in Fascist Italy*, Faber & Faber, London, 2014

Beevor, Anthony, *Crete: The Battle and the Resistance*, John Murray, London, 1991

Beevor, JG, *SOE: Recollections and Reflections 1940–1945*, Bodley Head, London, 1981

Beltrami, Michele, *Il governo dell'Ossola partigiana*, Sapere 2000, Rome, 1994

Bergwitz, Hubertus, *Die Partisanenrepublik Ossola. Vom 10. September bis zum 23. Oktober 1944*, Verlag für Literatur und Zeitgeschehen, Hannover, 1972

Bolger, WP, and JG Littlewood, *The Fiery Phoenix: The Story of the 2/7 Australian Infantry Battalion 1939–1946*, 2/7 Battalion Association, Melbourne, 1983

Bosworth, Richard, *Mussolini*, Edward Arnold, London, 2002

Bunbury, Bill, *Rabbits and Spaghetti: Captives and Comrades, Australians, Italians and the War*, Fremantle Arts Centre Press, Fremantle, 1995

Carver, Tom, *Where the Hell Have You Been?: Monty, Italy and One Man's Great Escape*, Short Books, London, 2010

Chabod, Federico, *A History of Italian Fascism*, Cedric Chivers, Bath, 1974

Ciavattone, Federico, 'Counterinsurgency in the Italian Social Republic, 1943–1945', in Daniel Macías Fernández and Fernando Puell de la Villa (eds), *David contra Goliat: Guerra y Asimetría en la Edad contemporánea*, Instituto Universitario General Gutiérrez Mellado, Madrid, 2014, pp. 253–80

Corni, Gustavo, 'Italy', in Bob Moore (ed.), *Resistance in Western Europe*, Berg, Oxford, 2000, pp. 157–87

Damer, Sean and Ian Frazer, *On the Run: Anzac Escape and Evasion in Enemy-occupied Crete*, Penguin (NZ), Northshore, 2007

Davin, Dan, *Crete: Official History of New Zealand in the Second World War 1939–1945*, War History Branch, Dept. of Internal Affairs, Wellington, 1953

Delzell, Charles F, *Mussolini's Enemies: The Italian Anti-Fascist Resistance*, Princeton University Press, Princeton, 1961

Dennis, Peter et al. (eds.), *The Oxford Companion to Australian Military History*, 2nd edn, Oxford UP, Melbourne, 2008

Ewer, Peter, *Forgotten Anzacs: The Campaign in Crete*, Scribe, Melbourne, 2008

Fenton, Ken, *Alamein to the Alps: War in the Piedmont with Mission Cherokee and the Lost Anzacs 1943–1945*, Frontier Press, Nelson, 2011

Fenton, Ken, *Anzacs at the Frontiers 1941–45. Northern Italy*, 2 vols, Ken Fenton, Nelson, 2008

Fenton, Ken, 'The Gold Mine in the Valley of the Widows', unpublished manuscript

Field, AE, 'Prisoners of the Germans and the Italians', in Barton Maughan, *Tobruk and El Alamein*, Australian War Memorial, Canberra, 1966, pp. 755–822

Foot, MRD, and JM Langley, *MI9: The British Secret Service that Fostered Escape and Evasion 1939–1945 and Its American Counterpart*, Bodley Head, London, 1979

Gentile, Carlo, *Wehrmacht und Waffen-SS im Partisanenkrieg: Italien 1943–1945*, Ferdinand Sch[[ningh, Paderborn, 2012

Ghini, Donatella, and Patrick Leech (eds), *No. 1 Special Force and Italian Resistance: Proceedings of the Conference held at Bologna, 28–30 1987,* vol. II, CLUEB, Bologna, 1988

Gordon, Harry, *The Embarrassing Australian: The Story of an Aboriginal Warrior*, Lansdowne Press, Melbourne, 1962

Henderson, Jim, *22 Battalion*, Official History of New Zealand in the Second World War, War History Branch, Department of Internal Affairs, Wellington, 1958

Hill, Maria, *Diggers and Greeks: The Australian Campaigns in Greece and Crete*, UNSW Press, Sydney, 2010

Holt, Thaddeus, *The Deceivers: Allied Military Deception in the Second World War*, Scribner, London, 2004

Howarth, Patrick, *Undercover: The Men and Women of the Special Operations Executive*, Routledge & Kegan Paul, London, 1980

Jacobs, Susan, *Fighting with the Enemy: New Zealand POWs and the Italian Resistance*, Penguin, Auckland, 2003

Kiriakopoulos, GG, *The Nazi Occupation of Crete 1941–1945*, Praeger, Westport CT, 1985

Klee, Ernst, *Personenlexikon zum Dritten Reich. Wer war was vor und nach 1945,* Fischer, Frankfurt am Main, 2005

Kokonas, NA (ed.), *The Cretan Resistance 1941–1945: The Official British Report of 1945 Together with Comments by British Officers Who Took Part in the Resistance*, NA Kokonas, Retimo, 1991

Laffin, John, *Anzacs at War: The Story of Australian and New Zealand Battles*, Abelard-Schuman, London, 1965

Lamb, Richard, *War in Italy 1943–1945: A Brutal Story*, Penguin, London, 1995

Long, Gavin, *Greece, Crete and Syria. Australia in the War of 1939–1945. Series 1 – Army. II*, Australian War Memorial, Canberra, 1953

Long, Gavin, *The Six Years War: A Concise History of Australia in the 1939–1945 War*, Australian War Memorial and Australian Government Printing Service, Canberra, 1973

MacDonald, Callum, *The Lost Battle: Crete, 1941*, Free Press, New York, 1993

Massara, Enrico, *Antologia dell'antifascismo e della resistenza novarese: Uomini ed episodi della lotta de liberazione*, Provincia di Novara Istituto Storico della Resistenza e della Società Contemporanea, Novara, 1984

Monteath, Peter, *POW: Australian Prisoners of War in Hitler's Reich*, Pan Macmillan, Sydney, 2011

Naftali, Timothy, 'The CIA and Eichmann's Associates', in Richard Breitman, Norman JW Goda, Timothy Naftali, Robert Wolfe (eds), *US Intelligence and the Nazis,* Cambridge University Press, Cambridge, 2005, pp. 337–74

Nascimbene, Giorgio, *Prigionieri di guerra. L'anabasi dei prigionieri alleati che nel 1943 fecero parte dei campi di lavoro nelle risaie vercellesi e dintorni*. Società Operaia di Mutuo Soccorso Villata 1884, Vercelli, 2004

Nicholls, DJ, 'A British PoW Becomes a Partisan, 1943–1945', WW2 People's War, <www.bbc.co.uk/history/ww2peopleswar/stories/41/a2001141.shtml>

Palazzo, Albert, *Battle of Crete*, Army History Unit, Canberra, 2007

Peck, Keith T, *'The Kemp Connection': The Family Story of George and Louisa Kemp*, Keith T Peck, Riverwood, 1993

Power, Graham, 'The Anzacs at 42nd Street', <www.grahampower.nz/media/battle-at-42nd-street--graham-power.pdf>

Rankin, Nicholas, *Churchill's Wizards: The British Genius for Deception, 1914–1945*, Faber & Faber, London, 2008

Schenk, Dieter, *Auf dem rechten Auge blind. Die braunen Wurzeln des BKA*, Kiepenheuer & Witsch, Cologne, 2001

Schreiber, Gerhard, 'Das Ende des nordafrikanischen Feldzugs', in Karl-Heinz Frieser (ed.), *Das Deutsche Reich und der Zweite Weltkrieg. Bd. 8. Die Ostfront 1943/44. Der Krieg im Osten und an den Nebenfronten*, Deutsche Verlagsanstalt, Munich, 2007, pp. 1100-63

Seaman, Mark (ed.), *Special Operations Executive: A New Instrument of War*, Routledge, London, 2006

Secchia, Pietro and Cino Moscatelli, *Il Monte Rosa è sceso a Milano: la Resistenza nel Biellese nella Valsesia e nella Valdossola*, Einaudi, Turin, 1958

Soggetto, Marco, *Braccati: Prigionieri di Guerra alleati in Piemonte e Valle D'Aosta*, Aviani & Aviani, Udine, 2013

Sogno, Edgardo, *Guerra senza bandiera: Cronaca della Franchi nella Resistenza*, Mursia, Milan, 1970

Stafford, David, *Mission Accomplished: SOE and Italy 1943–1945*, Vintage, London, 2012

Tenconi, Massimiliano, 'Prigionia, sopravvivenza e Resistenza: Storie di australiani e neozelandesi in provincia di Vercelli (1943–1945)', *L'impegno*, 28, 1 (June 2008), pp. 27–49

Thompson, Peter, *Anzac Fury: The Bloody Battle of Crete 1941*, Heinemann, Sydney, 2010

Travis, David, 'Communism and resistance in Italy, 1943–8', in Tony Judt (ed.), *Resistance and Revolution in Mediterranean Europe 1939–1948*, Routledge, London, 1989, pp. 80–109

Tudor, Malcolm, *Special Force: SOE and the Italian Resistance 1943–1945*, Emilia Publishing, Powys, 2004

Tzobanakis, Stella, *Creforce: The Anzacs and the Battle of Crete*, Black Dog, Melbourne, 2010

Vogel, Detlef, 'German Intervention in the Balkans', in Research Institute for Military History (ed.), *Germany and the Second World War. Volume III. The Mediterranean, South-east Europe, and North Africa 1939–1941*, transl. Dean S McMurry, Ewald Osers and Louise Wilmot, Clarendon Press, Oxford, 1995, pp. 449–555

West, Nigel, *Secret War: The Story of SOE, Britain's Wartime Sabotage Organisation*, Hodder & Stoughton, London, 1992

Wilkinson, Peter and Joan Bright-Astley, *Gubbins and SOE*, Leo Cooper, London, 1993

Windsor, John, *The Mouth of the Wolf*, Hodder & Stoughton, London, 1967

Selected websites

Anzac POW Freemen in Europe, <www.aifpow.com>
Associazione Nazionale Partigiani d'Italia,
Australian Dictionary of Biography, <http://adb.anu.edu.au/>
Department of Veterans' Affairs, <www.dva.gov.au>
Encyclopedia of the Australian War Memorial, <https://www.awm.gov.au/
    encyclopedia>

INDEX

Note: map references are italicised and photo references are indicated by *ps* (picture section)

42nd Street, battle of *ps*, 44–48, 51, 74

A Force (IS9) 80, 95, 146
Aborigines 46–47, 58, 93, 173, 242
Action Party 156, 168, 203, 206
Afrika Korps 20, 122
Agia Galini 59–60
Agia Roumeli 57
Agrati, Pino 150–151
Ajedabia 16
Alexander, Field Marshal 235
Alexandria 20–22, 28, 54, 81, 98
Alones 85
Amoore, Patrick 232–233
Andrew, Leslie 39–40
Anti-Partisan Week 224–225
Anzac forces 52, 89, 122, 125
   in Crete 44–48, 93, 116
   in Greece 21, 23, 24
Anzasca Valley 130, 214, 216–217

Aosta Valley 145, 171, 173, 233
Apollona 121
Armistice
   and Allied POWs 138–146, 147, 164–165, 171–172, 194–195
   resistance activity 156, 166, 170, 172, 177, 203
   and SOE 201–202, 209
Asi Gonia 81, 83, 107
Atock, Ken 'Bluey' 72
Australian Department of Foreign Affairs 240
Australian government 20, 194
Australian units
   1 AIF 4, 25
   2 AIF 4, 9, 25
   6 Division *ps*, 4, 9, 10, 14–15, 20–22
   7 Division 238
   9 Division 21
   16 Brigade 12, 15, 33
   17 Brigade (Victorian Brigade) 9, 11–12, 25
   19 Brigade 12
   2/2 Field Regiment 92

2/3 Field Regiment 60
2/1 Battalion 35, 37–38, 47, 59
2/2 Battalion 33
2/3 Battalion 33
2/4 Battalion 35, 38
2/5 Battalion 9
2/6 Battalion 9, 12, 25
2/7 Battalion 8–9, 237, 242–243
   battle of 42nd Street *ps*, 44–48, 51,
     74
   battle of Bardia 11–16, 25
   battle of Sidi Barrani 10–11
   battle of Tobruk 15–16
   C Company 12, 14, 45, 51–54, 69,
     178
   Costa Rica sinking 26–28
   Crete 35, 40–42, 44–49, 69, 72
   desert training 4–5, 9
   evacuations 32–33, 51–56, 60–64,
     88, 93, 114
   Greece 22–28
2/8 Battalion 9, 44, 94
2/11 Battalion 35, 37, 59, 61, 88, 98
2/15 Battalion 170
2/24 Battalion 153, 173, 197, 233
2/28 Battalion 123, 173, 197
2/32 Battalion 173, 197–198
Australian War Memorial *ps*, 61, 152
Avdou Pediados 113, 115
Ay Yiannis 118

Bacciagaluppi, Audrey 157, 161
Bacciagaluppi, Giuseppe 157–158,
   163, 192, 243–244
Badoglio, Marshal Pietro 5, 135–139
Balzarini 244
Bandiera, group 173
Bandouvas, Manoli *ps*, 102–103, 114, 116
Bandouvas, Nikos *ps*
Bandouvas, Yiannis *ps*
Baralle, Giuseppe 150
Barbero, Oreste 151, 183
Bardia 115
Bardia, battle of *ps*, 11–16, 25, 47
Bari 122
   PG 75 124, 126
Basilica di Sant'Andrea, Vercelli 150–
   151
Batt, Leslie George *ps*, 196–197
Battala 224

Bazeley, William Maynard 98
BBC 139
Beato Amedeo 133
Bellinzona 228
Benghazi 16, 20, 122, 173
Bertola, Ermenegildo 150
Biella 173, 197, 232
Birkbeck, Major John 194–195, 200,
   202, 205, 208, 222, 228
Bishop, Private 59–60
Black, Dan 173
Black Brigades 180
Black Watch 59–60
Blackshirts 193
Blain, Harry 197
Blake, Harry 60, 63
Blamey, General Thomas 8–9, 21
BLOs *see* British Liaison Officers (BLOs)
Bologna 156, 214
   PG 19 141
Bolton, Lieutenant Wilson 47
Bonardo, Filippo ('Nino') 150, 183
Borgosesia 154, 169, 247
Bowes, Frank 172, 196
Brallos Pass 23–24
Brenner Pass 135, 235
Brewer, Francis Neil Tudor 98
Brigate Fiamme Verdi (Green Flame
   Brigade) 168, 204
Brigate Nere (Black Brigades) 180
Brindisi 123, 137, 202
Britain
   battle for Crete 29, 31–35, 38
   evacuations from Crete 54–55, 78,
     79–80
   Greece 19–21
   Italian war 8, 11–16, 15–16
British Army 179, 238
British consulate, Lugano 194, 200,
   202
British Embassy, Berne 194, 200
British Liaison Officers (BLOs) *ps*,
   203–204, 206, 208–212, 213, 214–215,
   218, 222, 231–232, 234, 245–247
Brook, Douglas Andrew 129–132
Brown, George William 'Bomber'
   129–130
Burgess, George 58

Cadorna, General Raffaelle 206–207

Calcaterra, Colonel Vittorio 125–126, 141, 244
Calzavara, Armando (Arca) 161, 193
Camana, Piero 150
Campbell, Lieutenant-Colonel Ian 35, 37, 54, 59
Canberra, HMAS 238
Canea 59, 62, 68, 71, 74, 78, 236
  airfield defence 31, 35, 40–44
Carstairs, Lieutenant James De Mole 51, 93
Carta, General Angelo 115, 136
'Casa Rossi', house 204
Cascina Dallodi farm 133
CEMSA (Costruzioni Elettro Meccaniche di Saronno) 178
Ceppo Morelli 132, 154
Cerberus, HMAS 5
Cerutti, Vittoria 150
Cesare Battisti, group 161
Chappel, Brigadier BH 38
Cherokee mission 232–233
Chieta, PG 21 140
Christmas 10–11
Churchill, Winston 19–21, 31–32, 79–80, 95, 146
Cividale 124–125
Clark, JT *ps*, 196–197
Clarke, Lieutenant-Colonel Dudley 80, 95
CLNAI *see* Committees of National Liberation (CLNs)
CLNs *see* Committees of National Liberation (CLNs)
Comforts Fund 11
Committees of National Liberation (CLNs) 156–157, 162–163, 168, 203
  CLNAI 203, 206, 216–217, 231, 235, 246
Como 155, 159, 190, 201
Costa Rica, troopship 26–28, 54, 94, 121, 144
Cottington, Pat *ps*
Council for National Academic Awards 241
Creforce 32–34, 44
Cretan runners *ps*, 99, 242
Cretan wireless 81
Crete
  airfields defence 31–42

battle for Crete 29–49, 74
battle of 42nd Street 44–49
Crete in 1941 *30 map*
German occupation *ps*
history and topography 29–31
SOE operations 94–109, 114, 116, 236
war ends 235
Crib Point 1, 5–6, 195–196, 238
Crockatt, Brigadier Norman 79, 139, 140
Czechs 118–119, 121, 243

Dachau 244, 245
Dall'Orto, Nando 150
Dall'Orto, Volmano 150
Daphne 22, 62
Davies, Eric 39
Davis, Harry 173
D-Day landings 206
Defender, HMS 27
De-Grandi, - 244
Delzell, Charles 210
Demetrios 82–84
Derna 16, 170
Di Dio, Marco 228
Domodossola 219–221, 225–226, 228, 245
Domokos 22–23
Doran, Roy 61
Dorney, Kiernan 'Skipper' 111–117
Dulles, Allen 200, 202–205, 221, 223
Dunbabin, Tom 236
Dunkirk 78, 134–135
Dunn, Noel 87, 99–106, 113–118, 119, 121–122

Edwards, Geoffrey 88
El Alamein 123
Empress of Japan 4
Evans, Arthur 114
Evans, George 174

Fermor, Patrick Leigh 98, 108, 236
Ferramonti 243
Ferrari, Ines 186, 188, 244
Ferrari, Oreste *ps*, 155, 163, 185–186, 188, 244
Fielding, Xan ('Aleko') 89, 98, 102, 106–107
Flinders Naval Depot 5–6, 238

Fondo Toce 224
Fontanella Brigade 172
Force 133 99
Forde, Private NJ 153
Forth, - 212
Fossoli concentration camp 244
France 5, 78, 145, 195, 206, 230
Franchi organisation 204, 210–211
Free Republic of Ossola *ps*, 220–229,
 230–231, 240, 245
Freyberg, General Bernard 32–36, 40,
 42–43

Galatas, POW camp 42, 68–74, 97, 109,
 111, 116
Gamba, Pina 150, 183–184
Garibaldi, Giuseppe 168–169
Garibaldi brigades 211, 214–216, 219,
 232–233, 244
Garrett, Major R 56
Gavdos 56, 61
Geneva Convention on the Treatment
 of Prisoners of War 67, 118–119,
 124–125, 165, 181
Genoa 141, 156, 200
Georgioupoli 9, 35, 40, 43, 59, 61–63,
 74–76, 101, 118
German units
 5th Mountain Division 21
 141 Gebirgsjäger Regiment 45
 XI Fliegerkorps 36
Germany 5, 213–214
 Allied POWs 54–55, 118–119,
  122–123
 battle for Crete *ps*, 29–49
 defeat 230–236
 Greek campaign 19–28
 occupation of Italy 135–138, 140
 Operation Barbarossa 19–20, 79–80
 POW camps 65–72, 137, 141–142,
  164
 war crimes 244–245
Ghali, Paul *ps*
GHQ Middle East, Cairo 10, 31, 43, 78,
 80, 94
Giles, John Thomas (Jack) 129–130
Giustizia e Libertà (Justice and Liberty)
 brigades 168, 206
Gorton, Jim 61
Gothic Line 207

Gourevitch, Major Arnold 111–112,
 115
Grassi, Salvatore 150
Gravellona 218, 224, 225
Gravina, PG 65 124, 126, 128
Greece 30, 115
 communists 233–234
 evacuations *ps*, 24–28, 32–33, 55, 66,
  78, 95, 98
 German campaign 19–28, 32, 79
 Greece in 1941 *18 map*
 Italian campaign 17, 19–20
Green Flame Brigade 168, 204
Greenway, Lieutenant GJ 98
Gruppi d'Azione Patriottica (Patriotic
 Action Groups (GAPs)) 168
Gruppignano, PG *ps*, 124–128, 129, 132,
 141, 157, 170–173, 244
Gruppo Volontari per la Libertà (Corps
 of the Volunteers for Freedom (CVL)
 205–206
Gubbins, Major-General Colin 201–
 202
Gustav Line 206

Hargest, Brigadier James 35
Harvey, Bill 197
Headquarters, Australian Overseas
 Base 4–5, 8
Hedgehog, HMS 93, 114–115
Heraklion 96
 airfield defence 31, 35–36, 38, 40, 42
 evacuations 43, 59, 113–114, 116,
  171
Hereward, HMS 27, 171
Hero, HMS 27
Hill 107 39–42
Himmler, Heinrich 179
Hitler, Adolf 16, 19, 28, 29, 36, 80, 135,
 165, 213
 and Mussolini 17, 138, 166, 180
Hobart, HMAS 238

Ikingi Maryut 10–11
Imbros 43, 50, 52–53
Imbros Gorge 50–51, 55, 57
Intra 161, 193
Italian 10th Army 10
Italian Armistice *see* Armistice
Italian Embassy, Canberra 240

Italian General Staff 135
Italian Patriot Brigade 219, 239
Italian Social Republic (RSI) *see*
  Repubblica Sociale Italiana (RSI)
Italian units, Tagliamento Battalion
  196–197
Italian War Ministry 139
Italy
  Allied invasion 134–136
  Allied POWs 120–124, 134–136,
    151–159, 166
  Free Republic of Ossola 220–229
  German occupation 135–137,
    135–138, 142–143, 166–167
  Greek campaign 17–20
  Mussolini's RSI 138
  North African campaign 8–16, 17,
    19, 122
  occupation of Crete 40, 93–94, 115,
    117, 118
  partisans 166–175, 176–180, 184–
    188, 196–198, 232–233
  POW camps 124–129, 138–143
  POW escape networks 147–163,
    176, 179
  SOE operations 194–195, 199–212,
    231–234

Jager, Charles 92
Jarvis, LM 154
Jerusalem 7
Jews 111, 118–119, 159, 190–191, 211,
  243, 245
Jocumsen, Frank ('Butch') *ps*, 173–175,
  210, 211, 214–215, 217–218, 245–247
Jones, Keith Stanley 173, 232–233

Kalamata *ps*, 25–26, 28, 118
Kalithea prison 118
Kalives 66–67
Kastelli 113, 117
Kefalonia 135
Kesselring, General Field Marshal
  Albert 179, 181, 206–207, 213–215,
  224–225, 244
King of Italy 134–135, 137
Klima 62, 101
Knarakis family 113
Knossos 30, 113–114
Komitades 43, 51–54, 57, 58

Kontomari *ps*, 101
Kreipe, General Heinrich 108, 236
Kürti, Ladislao 243

Lago Maggiore 155, 157, 161, 177,
  178, 193, 224
Lago Mergozzo 224, 225
Lake Como 201, 235
Lambert, Arthur 93
Lamia 23–24
Langouvardos, Father Agathángelos
  87–88
Lasithi 93–94, 95, 115–116, 117
Lazzarini, - 185
Le Souef, Dr Leslie 55, 72, 111
Ledgerwood, Bill 61–63, 242–243
Lefka Ori (White Mountains) 31, 43, 61
Lewis-Heath, Ronald 243
Libya 10, 15, 20, 56, 122
Liddell, Clive 197
Limni beach 87–88
Livorno 233
Locarno 194
Lombardy *127 map*, 156–157, 168, 178,
  190–192, 206, 209
Lombardy Brigade 219, 223
London Radio 219
Longo, Luigi ('Gallo') 206
Luftwaffe 23, 24, 36–41, 43–44, 56
Lugano 194, 200, 202, 204–205, 228
Luino 154–156, 163, 177–178, 189–
  190, 200, 244
Lupano, partisan 184–185, 244

MacDonald, Major Alastair 232–233
Macugnaga 130–131
Mafia 202
Maleme 31, 35, 36, 38–42, 66, 74, 101
Mallaby, Dick 201
Mandelli, - 244
Marengo, Anna *ps*, 149–151, 183–184
Maryland, SOE base 202, 246
Maschietti, Adele 149, 162
Massingham, SOE base 201
Mastroviti, Luigi 150–151, 183
Matteotti brigades 168, 223
McCaffery, Jock ('Rossi') 194–195,
  200–205, 207, 208, 210–212, 214, 215,
  221–222, 223, 228, 232, 245, 246
McCaskey, Frank 118

McCracken, Private James 197–198
McGeoch, Lieutenant Beverley 45
McMillan, George 61
Megala Petra 103–104
Menzies, Robert 20
Mergozzo *ps*, 160, 223, 224
Metaxas Line 21–22, 36
MI6 246
MI9 79, 80, 94–95, 97–99, 139, 145–146
Milan 189–190, 192–193, 241, 244–245
   CLN 156–159, 203, 216, 231, 235
Military Intelligence Directorate, MI9 79, 80, 94–95, 97–99, 139, 145–146
Miller, Harry Herbert 'Mickey' 172, 196
Miller, Major Walter 45
Minoans 30, 113–114
Mobile Naval Base Defence Organisation 32
Monte Moro Pass 131, 151, 154, 214
Monte Rosa Division 227
Monte Rosa massif 130–131, 145
Monza 179, 182, 214
Moore, Bert 172
'Moosburg Express' 141
Moscatelli, Vincenzo (Cino) *ps*, 168–169, 174, 204, 210, 211, 214–219, 222–223, 232–233, 244–247
Moss, Billy 98, 236
Mountain, Brigadier Ronald 141
Muller, Freddie 149, 183, 200, 212, 213, 214–215, 217–218
Mussolini, Benito 120, 126
   death 235
   demise 134–135, 149
   Greek campaign 17, 19
   North African campaign 5–10
   RSI 138, 166–167, 177, 180, 234

Nascimbene, Giorgio 129
Nascimbene, Silvio 150
National Republican Guard (GNR) 180
   115th Montebello Battalion 196–197
Natusch, Roy 118
New Zealand government 20
New Zealand units
   5 Brigade 35, 39, 44
   19 Battalion 44

20 Battalion 41
21 Battalion 40–41, 44, 47
22 Battalion 35, 39–40, 44, 83
23 Battalion 40
28 Battalion (Maori Battalion) 40–41, 44–48
Newnham, Arnold 44, 74–75
Nicholls, Jack 'Tricker' 197
Nino Bixio 123
No. 1 Special Force, SOE 202, 205
Non-Commissioned Officers (NCOs) 124–125, 142
Novara *ps*, 155, 193, 214, 228

Office of Strategic Services (OSS) 200, 202, 221, 223
O'Gorman, Pat 3
O'Gorman family 3
O'Leary, Ken 153
Operation Avanti 225
Operation Barbarossa 19–20, 79–80
Operation Compass 10
Operation Husky 134
Operation Marita 21
Operation Merkur 36
Osoppo brigades 168
Ossola Valley 130, 219–220, 222, 223, 224, 231, 232
Other Ranks (ORs) 98, 124–125, 239
Ottomans 30, 85

Paglierini, Clia 150
Palestine 4–9
Parker, Les 196
Parker, Private JH 153
Parri, Ferruccio 156–157, 203, 206
Partito d'Azione (Action Party) *see* Action Party
Paterson, George 192, 211–212, 222–223, 228–229, 243
Patriot Battalion 219, 239
Patriotic Action Groups (GAPs) 168
Peck, Bert 2–3, 238
Peck, Brenda 238, 240, 241
Peck, Harry 3
Peck, Jean 2–3
Peck, Joffre 238
Peck, John Desmond ('Johnny') *ps*
   age 4, 8
   education 241–242

family 1, 4–6, 189, 195–196, 199,
    238, 240–242
  health 103–109
  honours 239–240, 241
  later life 231–232
Peck, Lock 5, 238
Peck, Mervin 238
Peck, Phyllis 2
Peck, Tony 238, 240–241
Peebles, Stan 173
Pendlebury, JDS 95–96
Pensotti, Aldo 150
Perazzi, Claudio ('Nebbia') 227–228
Pestarena 131, 216
Pettigrew, Dave 60–63, 242–243
PG 19 Bologna 141
PG 21 Chieti 140
PG 57 Gruppignano 13 ps, 124–128, 129,
    132, 141, 157, 170–173, 244
PG 65 Gravina 124, 126, 128
PG 75 Bari 124, 126
PG 78 Sulmona 124, 141
PG 106 Vercelli 128–133, 142
Philby, Kim 245–246
Piave group 173
Piedmont 127 map
  partisan activities 167–168, 169, 172,
    177, 178–179, 181–183, 192, 196,
    219–220, 222, 224–225, 235
  POW escape network 151, 155–
    157, 161
  SOE 209, 211, 232–233, 246–247
Pirgos 41
Pool, Francis ('Skipper') 80–81, 83, 87,
    96, 97, 100–103
Pozzati, Maria 150
Preveli 58, 76, 81, 85–89, 92, 99
Preveli Monastery 58, 81, 85–89, 92
Prison Valley 42, 74
Psychoundakis, George ps, 99, 105,
    107–109, 242
Puckapunyal 9

Reiter, Frank ('Blue') 58
Repubblica Sociale Italiana (RSI) 138,
    166–167, 177, 180, 204, 205, 219,
    234–235
Retimo 62–63
  airfield defence 31, 35–38, 40, 42,
    43, 59

Rhodes 118–122, 120–122, 243
Richards, Harry 56, 61
Rigoni, Sergio 142
Riordan, Esca 144
Rome 136–7, 206–207, 246–247
Rommel, General Erwin 16, 20,
    122–123
Ronco Biellese 173
Rossi, Bianca 163, 183–184
Rowe, Jack 172, 196
Royal Air Force (RAF) 22, 33, 207–208
Royal Australian Navy 4–5, 238
Royal Engineers, 42 Field Company ps,
    44
Royal Navy 12, 123
  battle for Crete 32, 34, 40
  evacuations from Crete 43–44,
    54–55, 57–59, 78
  evacuations from Greece 24, 26
  sinking of Costa Rica 26–28, 54
RSI see Repubblica Sociale Italiana (RSI)
Ruin Ridge 123, 172, 233

Sachs, Johnny 118
Saevecke, Theo ps, 190–191, 245
Salerno 136–137
Salonika 21, 66, 111
Samaria Gorge 57
San Donnino prison, Como 201
San Germano Vercellese 128, 133
San Martino 177–178
'San Vittore,' house 189, 242
San Vittore prison, Milan 189–192,
    209, 211–212, 228, 243–244
Sandover, Major Ray 59–60, 88
Santuario d'Oropa, Biella 171
Satriani, - 244
Saunders, Reg 46–47, 52, 54, 58, 81,
    93, 114–115, 173, 242
Savige, Brigadier Stanley G 9, 15, 25
Scott, Norm 93–94
Sedgman, Corporal NF 153
Senior British Officers (SBOs) 139–140
Senter, John 246
Sfakia ps, 43–44, 50–64, 65, 83, 111
Sicily 134
Sidi Barrani 61
Sidi Barrani, battle of 10–11, 16
Sidi Haneish 11
Simonds, Major Anthony 95–96, 146

Simplon tunnel 220–221
Skines 66
Skorzeny, Otto 138
Skylark 54
Sloane, Neil 144
Smedley, Douglas *ps*, 196–197
Smith, Audrey 157, 161
Smith, Edward Althey 'Big Bill' 233
Smith-Hughes, Jack 97
Soddini, Corporal 126
Sogno, Edgardo 174, 210–211
Soviet Union 19–20, 29, 79–80, 168,
   214, 230, 246
Special Operations Executive (SOE)
   136
   bases 200–202
   BLOs 203, 208–212, 214–215, 222,
      231–232, 234, 245–247
   Cherokee mission 223–224
   and Free Republic of Ossola 220–
      223, 228–229
   and MI9 94–95
   operations in Greece 233–234
   operations on Crete 94–97, 99, 114,
      116, 236
   relations with Italian resistance
      groups 203–211, 232–234
   relations with OSS 202–205, 221,
      223
   resistance activity 232–234
Spriggs, Tom 93–94
Sproule, Ian 170, 196
Squires, Private W 153
Steele, Don 153
Stockbridge, Ralph 97
Student, General Kurt 36
Suda Bay *ps*, 28, 31, 32, 34–37, 40, 42–44,
   58, 63
Suez Canal 6, 10
Sulmona, PG 78 124, 141
Superti, Dionigi *ps*, 223, 226–227
Swinburne, Wally 93–94
Switch Line 12
Symons, Edward William 'Sox' 126

Tabram, Bert 233
Tensfeld, SS-Brigadeführer Willi *ps*, 214,
   225, 245
Thomson, John ('Jack') *ps*, 61
Thrasher 81

Thunderbolt, HMS 102
Tibaldi, Ettore 220–221
Timbaki 100–101, 103, 109
Tobruk 243
Tobruk, battle of *ps*, 15–16, 21, 23, 25,
   122, 233
Torbay, HMS 88
Treis Ekklisies (Three Churches) 89, 93,
   110–112
Triffett, Edgar 170–171
Triple Entente 135
Trofalos 114
Turbulent, HMS 123
Turin 155–156, 159, 168, 184
Turkey 71, 98, 113, 120–121
Tyrakis, George 108–109

Ufficio Assistenza Prigionieri di Guerra
   Alleati 156
'Ultra' 34, 36
Union Jack *ps*, 61, 70, 157
United States 179, 206, 234
United States Central Intelligence
   Agency (CIA) 191, 200, 245
United States Office of Strategic
   Services (OSS) 200, 202–205, 221,
   223

Vafes 106
Val Formazza 227–228
Val Toce Division 226, 228
Valdossola Division *ps*, 219, 223–224,
   226, 240
Valiani, Leo 203
Valley of Butterflies 121
Valsesia 169, 173–174, 214, 217–218
Vandoulakis, - 106–107
Varallo 130, 174, 197–198
Varese 155, 178, 190
Vasey, Brigadier George 33, 35
Venezelos, George 101
Venezelos family 62–63, 75–76, 81,
   101
Vercelli
   escaped POWs 142–145, 169, 176
   partisans 170-2
   PG 106 128–133, 142
   POW escape networks *ps*, 147–155,
      162–163, 182–184
Victor, Saint 190

Victory Parade, London 240–241
Vilandredo 84–85
Vincent, Les 58
Von Ryan's Express, film 142

Wainewright, Bert 181–182
Waler , - 212
Walker, Lieutenant-Colonel Theo G 9,
    15, 22, 24, 25, 41, 44–45, 48, 52–55, 60
Waltzing Matilda 89
War Office, London 140, 239
Warner, Steve 44, 74–75
Wavell, Lieutenant-General Archibald
    10, 20, 31–32, 43, 80
Webb, Claude *ps*, 148–149, 150

Webster, Malcolm 171–172
Wehrmacht 21, 42, 137, 179, 231
Wil 195, 199, 209
Wilson, Henry Maitland ('Jumbo') 21
Wolfe, Ernie 197
Wolff, General Karl 179–180, 190–191,
    214–215, 235, 244–245
Woodhouse, Monty 97, 114
Woollahra 2
World War I 135
Wrigglesworth, Bill 172
Wrigley, Hugh 25

Yugoslavia 19, 21, 115, 124, 207